GERD GIGERENZER

Risk Savvy

How to Make Good Decisions

PENGUIN BOOKS

PENGUIN BOOKS

UK | USA | Canada | Ireland | Australia
India | New Zealand | South Africa

Penguin Books is part of the Penguin Random House group of companies
whose addresses can be found at global.penguinrandomhouse.com.

First published in the United States of America by Viking Penguin,
a member of Penguin Group (USA) LLC 2014
First published in Great Britain by Allen Lane 2014
Published in Penguin Books 2015

001

Printed in Great Britain by Clays Ltd, St Ives plc

A CIP catalogue record for this book is available from the British Library

ISBN: 978-0-241-95461-4

www.greenpenguin.co.uk

Penguin Random House is committed to a
sustainable future for our business, our readers
and our planet. This book is made from Forest
Stewardship Council® certified paper.

For Raine and Thalia

CONTENTS

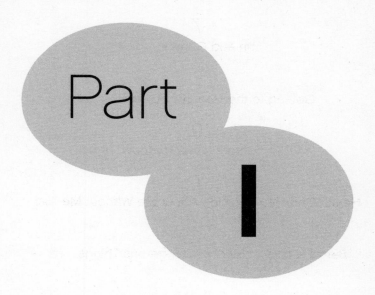

Part I

The Psychology of Risk

Creativity requires the courage to let go of certainties.

Erich Fromm

To be alive at all involves some risk.

Harold Macmillan

1

Are People Stupid?

Knowledge is the antidote to fear.

Ralph Waldo Emerson

Remember the volcanic ash cloud over Iceland? The subprime disaster? How about mad cow disease? Each new crisis makes us worry until we forget and start worrying about the next one. Many of us found ourselves stranded in crowded airports, ruined by vanishing pension funds, or anxious about tucking into a yummy beef steak. When something goes wrong, we are told that the way to prevent further crisis is better technology, more laws, and bigger bureaucracy. How to protect ourselves from the next financial crisis? Stricter regulations, more and better advisers. How to protect ourselves from the threat of terrorism? Homeland security, full body scanners, further sacrifice of individual freedom. How to counteract exploding costs in health care? Tax hikes, rationalization, better genetic markers.

One idea is absent from these lists: risk-savvy citizens. And there is a reason.

"Human beings are fallible: lazy, stupid, greedy and weak," an article in the *Economist* announced.[1] We are said to be irrational slaves to our whims and appetites, addicted to sex, smoking, and electronic gadgets. Twenty-year-olds drive with their cell phones glued to their ears, oblivious to the fact that doing so lowers their reaction time to that of a seventy-year-old. A fifth of Americans believe that they are in the top 1 percent income group and just as many believe that they will soon be there. Bankers have little respect for people's ability to invest money, and some doctors tell me that most of their patients lack intelligence, making it pointless to

1

disclose health information that might be misunderstood in the first place. All of this points to the conclusion that Homo sapiens ("man the wise") is a misnomer. Something has gone wrong in our genes. Evolution seems to have cheated us with shabby mental software and miswired our brains. In short, John and Jane Q. Public need continuous guidance, as a child needs a parent. Although we live in the high-tech twenty-first century, some form of paternalism is the only viable strategy: Close the doors, collect the experts, and tell the public what's best for them.

This fatalistic message is not what you will read in this book.[2] The problem is not simply individual stupidity, but the phenomenon of a *risk-illiterate society*.

Literacy—the ability to read and write—is the lifeblood of an informed citizenship in a democracy. But knowing how to read and write isn't enough. *Risk literacy* is the basic knowledge required to deal with a modern technological society. The breakneck speed of technological innovation will make risk literacy as indispensable in the twenty-first century as reading and writing were in previous centuries. Without it, you jeopardize your health and money, or may be manipulated into unrealistic fears and hopes. One might think that the basics of risk literacy are already being taught. Yet you will look in vain for it in most high schools, law schools, medical schools, and beyond. As a result, most of us are risk illiterate.

When I use the general term *risk savvy* I refer not just to risk literacy, but also more broadly to situations where not all risks are known and calculable. Risk savvy is not the same as risk aversion. Without taking risks, innovation would end, as would fun, and courage would belong to the past. Nor does risk savvy mean turning into a reckless daredevil or BASE jumper, denying the possibility of landing on one's nose. Without a beneficial degree of caution, humans would have ceased to exist long ago.

You might think, why bother if there are experts to consult? But it isn't that simple. Bitter experience teaches that expert advice may be a dangerous thing. Many doctors, financial advisers, and other risk experts themselves misunderstand risks or are unable to communicate them in an understandable way. Worse, quite a few have conflicts of interest or are so afraid of litigation that they recommend actions to clients they would never recommend to their own families. You have no choice but to think for yourself.

I'd like to invite you into the world of uncertainty and risk, beginning with weather reports and a very humble hazard, getting soaked.

Chances of Rain

A weathercaster on U.S. television once announced the weather this way:

> *The probability that it will rain on Saturday is 50 percent. The chance that it will rain on Sunday is also 50 percent. Therefore, the probability that it will rain on the weekend is 100 percent.*

Most of us will smile at this.[3] But do you know what it means when the weather report announces a 30 percent chance of rain tomorrow? 30 percent of what? I live in Berlin. Most Berliners believe that it will rain tomorrow 30 percent *of the time*; that is, for seven to eight hours. Others think that it will rain in 30 percent *of the region*; that is, most likely not where they live. Most New Yorkers think both are nonsense. They believe that it will rain on 30 percent *of the days* for which this announcement is made; that is, there will most likely be no rain at all tomorrow.[4]

Are people hopelessly confused? Not necessarily. Part of the problem is the experts who never learned how to explain probabilities in the first place. If they clearly stated the class to which a chance of rain refers, the confusion would disappear. Time? Region? Days? What meteorologists intend to say is that it will rain on 30 percent of the days for which this prediction is made. And "rain" refers to any amount above some tiny threshold, such as 0.01 inches.[5] Left on their own, people intuitively fill in a reference class that makes sense to them, such as how many hours, where, or how heavily it rains. More imaginative minds will come up with others still. As one woman in New York said, "I know what 30 percent means: Three meteorologists think it will rain, and seven not."

Here is my point. New forecasting technology has enabled meteorologists to replace mere verbal statements of certainty ("it will rain tomorrow") or chance ("it is likely") with numerical precision. But greater precision has *not* led to greater understanding of what the message really is. The confusion over probabilities of rain has persisted in fact since the very first time

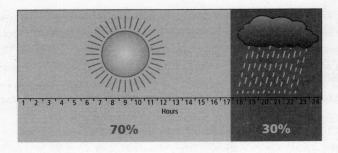

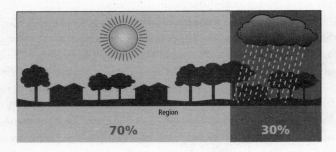

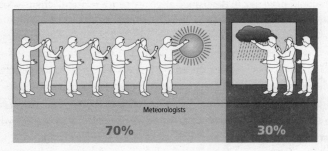

Figure 1-1. What does a "30 percent chance of rain tomorrow" mean? Some believe it will rain tomorrow 30 percent of the time (upper panel). Others believe it will rain tomorrow in 30 percent of the region (middle panel). Finally, some believe that three meteorologists think that it will rain and seven do not (lower panel). What meteorologists in fact intend to say is something different: that it will rain on 30 percent of the days for which this announcement is made. The problem is not simply in people's minds, but in the failure of experts to state clearly what they mean.

they were broadcast to the public in 1965 in the United States. This confusion is not just limited to rain, but occurs whenever a probability is attached to a single event—such as "if you take an antidepressant, you have a 30 percent chance of developing a sexual problem." Does that mean that 30 percent of all people will develop a sexual problem, or that you yourself will have a problem in 30 percent of your sexual encounters? The solution to clearing this widespread and long-standing muddle is surprisingly simple:

Always ask for the reference class: Percent of what?

If weathercasters were taught how to communicate to the public, you wouldn't even have to ask.

Getting soaked is a minor risk, although for some, from the farmer to Ferrari, the chances of rain matter. Before the Formula 1 Grand Prix, one of the most-discussed issues is the weather forecast—choosing the right tires are the key to winning the race. The same holds for NASA: The weather forecast is essential for approving or canceling a space shuttle launch, as the Challenger disaster tragically illustrates. Yet for most of us, all that is at stake is canceling a family outing unnecessarily or getting wet feet. People may not make a special effort to understand chances of rain simply because the hazards are modest. Are we more risk savvy when something truly important is at stake?

Pill Scare

Great Britain has many traditions, one of them being the contraceptive pill scare. Since the early 1960s, women are alarmed every couple of years by reports that the pill can lead to thrombosis, potentially life-threatening blood clots in the legs or lungs. In the most famous scare, the UK Committee on Safety of Medicines issued a warning that third-generation oral contraceptive pills increased the risk of thrombosis twofold—that is, by 100 percent. How much more certain can you get? This terrifying information was passed on in "Dear Doctor" letters to 190,000 general practitioners, pharmacists, and directors of public health and was presented in an emergency announcement to the media. Alarm bells rang around the country. Distressed women stopped taking the pill, which caused un-wanted pregnancies and abortions.[6]

Just how big is 100 percent? The studies on which the warning was based had shown that of every seven thousand women who took the ear-lier, second-generation pill, about one had a thrombosis; and that this number increased to two among women who took third-generation pills. That is, the *absolute risk* increase was only one in seven thousand, whereas the *relative risk* increase was indeed 100 percent. As we see, in contrast to absolute risks, relative risks appear threateningly large and can cause a great stir. Had the committee and the media reported the absolute risks, few women would have panicked and dropped the pill. Most likely, no one would have even cared.

This single scare led to an estimated thirteen thousand (!) additional abortions in the following year in England and Wales. But the fallout lasted for longer than one year. Before the alert, abortion rates had been steeply on the decline, but afterward, this trend was reversed and abortion rates increased for years to come. Women's confidence in oral contracep-tives was undermined, and pill sales fell sharply. Not all unwanted preg-nancies were aborted; for every abortion there was also one extra birth. The increase in both abortions and births was particularly pronounced among girls under sixteen, with some eight hundred additional conceptions.

Ironically, pregnancies and abortions are associated with a risk of thrombosis that exceeds that of the third-generation pill. The pill scare hurt women, hurt the National Health Service, and even brought down the stocks of the pharmaceutical industry. The resulting increase in costs to the National Health Service for abortion provision has been estimated at £4–6 million. Among the few who profited were the journalists who got the story on the front page.

An unwanted pregnancy and abortion is not something to be taken lightly. As one woman reports:

> When I learned that I was pregnant, my partner and I were together
> for two years. His first reaction was: "Come back when it's gone." I
> threw him out and tried to find a solution. I wanted so much to begin
> with college. I fought for building a future for us, but I began to realize

there was none. The one thing I did not want was to become dependent on the government, or—even worse—on a man. Therefore I decided last minute for an abortion. It's now two days ago, and I have one nervous breakdown after the other. My mind says, it was the best decision, but my heart weeps.

The tradition of pill scares continues to the present day, and always with the same trick. The solution is not better pills or more sophisticated abortion technology, but risk-savvy young women and men. It would not be so difficult to explain to teenagers the simple distinction between a relative risk ("100 percent") and an absolute risk ("one in seven thousand"). After all, batting averages and other sports statistics are common knowledge for many, young and old. Yet to the present day journalists have succeeded in causing scares with BIG numbers, and the public predictably panics, year after year.

Once again, the remedy is a simple rule:

Always ask: What is the absolute risk increase?

Journalists are not the only ones who play on our emotions with the help of numbers. Top medical journals, health brochures, and the Internet also inform the public in terms of relative changes, because bigger numbers make better headlines. In 2009 the prestigious *British Medical Journal* published two articles on oral contraceptives and thrombosis: One made the absolute numbers transparent in its abstract, while the other again touted relative risks, reporting that "oral contraceptives increased the risk of venous thrombosis fivefold."[7] The "fivefold" increase of course made for more spectacular headlines, and some newspapers, such as the *London Evening Standard,* didn't even bother mentioning the absolute numbers. As a rule, although we have high-tech medicine, understandable information for patients and doctors remains the exception.

It should be the ethical responsibility of every editor to enforce transparent reporting and it should be on the agenda of every ethics committee and every department of health. But it is not. After publication of my book *Calculated Risks,* which explains how to help both the public and doctors understand numbers, the neuroscientist Mike Gazzaniga, then dean of the faculty at Dartmouth College, paid me a visit. Outraged by the tricks played on the public by the use of relative risks and other means, he said that he would propose this issue to the President's Council on Bioethics, of which he was a member. After all, he argued, misleading the public with numbers happens in the United States just as often as in the United Kingdom, and is one of the few ethical problems to which a solution is known. Other less clear-cut issues, such as abortion, stem cells, and genetic testing, tend to occupy the council with endless discussions. I am grateful to Gazzaniga for trying. Yet the ethics committee did not recognize misleading the public as a significant issue and never took it up.

If ethics committees don't protect people, why don't doctors do it? The surprising answer is that many doctors themselves don't know how to communicate risks, a skill rarely taught at medical schools. The damaging effect of the "Dear Doctor" letters illustrates that many of them were taken in by relative risks. Once again, the experts are in need of training. Otherwise, when the next pill scare arrives, they and those affected may be as unprepared as ever.

I have explained the difference between relative and absolute risks to hundreds of journalists, and many have stopped alarming the public and reported absolute risks—only to see their editors often reintroduce the BIG numbers. We may not always be able to halt those who like to play with our fears, but we can learn to see through their tricks.

Terrorists Use Our Brains

Most of us remember exactly where we were on September 11, 2001. The pictures of the planes crashing into the twin towers of the World Trade Center have been ingrained into our memories. In the meantime, everything appears to have been said about the tragic attack. *The 9/11 Commission Report*, which appeared three years later, focused on how al-Qaeda terrorism evolved and on diplomatic strategies, legal reform, and technological measures. The one measure the 636-page report did not pay attention to, however, was risk-savvy citizens.

Let us turn the clock back to December 2001. Imagine you live in New York and want to travel to Washington. Would you fly or drive?

We know that after the attack, many Americans stopped flying. Did they stay home or jump into their cars? I have looked for an answer in the transportation statistics. In the months after the attack, the miles driven increased substantially. The increase was particularly strong on the rural interstate highways where long-distance travel happens, jumping by as much as 5 percent in the three months after the attack.[8] For comparison, in the months before the assault (January to August), individual monthly vehicle miles were up only less than 1 percent compared to 2000, which reflects the normal increase from year to year. All this extra driving lasted for twelve months; thereafter, car driving went back to normal. By then the images of the burning twin towers were no longer a daily feature in the media.

The increase in road travel had sobering consequences. Before the attack, the number of fatal traffic accidents remained closely around the average of the previous five years (the zero line in Figure 1-2). Yet in each of the twelve months after 9/11, the number of fatal crashes was above average, and most of the time, even higher than anything that happened in the previous five years. All in all, an estimated sixteen hundred Americans lost their lives on the road due to their decision to avoid the risk of flying.

This death toll is six times higher than the total number of passengers (256) who died on board the four fatal flights. Every one of those traffic victims might still be alive if they had flown instead. From 2002 to 2005, 2.5 billion passengers took to the air on U.S. commercial flights. Not a single one died in a major airline crash. Thus, although the 9/11 attacks were reported to have cost the lives of about three thousand Americans, the number is at least half as many more.

Let's give the statistic a face, but a lucky one—one who barely escaped death.

Justin Klabin, a twenty-six-year-old competitive rugby player and volunteer firefighter, watched the twin towers collapse from across the Hudson River. With his fire department, he rushed to Ground Zero. After this deeply emotional experience, he decided to stop flying. A month later, he and his girlfriend went on a trip to Florida—by car. Their pickup truck mastered the thousand-mile distance. But at the end of a long day on the road back home, they heard a loud pop: Both front tires turned toward

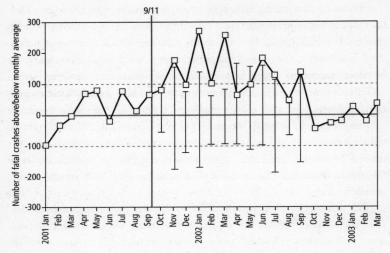

Figure 1-2. Terrorists' second strike. After the attacks on September 11, 2001, the number of fatal traffic accidents increased in the United States for a period of twelve months, resulting in an estimated sixteen hundred Americans losing their lives on the road in the attempt to avoid the risk of flying. Numbers are expressed as deviations from the five-year baseline 1996–2000 (the zero line). Before September 2001, the monthly fatal crashes were close to the zero line. In the twelve months following the attack, the number of fatal crashes was higher than the zero line for every month, and in most cases exceeded the maximum of the previous years (the vertical bars show the maximum and minimum). The peaks after 9/11 correspond to terrorism alerts.

Source: Gigerenzer (2004, 2006).

each other, like snowplowing skis. The tie-rod that connected the steering column to the wheel had snapped, and the truck could not drive a foot farther. They were lucky that the disaster happened when they pulled into a parking space in South Carolina. Had the rod snapped minutes earlier on the highway at a speed of seventy miles per hour, it is likely that Klabin and his girlfriend would have joined those unfortunate travelers who lost their lives by avoiding the risk of flying.

Terrorists strike twice. First they assault with physical force, and then they assault us with the help of our brains. The first strike gains all the attention. Billions of dollars have been poured into developing gigantic bureaucracies, including Homeland Security, and new technologies, such as full body scanners that make visible the nude surface of skin beneath clothing. The second strike, in contrast, has received almost no attention. In fact, when I gave talks on risk management to international intelligence services and counterterrorism agencies across the world, from Singapore to Wiesbaden, my hosts were repeatedly surprised, having never even considered it. Osama bin Laden once explained with relish how little money he used to cause such huge damages: "Al-Qaeda spent $500,000 on the event, while America, in the incident and its aftermath, lost—according to the lowest estimate—more than $500 billion, meaning that every dollar of al-Qaeda defeated a million dollars."[9] It's hard to prevent terrorists' suicide missions, but it should be easier to put a stop to the dangerous reactions based on fears that their attacks create within us in their aftermath.

What exactly is our brain's psychology that terrorists exploit? Low-probability events in which many people are suddenly killed, so-called *dread risks*,[10] trigger an unconscious psychological principle:

If many people die at one point in time, react with fear and avoid that situation.

Note that the fear is not about dying per se. It is about dying in a specific manner, namely together *at one point in time*, or in a short interval. When many die spectacularly at one point in time, as in the 9/11 attacks, our evolved brain reacts with great anxiety. But when as many or more die *distributed over time*, such as in car and motorbike accidents, we are less likely to be afraid. In the United States alone, where about 35,000 people die on the road every year, few worry about dying while driving. What matters psychologically is not, as sometimes claimed, that people have control when driving but not when flying. Passengers sitting next to the driver, not to speak of those in the back seats, have no control either, yet show little fear. We don't really fear dying in the steady stream of everyday incidents; we fear dying together suddenly with lots of others. We dread the rare nuclear power plant accident, not the steady death toll caused by pollution from coal power plants. We dreaded the swine flu pandemic after hearing the forecast of possibly tens of thousands of deaths—which never occurred—while few worry about being among the actual tens of thousands of people killed every year by the regular flu.

Where does this tendency to fear dread risks come from? In human history, it was likely a rational response. For most of our evolution, humans lived in small hunter-gatherer bands that may have consisted of up to twenty to fifty individuals and rarely exceeded one hundred people, similar to such bands in the world today. In small bands, the sudden loss of many lives could increase the risk of predation and starvation, and thus threaten survival of the whole group.[11] But what was rational in the past is not rational today. In modern societies, an individual's survival is no longer dependent on the support and protection of a small group or tribe. Yet the psychological response can still be easily elicited. To this day, real or imagined catastrophes have the potential to trigger panicky reactions.

The "old-brain" fear of dread risks can suppress any flash of thought in the new parts of our brains. As a professor from Loyola University Chicago wrote to me, "After 9/11, I explained the greater risk of driving compared to flying to my wife; that did not do the trick." Rational argument does not always win over old-brain fear, particularly if one spouse tries to educate the other. Yet there is a simple rule of thumb that could have helped that professor:

If reason conflicts with a strong emotion, don't try to argue. Enlist a conflicting and stronger emotion.

One such emotion that conflicts with dread-risk fear is parental concern. The professor might remind his wife that by making them drive long distances she puts the lives of her children—not just that of her husband—at risk. Parental emotions stand a better chance of overcoming the lingering fear of flying. A smart "new brain" can play one evolved fear against another to better survive in a modern world. Evolution is not destiny.

Terrorists' second strike goes beyond the story told here. It has led to an erosion of civil liberties: Before 9/11, strip searches without probable cause were seen to violate human rights; they are now seen as citizens' duty. Dread-risk fear makes us willing to tolerate long lines at the airport, put liquids in plastic bags, remove our shoes and belts and jackets, have our bodies touched by strangers. Higher security expenses in turn have gone hand in hand with reduced service and cramped seating, as if the airlines were competing for the worst customer service. People have become less lighthearted and more fearful. Last but not least, the wars in Afghanistan and Iraq have cost more than a trillion dollars together with the lives of thousands of soldiers and many more civilians. This financial strain also likely played a part in the financial crisis of 2008.[12]

If a similar attack ever repeats itself, we should not let our brains be misused again for a second strike. Only when we are risk savvy can we resist terrorist manipulation and create a safer and more resilient society. To get there, three tools are essential: understanding the nature of dread-risk fear, controlling it by enlisting conflicting emotions if reasons don't work, and knowing the actual risk of flying.

Let's go back to the question I posed before: Should you fly or drive? Assume again you live in New York and want to travel to Washington. You have only one goal, to arrive alive. How many miles would you have to drive by car until the risk of dying is the same as in a nonstop flight? I have asked this to dozens of expert audiences. The answers are all over the place: one thousand miles, ten thousand miles, driving three times around the world. However, the best estimate is twelve miles. Yes, only twelve. If your car makes it safely to the airport, the most dangerous part of your trip is likely already behind you.

Are People Hopeless in Dealing with Risk?

How can so many people not notice that they don't understand probabilities of rain? Or end up with unwanted pregnancies and abortions because they don't know the difference between relative and absolute risks? After all, probabilities of rain and pill scares have been around since the mid-1960s, and the fear of dread risks repeats itself with every new threat, from mad cow disease to SARS to bird flu, in an apparently endless circle. Why don't people learn?

Many experts think the answer is that people are basically incapable of understanding such things. Attempts to educate people out of their errors, so the argument goes, have mostly failed. Based on this dismal view of the general public, a publication by Deutsche Bank Research features a list of errors that we "Homer Simpsons" commit against rationality.[13] Popular books rehearse this message, portraying Homo sapiens as "predictably irrational" and in need of "nudges" into behaving sensibly by the few sane people on earth.[14]

My story is different. People aren't stupid. The problem is that our educational system has an amazing blind spot concerning risk literacy. We teach our children the mathematics of certainty—geometry and trigonometry—but not the mathematics of uncertainty, statistical thinking. And we teach our children biology but not the psychology that shapes their fears and desires. Even experts, shockingly, are not trained how to communicate risks to the public in an understandable way. And there can be positive interest in scaring people: to get an article on the front page, to persuade people to relinquish civil rights, or to sell a product. All these outside causes contribute to the problem.

The good news is that there is a solution. Who would have thought, a few hundred years ago, that so many people on earth would learn to read and write? We will see that everybody who wants to can also become risk savvy. Based on my and other colleagues' research, I will argue that:

1. *Everyone can learn to deal with risk and uncertainty.* In this book, I will explain principles that are easily understood by everyone *who dares to know.*

2. *Experts are part of the problem rather than the solution.* Many experts themselves struggle with understanding risks, lack skills in communicating them, and pursue interests not aligned with yours. Giant banks go bust for exactly these reasons. Little is gained when risk-illiterate authorities are placed in charge of guiding the public.

3. *Less is more.* When we face a complex problem, we look for a complex solution. And when it doesn't work, we seek an even more complex one. In an uncertain world, that's a big error. Complex problems do not always require complex solutions. Overly complicated systems, from financial derivatives to tax systems, are difficult

to comprehend, easy to exploit, and possibly dangerous. And they do not increase the trust of the people. Simple rules, in contrast, can make us smart and create a safer world.

"Savvy" means acute, astute, and wise. But being risk savvy is more than being well informed. It requires *courage* to face an uncertain future as well as to stand up to authority and ask critical questions. We can take the remote control for our emotions back into our own hands. Using one's mind without another's guidance entails an inner psychological revolution. Such a revolt makes life more enlightening and less anxiety-ridden. I have written this book to encourage risk-savvy citizens.

Becoming Risk Savvy

In his essay "What Is Enlightenment?" the philosopher Immanuel Kant begins thus: [15]

> *Enlightenment is man's emergence from his self-imposed nonage. Non-age is the inability to use one's own understanding without another's guidance. This nonage is self-imposed if its cause lies not in lack of understanding but in indecision and lack of courage to use one's mind without another's guidance. Dare to know!*

Freedom of speech, the right to vote, and protection against harm are among the most important achievements since the Enlightenment. These liberties are a treasure. They refer to what doors are open to you, to your opportunities. Today, every Internet user has free access to more information than humankind ever had before. Yet the idea of open doors is a passive or "negative" concept of liberty. *Positive liberty*, in contrast, entails more than free access. The question is whether you are able to walk through these doors, whether you can master your life without the constant guidance of others.[16] Now that people in democratic societies have vastly enlarged their opportunities, positive liberty has become the next challenge.

Risk-savvy citizens are indispensable pillars of a society that is ready for positive liberty. Whether the context is a weather forecast, a medical decision, or a large-scale disaster, being risk savvy requires a basic knowledge of our intuitive psychology as well as an understanding of statistical information. Only with both skills, and a portion of curiosity and courage, will we be able to take our lives in our own hands.

2

Certainty Is an Illusion

---

*Nothing will ever separate us. We will probably
be married another ten years.*

Elizabeth Taylor, 1974, five days before
she and Richard Burton announced their divorce

We think of uncertainty as something we don't want. In the best of all worlds, all things should be certain, absolutely certain. So we buy insurance against everything, swear by horoscopes, or pray to God. We collect terabytes of information to turn our computers into crystal balls. Yet think of what would happen if our wishes were granted. If we knew everything about the future with certainty, our lives would be drained of emotion. No surprise and pleasure, no joy or thrill—we knew it all along. The first kiss, the first proposal, the birth of a healthy child would be about as exciting as last year's weather report. If our world ever turned certain, life would be mind-numbingly dull.

The Illusion of Certainty

Nonetheless many of us ask for certainty from our bankers, our doctors, and our political leaders. What they deliver in response is the *illusion* of certainty, the belief that something is certain even when it isn't. Every year we support a multibillion-dollar industry that calculates future predictions, mostly erroneous, from market tips to global flu pandemics. Many of us smile at old-fashioned fortune-tellers. But when the soothsayers work with computer algorithms rather than tarot cards, we take their predictions seriously and are prepared to pay for them. The most astounding part is our collective amnesia: Most of us are still anxious to see stock market predictions even if they have been consistently wrong year after year.

Throughout history, humans have created belief systems that promise certainty, such as astrology and divination. A glance on the Internet reveals that these systems are still in high demand. Modern technology has added further vehicles of apparent certainty, from genetic tests to personalized medicine to risk measures in banking.

Blind Faith in Tests

If a genetic test shows that the defendant's DNA matches with the traces found on the murdered victim, isn't this certain evidence that he is the murderer? If a woman who is pregnant takes an HIV test and the test comes out positive, isn't this certain evidence that she—and likely her baby—is infected? In a word, no. To find out how widespread the illusion of certainty actually is, I surveyed a representative sample of one thousand German adults. They were asked in face-to-face interviews: "Which of the following tests are absolutely certain?" The result is shown in Figure 2-1.

When an astrologer calculates an expert horoscope for you and foretells that you will develop a serious illness and might even die at age forty-nine, will you tremble when the date approaches? Some 4 percent of Germans would; they believe that an expert horoscope is absolutely certain.[1] Yet there is no evidence that horoscopes do better than a good friend asked to predict your future. But when technology is involved, the illusion of certainty is amplified. Forty-four percent of people surveyed think that the result of a screening mammogram is certain. In fact, mammograms fail to detect about ten percent of cancers, and the younger the women being tested, the more error-prone the results, because their breasts are denser.

Finally, nearly two thirds of Germans believe that HIV tests and fingerprints are absolutely certain, and an even higher number place their faith in DNA tests. These tests are indeed much more accurate than mammograms, but none of their results are certain. Fingerprints, for instance, are unique features of an individual, even for identical twins who share the same genes. If the fingerprints of a suspect matched with those found on

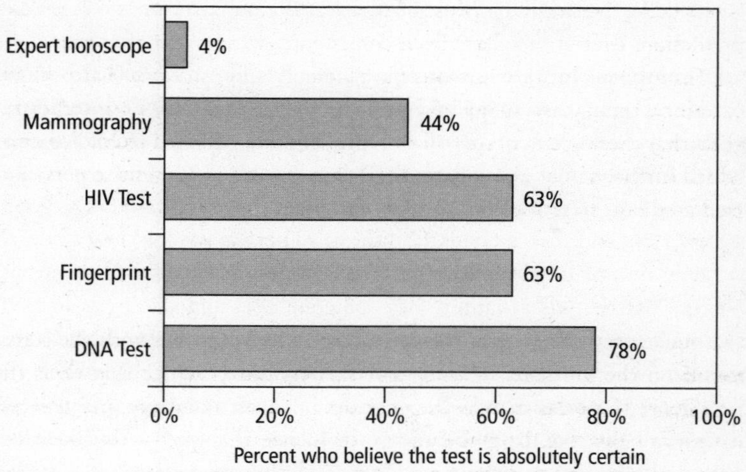

Figure 2-1. Which test is absolutely certain? Among a representative sample of one thousand Germans, 4 percent believed that an expert horoscope is absolutely certain. When modern technology is involved, the illusion of certainty is amplified. All of these tests make errors.

the scene of a crime, what jury would acquit the suspect? But is our system for fingerprint identification infallible? Fingerprints were believed to be "foolproof" until 1998, when the FBI sent two fingerprints found on a getaway car to be matched with the fingerprints of the convicted perpetrator to labs at several U.S. state law enforcement agencies. From thirty-five laboratories, eight could not match one of the prints and six more found no match for the other.[2] Clearly, this is not the exact science many believe it to be.

Not understanding a new technology is one thing. Believing that it delivers certainty is another. For those of us who suffer from the illusion of certainty, there is a simple remedy. Always remember what Benjamin Franklin said:

"In this world nothing can be said to be certain, except death and taxes."

My Security Blanket, Please

Humans appear to have a *need for certainty*, a motivation to hold on to something rather than to question it. People with a high need for certainty are more prone to stereotypes than others and are less inclined to remember information that contradicts their stereotypes.[3] They find ambiguity confusing and have a desire to plan out their lives rationally. First get a degree, a car, and then a career, find the most perfect partner, buy a home, and have beautiful babies. But then the economy breaks down, the job is lost, the partner has an affair with someone else, and one finds oneself packing boxes to move to a cheaper place. In an uncertain world, we cannot plan everything ahead. Here, we can only cross each bridge when we come to it, not beforehand. The very desire to plan and organize everything may be part of the problem, not the solution. There is a Yiddish joke: "Do you know how to make God laugh? Tell him your plans."

To be sure, illusions have their function. Small children often need security blankets to soothe their fears. Yet for the mature adult, a high need for certainty can be a dangerous thing. It prevents us from learning to face the uncertainty pervading our lives. As hard as we try, we cannot make our lives risk-free the way we make our milk fat-free.

At the same time, a psychological need is not entirely to blame for the illusion of certainty. Manufacturers of certainty play a crucial role in cultivating the illusion. They delude us into thinking that our future is predictable, as long as the right technology is at hand. Yet the future can be one damned thing after another. False certainty is disseminated by many an expert, and sometimes shamelessly. "I am sure I have found the Holy Grail," a financial expert divulged to an eager-looking client at a fancy Zurich hotel in such a bellowing baritone that I could not help but listen. After an hour of plugging a supposedly fail-safe investment without a waver of a doubt, he won over the client—and his money.

The quest for certainty is an old human endeavor. Magical cults, soothsayers, and authority figures who know what's right and wrong are its proponents. Similarly, for centuries many philosophers have been misled by looking for certainties where none exist, equating knowledge with certainty and belief with uncertainty, as John Dewey, the great pragmatist philosopher, pointed out.[4] Today, modern technologies, from mathematical stock prediction methods to medical imaging machines, compete for the confidence promised by religion and authority.

The quest for certainty is the biggest obstacle to becoming risk savvy. While there are things we can know, we must also be able to recognize when we *cannot* know something. We know almost for sure that Halley's Comet will return in the year 2062, but we can rarely predict natural disasters and stock crashes. "Only fools, liars, and charlatans predict earthquakes," said Charles Richter, namesake of the scale that measures their magnitude.[5] Similarly, an analysis of thousands of forecasts by political and economic experts revealed that they rarely did better than dilettantes or dart-throwing chimps.[6] But what the experts were extremely talented at was inventing excuses for their errors ("I was almost right"). The problem is that false certainty can do tremendous damage. As we will see, blind faith in tests and financial forecasts can lead to misery. Not only can it endanger your physical and mental health, but it can also ruin your bank account and the economy as a whole. We have to learn to live with uncertainty. It's time to face up to it. A first step toward doing so is to understand the distinction between known risks and unknown risks.

Risk and Uncertainty

Two magnificently dressed young women sit upright on their chairs, calmly facing each other. Yet neither takes notice of the other. Fortuna, the fickle, wheel-toting goddess of chance, sits blindfolded on the left while human figures desperately climb, cling to, or tumble off the wheel in her hand (Figure 2-2). Sapientia, the calculating and vain deity of science, gazes into a hand-mirror, lost in admiration of herself. These two allegorical figures depict a long-standing polarity: Fortuna brings good or bad luck, depending on her mood, but science promises certainty.

This sixteenth-century woodcut was carved a century before one of the greatest revolutions in human thinking, the "probabilistic revolution," colloquially known as the taming of chance. Its domestication began in the mid-seventeenth century. Since then, Fortuna's opposition to Sapientia has evolved into an intimate relationship, not without attempts to snatch each other's possessions. Science sought to liberate people from Fortuna's wheel, to banish belief in fate, and replace chances with causes. Fortuna struck back by undermining science itself with chance and creating the vast empire of probability and statistics.[7] After their struggles, neither remained the same: Fortuna was tamed, and science lost its certainty.

Today, we live in the mesmerizing world these two allegorical figures

Figure 2-2. Fortuna, the wheel-toting goddess of chance (left), facing Sapientia, the divine goddess of science (right). In this sixteenth-century woodcut, the two women are pictured in their traditional opposition: Fortune's luck makes people climb and fall from her wheel, while science promises certainty. A century later, in one of the greatest scientific revolutions, chance became tamed and science lost its certainty. Courtesy of the Bridgeman Art Library, London.

created. Our minds have become crowded with numbers and probabilities. Baseball grew out of sandlots and city streets, supported by a culture of working men and farm boys. Now it is unthinkable without statistics: batting averages, strikeout averages, and playing the percentages. If forced to choose, many a fan would prefer seeing the numbers to the game. Markets and trading emerged from daring, worldly-wise men who voyaged across empires and made their fortunes, surpassing the ruling aristocracy in wealth and eventually initiating a revolution so that others without titles of nobility could live a decent life. Today, traders no longer venture to make their fortunes on the road but on their high-speed computers with the help of mathematical models aimed at predicting the stock market. All the while blindfolded Fortuna is still at work, calmly spinning her wheel, fooling forecasters and plunging Nobel laureates' hedge funds into ruin.

The twilight of uncertainty comes in different shades and degrees. Beginning in the seventeenth century, the probabilistic revolution gave humankind the skills of statistical thinking to triumph over Fortuna, but these skills were designed for the palest shade of uncertainty, a world of *known risk*, in short, *risk* (Figure 2-3, center). I use this term for a world where all alternatives, consequences, and probabilities are known. Lotteries and games of chance are examples. Most of the time, however, we live in a changing world where some of these are unknown: where we face unknown risks, or *uncertainty* (Figure 2-3, right). The world of uncertainty is huge compared to that of risk. Whom to marry? Whom to trust? What to do with the rest of one's life? In an uncertain world, it is impossible to determine the optimal course of action by calculating the exact risks. We have to deal with "unknown unknowns." Surprises happen. Even when calculation does not provide a clear answer, however, we have to make decisions. Thankfully we can do much better than frantically clinging to and tumbling off Fortuna's wheel. Fortuna and Sapientia had a second brainchild alongside mathematical probability, which is often passed over: rules of thumb, known in scientific language as heuristics.[8] When making decisions, the two sets of mental tools are required:

• RISK: If risks are known, good decisions require logic and statistical thinking.

- UNCERTAINTY: If some risks are unknown, good decisions also require intuition and smart rules of thumb.

Most of the time, a combination of both is needed. Some things can be calculated, others not, and what can be calculated is often only a crude estimate.

Figure 2-3. Certainty, risk, and uncertainty. In everyday language, we make a distinction between "certainty" and "risk," but the terms "risk" and "uncertainty" are mostly used as synonyms. They aren't. In a world of known risks, everything, including the probabilities, is known for certain. Here, statistical thinking and logic are sufficient to make good decisions. In an uncertain world, not everything is known, and one cannot calculate the best option. Here, good rules of thumb and intuition are also required.

Known Risk

The taming of chance created mathematical probability. I will use the term *known risk* or simply *risk* for probabilities that can be measured empirically, as opposed to uncertainties that cannot.[9] Probabilities of rain, for instance, can be measured on the basis of observed frequencies, as can batting averages and the risk of thrombosis. Originally, the word "risk" referred not just to dangers or harms but also to both good or bad fortunes in Fortuna's hands: A risk can be a threat or a hope. I will retain the original use of the word. After all, without risk taking there would be little innovation. And in many situations, a negative outcome can be viewed as positive from another perspective: A probability of rain can refer to a dangerous event, such as heavy rain causing car accidents, but also to a positive outcome, such as rain ending drought and famine. The risk of losing your fortune in a gambling casino is a calamity for you but a welcome one for the casino owners.

The Three Faces of Probability

One important fact is often overlooked. Probability is not one of a kind; it was born with three faces: frequency, physical design, and degrees of belief.[10] And these have persisted to this day.

Frequency. In the first of its identities, probability is about counting. Counting the number of days with rainfall or the number of hits a baseball player makes and dividing these by the total number of days or strikes results in probabilities that are relative frequencies. Their historical origins lie in seventeenth-century mortality tables, from which life insurances calculated probabilities of death.

Physical Design. Second, probability is about constructing. For example, if a die is constructed to be perfectly symmetrical, then the probability of rolling a six is one in six. You don't have to count. Similarly, mechanical slot machines are physically designed to pay out, say, 80 percent of what people throw in, and electronic machines have software that determines the probabilities. Probabilities by design are called *propensities.* Historically, games of chance were the prototype for propensity. These risks are known because people crafted, not counted, them.

Degrees of Belief. Third, probability is about degrees of belief. A degree of belief can be based on anything from experience to personal impression. Historically, its origin is in eyewitness testimony in courts and, more spectacularly, in the Judeo-Christian lore of miracles.[11] To this day, the testimony of two independent witnesses counts more than that of two who talked with each other beforehand, and the same holds for the testimony of a witness who did not know the defendant than that of his brother. But how to quantify these intuitions? That was the question that gave rise to degrees of belief expressed as probabilities.

Unlike known risks based on measurable frequencies or physical design, degrees of belief can be quite subjective and variable. Frequencies and design limit probability to situations involving large amounts of data or a design that is clearly understood. Degrees of belief, in contrast, are more expansive, suggesting that probability can be applied to any and every problem. The danger is that by extending probability to everything, it is easy to be seduced into thinking that one tool—calculating probabilities—is sufficient for dealing with all kinds of uncertainty. As a consequence, other important tools, such as rules of thumb, are left in the cupboard.

Does this multiplicity of identities matter? Not much when playing dice, but it certainly does when it comes to modern technology. The risk of a major accident in a nuclear power plant can be estimated by counting earlier accidents, or by the physical design of the plant, or by experts' degrees of belief, or some mixture of these. The resulting estimates can be strikingly different. While counting nuclear accidents is straightforward, propensities are hard to determine for the design of a power plant, allowing for widely diverging estimates that may depend on the estimators' political attitudes and on their financial backer. For that reason, it is always important to ask how the risk of a nuclear meltdown, or any other risk, was actually calculated.

The Art of Risk Communication

To calculate a risk is one thing, to communicate it is another. Risk communication is an important skill for laypeople and experts alike. Because it's rarely taught, misinterpreting numbers is the rule rather than the exception. Each of the three kinds of probability—relative frequency, design, or degree of belief—can be framed in either a confusing or a transparent way. So far we have seen two communication tools for reporting risks:

- Use frequencies instead of single-event probabilities.
- Use absolute instead of relative risks.

These "mind tools" are relatively easy to learn and apply. The first helps to understand the chance of a risk, such as rain. As noted in chapter 1, "a 30 percent chance of rain tomorrow" is a single-event probability, while "it will rain on 30 percent of the days for which this announcement is made" is a frequency statement that makes the reference class clear (days, not region or time). The second mind tool helps to understand the change in a risk, such as when using a new contraceptive pill. While a 100 percent increase in the risk of a thrombosis is a relative risk that frightens many people, the absolute risk increase, one in seven thousand, puts the actual risk in perspective.

You will find more helpful tools throughout this book. Yet I should warn you that nothing works all the time; it may require some practice. Lorin Warnick, associate dean of the College of Veterinary Medicine at Cornell University, wrote me about an unsuccessful attempt to use transparent frequencies instead of single-event probabilities.

> *A few years ago I performed surgery to correct a displaced abomasums ["twisted stomach"] in a dairy cow at a dairy farm near Ithaca, NY. We know from previous studies that approximately 85 percent of cows treated by the technique recover and return to normal milk production. Ben, the owner of the farm, asked how likely the cow was to have problems after the surgery. Trying to put it in terms that he could relate to I said, "If we did this procedure on 100 cows, I expect about 10 to 15 would not completely recover within a few weeks of surgery." He paused a moment and said, "Well that's good because I only have 35 cows."*

Uncertainty

In an uncertain world, statistical thinking and risk communication alone are not sufficient. Good rules of thumb are essential for good decisions.

Miracles Happen

On a sunny January afternoon in 2009, 150 passengers boarded US Airways Flight 1549. Three minutes after they took off from LaGuardia airport in New York City, something happened out of the blue. A flock of Canada geese approached the plane, in perfect formation. At an altitude of twenty-eight hundred feet, passengers and cabin crew suddenly heard loud bangs. The geese had collided with the engines. A jet engine can "ingest" smaller birds but not Canada geese weighing ten pounds or more. If the bird is too big, the engine shuts down rather than exploding. But this time the improbable event had happened: The geese had flown into not just one but both engines, and both were silenced. When it dawned on the passengers that they were gliding toward the ground, it grew quiet on the plane. No panic, only silent prayer. Captain Chesley Sullenberger called air traffic control: "Hit birds. We've lost thrust in both engines. We're turning back towards LaGuardia."

But landing short of the airport would have catastrophic consequences, for passengers, crew, and the people living below. The captain and the co-pilot had to make a good judgment. Could the plane actually make it to LaGuardia, or would they have to try something more risky, such as a water landing in the Hudson River? One might expect the pilots to have measured speed, wind, altitude, and distance and fed this information into a calculator. Instead, they simply used a rule of thumb:

Fix your gaze on the tower: If the tower rises in your windshield, you won't make it.

No estimation of the trajectory of the gliding plane is necessary. No time is wasted. And the rule is immune to calculation errors. In the words of copilot Jeffrey Skiles: "It's not so much a mathematical calculation as visual, in that when you are flying in an airplane, things that—a point that you can't reach will actually rise in your windshield. A point that you are going to overfly will descend in your windshield."[12] This time the point they were trying to reach did not descend but rose. They went for the Hudson.

In the cabin, the passengers were not aware of what was going on in the cockpit. All they heard was: "This is the captain: Brace for impact." Flight attendants shouted: "Heads down! Stay down!" Passengers and crew later recalled that they were trying to grasp what death would be like, and the anguish of their kids, husbands, and wives. Then the impact happened, and the plane stopped. When passengers opened the emergency doors, sunlight streamed in. Everyone got up and rushed toward the openings. Only one passenger headed to the overhead bin to get her carry-on but was immediately stopped. The wings of the floating but slowly sinking plane were packed with people in life jackets hoping to be rescued. Then they saw the ferry coming. Everyone survived.

All this happened within the three minutes between the geese hitting the plane and the ditch in the river. During that time, the pilots began to run through the dual-engine failure checklist, a three-page list designed to be used at thirty thousand feet, not at three thousand feet: turn the ignition on, reset flight control computer, and so on. But they could not finish it. Nor did they have time to even start on the ditching checklist. While the evacuation was underway, Skiles remained in the cockpit and went through the evacuation checklist to safeguard against potential fire hazards and other dangers. Sullenberger went back to check on passengers and left the cabin only after making sure that no one was left behind. It was the combination of teamwork, checklists, and smart rules of thumb that made the miracle possible.

The Secret of Intuition: Unconscious Rules of Thumb

A rule of thumb, or *heuristic*, enables us to make a decision fast, without much searching for information, but nevertheless with high accuracy. The rule used by the pilots to find out whether the plane would make it to the next airport is a case in point. Pilots are trained to use the rule consciously. Yet others use the same rule intuitively; that is, without awareness. The rule is a special instance of the *gaze heuristic*, which helps to intercept objects in three-dimensional space:

> *Fix your gaze on an object, and adjust your speed so that the angle of gaze remains constant.*

Professional baseball players rely on this rule, although most are not aware of it. If a fly ball comes in high, the player fixates his eyes on the ball, starts running, and adjusts his running speed so that the angle of gaze remains constant.[13] The player does not need to calculate the trajectory of the ball. To select the right parabola, the player's brain would have to estimate the ball's initial distance, velocity, and angle, which is not a simple feat. And to make things more complicated, real-life balls do not fly in parabolas. Wind, air resistance, and spin affect their paths. Even the most sophisticated robots or computers today cannot correctly estimate a landing point during the few seconds a ball soars through the air. The gaze heuristic solves this problem by guiding the player toward the landing point, not by calculating it mathematically. That's why players don't know exactly where the ball will land, and often run into walls and over the stands in their pursuit.

Every rule of thumb I am aware of can be used consciously and unconsciously. If it is used unconsciously, the resulting judgment is called intuitive. An intuition, or gut feeling, is a judgment:

1. that appears quickly in consciousness,
2. whose underlying reasons we are not fully aware of, yet
3. is strong enough to act upon.

A gut feeling is neither caprice nor a sixth sense, nor is it clairvoyance or God's voice. It is a form of unconscious intelligence. To assume that intelligence is necessarily conscious and deliberate is a big error. Most parts of our brain are unconscious, and we would be doomed without the vast experience stored there. Calculated intelligence may do the job for known risks, but in the face of uncertainty, intuition is indispensable. Our society, however, often resists acknowledging intuition as a form of intelligence, while taking logical calculations at face value as intelligent. Similarly, some social scientists view intuition with suspicion and consider it the main source of human error. Some even postulate the existence of two cognitive systems, one conscious, logical, calculative, and rational and the other unconscious, intuitive, heuristic, and error-prone, each working by different principles.[14] The example I just gave contradicts this story. A heuristic can be safer and more accurate than a calculation, and the same heuristic can underlie both conscious and unconscious decisions.

Granted, one rule of thumb cannot possibly solve all problems; for that reason, our minds have learned a "toolbox" of rules. Just as a hammer is best for nails while a screwdriver is needed for screws, these rules of thumb need to be used in an adaptive way. Intelligent decision making entails knowing what tool to use for what problem. Intelligence is not an abstract number such as an IQ, but similar to a carpenter's tacit knowledge about using appropriate tools. This is why the modern science of intelligence studies the "adaptive toolbox" that individuals, organizations, and cultures have at their disposal; that is, the evolved and learned rules that guide our deliberate and intuitive decisions.[15]

Where do these rules of thumb come from? Some of them have accompanied humans and animals for a long time. Bats, dogs, and fish rely on the gaze heuristic to intercept prey and mates. Fish catch prey by holding a constant angle between their line of motion and that of the target. When a dog chases after a sailing Frisbee, it is guided by the same rule, trying to maintain a constant angle of vision while running. We will encounter more of these rules of thumb in the course of this book.

Simple Solutions to Complex Problems

The gaze heuristic illustrates how the mind can discover simple solutions to complex problems. It is called a heuristic because it focuses on the one or few pieces of information that are important and ignores the rest. Experts often search for less information than novices do, using heuristics instead. In the case of the US Airways pilots, they ignored all the information needed to calculate the trajectory of the sailing plane and relied on only one piece of information: the image of the tower in the windshield. The important point is that ignoring information can lead to better, faster, and safer decisions.

The gaze heuristic is successful because of our evolved brains. That's why pilots, outfielders, or dogs can rely on it, while it is of limited use for robots and computers. These do not have the evolved capability to keep an eye on a moving object against a noisy background. In lieu of this mental capacity, they have to calculate trajectories. What's simple for a human is not so simple for a computer, and vice versa—the human ability to decipher distorted letters and numbers is used as a safety feature against web robots, whereas computers will beat every mathematical whiz in calculating the seventh root of a seventeen-digit number.

One might think that the study of smart heuristics must be a central activity in many fields. But it isn't. Oddly, most theories of rational decision making, from economics to philosophy, still assume that all risks are knowable. Much brainpower in the social sciences has gone into sophisticated versions of logic and statistics. Almost none has been devoted to heuristic thinking, and when it has, it is mostly used to argue that heuristics are the reason for human error and disaster.

After the probabilistic revolution we need a second revolution, one that takes heuristics seriously and that will eventually provide humankind with skills for dealing with the entire palette of uncertainty. The American polymath Herbert Simon was one of the first to call for this revolution, and I have devoted much of my research to contributing to it in terms of mathematical models for decision making under uncertainty. This next step is what I call the "heuristic revolution."[16] It requires learning how to deal with uncertain worlds with the help of smart rules of thumb.

Don't Confuse Risk and Uncertainty

Given the many unknowns, few situations in life allow us to calculate risk precisely. In most cases the risks involved are a mixture of more or less well known ones. After 9/11, for instance, the risk of driving remained about the same as before the terrorist attack, but the risk of flying became much less certain: Another plane might have been hijacked. Here it was less clear whether the future was like the past. In health care, another world with a high degree of uncertainty, a doctor needs statistical thinking to understand the results of medical research, but also good intuitions to understand the patient. Similarly, in the world of business, statistical calculation is not enough; to know whom to trust, one needs good intuitions about other people. As one of the world's most successful executives, Jack Welch of General Electric, explained, good decisions are made "straight from the gut."[17]

The illusion of certainty has two faces. Whenever known risks are mistaken for absolute certainty, the *zero-risk* illusion occurs (Figure 2-4, left arrow). Modern technologies that many of us believe to be all but infallible, such as HIV tests, genetic analyses, and imaging tests, provide high-tech vehicles for illusory certainty. The *calculable risk* illusion (or turkey illusion;

see below) is different. It mistakes uncertainty for known risks. Like the zero-risk illusion, it is shown as a move to the left-hand side in Figure 2-4 (right arrow). In both cases, there is a clash between the real world and the perceived one. Let's begin with risks that are mistaken for certainty.

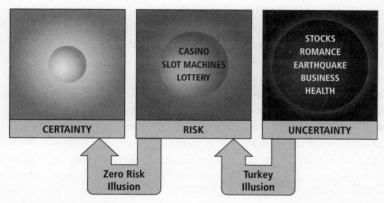

Figure 2-4. Two kinds of illusions of certainty. The first is to confuse a world of risk with one of certainty—the zero-risk illusion. The second is to confuse a world of uncertainty with one of known risk—the turkey illusion (calculable-risk illusion). In each case, the illusion corresponds to an arrow moving from the right side to the left.

The Zero-Risk Illusion

People who have unprotected sex with varying partners run a risk of being infected with HIV (human immunodeficiency virus). Those who believe that it can't happen to them incur the zero-risk illusion. But there is another dangerous risk that is less known: when people take a routine HIV test, the risk of a false positive.

Illusory Certainty Can Ruin Your Life

Screening for HIV is widespread and not always voluntary. Blood banks screen potential donors, armed forces screen recruits and personnel on active duty, and immigration offices screen immigrants. Men and women who want to marry are advised to take HIV tests, as are pregnant women. Billboards on U.S. highways advertise happy girls and the message "Do it for Mom. Free HIV test.net." To test for HIV, an ELISA (enzyme-linked immunosorbent assay) test is done first. If it's negative, the person is notified about the good news. If it's positive, another ELISA, preferably from a different manufacturer, is performed. If this test is also positive, a more expensive Western blot test is done, which is called a "confirmatory test." If the Western blot is also positive, then the person is typically considered to be HIV-positive. Procedures vary.

In my book *Calculated Risks*, I explained something you should know before taking an HIV test. If you are not at risk for AIDS but test positive for it, you are not necessarily infected. False positives occur. A false positive is like a false alarm: A person who is not infected nevertheless receives a positive result. As we can see from Figure 2-1, years later, a majority of the public is still not informed about the possibility of false positive HIV tests. Lives have been destroyed by false alarms. In the early days of HIV testing, twenty-two blood donors in Florida were notified that they had tested HIV-positive on the ELISA; seven of them committed suicide without knowing whether the results were true.[18]

A few years after I wrote *Calculated Risks*, Dr. Eileen Munro presented my analysis of HIV testing in an article. Not long afterward, she forwarded me this letter:[19]

Dear Dr. Munro,

Two weeks ago, I had an HIV test. I'm newly married and newly pregnant, and the test is a standard procedure now for pregnant women. They called me in a week later and said I had tested positive for HIV. I asked about the false positive rate; the doctor told me it was 5/100,000. They gave me some handouts from the Internet about living with HIV, and sent me off to tell my husband and my family the news.

It was a bad evening and next morning, but at work the next day I got to thinking. I did some research and saw they had not followed standard protocol (two ELISAs and then a Western Blot). They had only done the

*Western Blot, explaining that it was the confirmatory test, so they had not
bothered with the ELISAs. I reread your article, considered my low-risk
lifestyle, and began to feel some hope. I went with my husband that weekend to a different clinic, where they had the 20-minute pinprick test, and
we both tested negative; every subsequent test has been negative.*

*Your article saved me from a degree of despair I cannot even put
into words; it gave me enough stamina to continue to research the issue
and get tested again immediately. I appreciate the article for its contribution to the risk assessment arena, but I also wanted to tell you how
important it was to me on a much deeper level.*

> *Sincerely,*
> *Amy D.*
> *Berkeley, CA*

After reading this letter, I knew that all the hours I had put into writing
Calculated Risks had paid off. Let's go through the argument. What does a
positive test really mean? Assume her doctor was right and the false-positive
rate was five in one hundred thousand (see Figure 2-5, left). Consider one
hundred thousand women from the general public who are screened for
HIV. Statistics suggest that about ten are infected (which is called the prevalence) and that the test detects these with near certainty.[20] Out of the
majority of women who are *not* infected, five additional women can be
expected to test positive, according to Amy's doctor. That adds up to ten
correct positives and five incorrect ones, resulting in a two-to-one chance
of being infected, far from absolute certainty. Only if Amy had practiced a
high-risk lifestyle would the odds be poor.

The lesson is: If you are not at risk for HIV, *don't panic*. Think about
what the numbers mean, and go back for a second, independent test.

As we have seen, the meaning of a positive HIV test depends largely on
the prevalence and the false-positive rate. The best tests available have a
smaller false-positive rate than what Amy's doctor told her, only about 1 in
250,000. If the prevalence is 1 in 10,000 (or 25 in 250,000), as before,
then one can expect one false positive for every twenty-five true positives
(Figure 2-5, right). That is, the chance of being infected given a positive

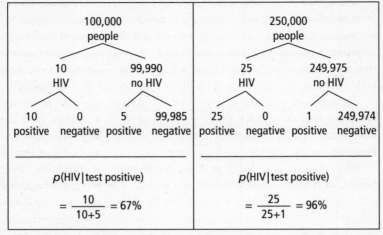

Figure 2-5. What does a positive HIV test mean? The answer depends on the prevalence and the false-positive rate. Left tree: The false-positive rate is 5 in 100,000 according to Amy's doctor. The prevalence is 1 in 10,000 for women with no known risk factors. Among 100,000 women who take the test, 10 will likely be infected, and also correctly test positive. Among the 99,990 not infected, the test is likely to err in five cases—that is, result in a false positive. Thus, we expect that 15 persons will test positive but only 10 will actually be infected. Right tree: Here, the false-positive rate is 1 in 250,000, corresponding to the most recent studies using better tests. Among 250,000 women who take the test, 25 are likely to be infected, and also correctly test positive. Among the 249,975 not infected, the test is likely to err in one case. In other words, out of every 26 who test positive, we expect that 1 will in fact not be infected. The numbers vary by country, risk group, and quality of test.

test is about 96 percent. This is high but still far from certain. It's an ethical imperative that AIDS counselors explain to their clients what their risk of being infected actually is, given the prevalence and false-positive rate of the test used. The majority of AIDS counselors I have studied, however, were confused by probabilities and told their low-risk clients that the result is 100 percent certain.[21]

In our examples, the test caught all those who were infected; nevertheless, misses do occur. The world record appears to be held by an American construction worker, who tested negative about thirty times despite being infected.

The problem is compounded by the fact that many authoritative institutions—not only in California—propagate the illusion of certainty. For instance, if you live in Chicago and consult the website of the Illinois Department of Public Health, you'll read: "A positive test result means that antibodies to HIV were found in your blood. That means you have HIV infection. You are infected for life and can spread HIV to others."[22]

The statement provides false certainty. The doctors who sent Amy home to tell her husband and family the news appear to have suffered from the same illusion. No ifs, no buts, no mention of the possibility of false positives. Pregnant women, like the rest of us, deserve better information than that.

Not everyone is as lucky as Amy. People have lost their jobs, their homes, their health, their children, and friends after being misdiagnosed and wrongly treated with medical cocktails. Some have committed suicide, others embarked on a downward spiral of self-destructive behavior, including unprotected sex with others infected with HIV, thinking that it wouldn't matter anymore.[23]

The Turkey Illusion

It is not always easy to know how uncertain the situation is in which we find ourselves, whether it contains known risks or is largely unpredictable. Let's begin with a story by writer Nassim Taleb.[24] Put yourself into the mind of a turkey. On the first day of your life a man came. You were afraid that he might kill you, but he was kind and gave you food. Next day, you see the man approach you once more. Will he feed you again? Using probability theory, you can calculate the chance that this will happen. The *rule of succession*, derived by the great mathematician Pierre-Simon Laplace, provides the answer:

> *Probability that something happens again if it happened* n *times before*
> $= (n+1)/(n+2)$

Here, n is the number of days the farmer fed you. That is, after the first day, the probability that the farmer will feed you the next day is 2/3, after the second day it increases to 3/4, and so on, growing more and more certain every day. At the same time, the alternative that he might kill you becomes less and less likely. On day one hundred, it is almost certain the farmer will come to feed you, or so you might think. But unknown to you, that day is the day before Thanksgiving. Just when the probability of being fed is higher than ever before, you're dead meat.

Thanksgiving was an unknown to the turkey. If the turkey had known all possible risks, updating probabilities would in fact have been rational. But the turkey found out the hard way that it was missing one important piece of information.

While many AIDS counselors misleadingly suggest absolute certainties, the turkey at least tried to calculate the probabilities. However, wrongly assuming that a risk can be calculated is another illusion of certainty (Figure 2-4). Let's call it the *turkey illusion*, although it probably happens more often to people than to turkeys.

Bad Luck or Illusory Certainty?

There is a similarity between the turkey's unexpected disaster and experts' inability to anticipate financial crises: Both use models that might work in the short run, but cannot foresee the disaster looming ahead. As in the case of the turkey, the risk estimates in the U.S. housing market were based on historical data and on models similar in spirit to the rule of succession. Because the housing prices kept rising, the risk seemed to decline. Confidence in stability was highest before the onset of the subprime crisis. As late as March 2008 Henry Paulson, the U.S. Secretary of the Treasury, declared: "Our financial institutions, banks and investment banks, are strong. Our capital markets are resilient. They're efficient. They're flexible."[25] Shortly thereafter, the entire economy was in turmoil. The risk models influencing Paulson's belief did not anticipate the scale of the bubble, similar to the turkey not anticipating the concept of Thanksgiving. The only difference was that instead of being slaughtered, the banks were bailed out by taxpayers. By suggesting a false sense of certainty, models of known risk can promote rather than prevent disaster.

For instance, David Viniar, chief financial officer of Goldman Sachs, reported that their risk models were taken totally by surprise by unexpected "twenty-five-sigma events" several days in a row, resulting in huge losses. How unlikely is a twenty-five-sigma event? According to the risk models used (known as "value at risk"), a three-sigma event is expected to occur on one day every two years, a five-sigma event just once since the last ice age, and a seven-to-eight-sigma event only once since the big bang; a twenty-five-sigma event is beyond anything the models could imagine. Yet this unthinkable event occurred not only once but several times. Was it bad luck or bad risk calculations? Bad luck is unlikely. The problem is improper risk measurement: methods that wrongly assume known risks in a world of uncertainty. Because these calculations generate precise numbers for an uncertain risk, they produce an illusory certainty.[26]

Banks are sometimes criticized for operating like casinos. If only that were true! As Mervyn King, the former governor of the Bank of England, noted, if they did, it would at least be possible to calculate the risk. But investment banks play in the real, ever-changing, and uncertain world. Here, not everyone can be trusted, surprises happen, and trying to calculate precise risks can lead to disaster. In fact, the use of theories of finance designed for a world of known risks is suspected to be one of the causes of financial crises. As Joseph Stiglitz observed regarding the crisis of 2008: "It simply wasn't true that a world with *almost* perfect information was very similar to one in which there was perfect information."[27]

The Quest for Certainty

Absolute certainty is a mental state that precludes doubt of any nature. Much of human history was molded by people who were absolutely certain that their religion, kin, or race was the most valued by God or destiny, which made them believe they were entitled to get rid of conflicting ideas, together with the people that were polluted by them. Most important, the zero-risk illusion does not simply originate in people's minds. It is marketed, carefully tailored to audiences, and heavily advertised. Business bestsellers promise to teach their readers how to suggest absolute certainty to clients, and health brochures forego mentioning known risks to patients.

The quest for certainty is a deep human desire. The dream that all thinking can be reduced to calculation is an old and beautiful one. In the seventeenth century, the philosopher Gottfried Wilhelm Leibniz envisioned establishing numbers or symbols for all ideas, which would enable determining the best answer for every question. That would put an end to all scholarly bickering: If a dispute arose, the contending parties could settle it quickly and peacefully by sitting down and saying, "Let's calculate."[28] The only problem was that the great Leibniz never managed to find this universal calculus—nor has anyone else. What he overlooked was the distinction between risk and uncertainty. Yet, extending into our century, smart scholars have invented many tricks to treat uncertainty as if it were a known risk so that they can apply their standard mathematical models rather than face the real world.

Some advice is considered so obvious that it cannot be but true. More information is always better. More calculation is always better. As we will see, this is a big mistake. In an uncertain world, complex decision making methods involving more information and calculation are often worse and can cause damage by invoking unwarranted certainty.

This message has not yet sunk in. For many experts and the public alike, the popular conviction is that more is always better. Who would reject more information and fancy calculations if they were offered for free? The perception among many is that rules of thumb are "quick and dirty" shortcuts that save time and effort, but at the cost of quality—a claim called the *accuracy-effort tradeoff*. When making decisions, so the argument continues, rules of thumb are always second best. Yet that is only true in a world of known risk, not in an uncertain world. To make good decisions in an uncertain world, one has to ignore part of the information, which is exactly what rules of thumb do. Doing so can save time and effort and lead to better decisions.

Let's sum up:

1. *RISK ≠ UNCERTAINTY.* The best decision under risk is not the best decision under uncertainty.

2. *RULES OF THUMB ARE NOT DUMB.* In an uncertain world, simple rules of thumb can lead to better decisions than fancy calculations.

3. *LESS IS MORE*. Complex problems do not always require complex solutions. Look for simple solutions first.

I will illustrate these insights in the next chapters.

The Uncertain Future Is Hard to Predict

"Predictions are hard, especially about the future."

Niels Bohr (also attributed to Mark Twain, Yogi Berra, and a host of others)

Telephones

In 1876 Western Union, the largest American telegraph company, refused to buy Graham Bell's patent for one hundred thousand dollars, arguing that people are not savvy enough to handle a phone: "Bell expects that the public will use his instrument without the aid of trained operators. Any telegraph engineer will at once see the fallacy of this plan. The public simply cannot be trusted to handle technical communications equipment."[29]

A group of British experts thought somewhat differently: "The telephone may be appropriate for our American cousins, but not here, because we have an adequate supply of messenger boys."

Lightbulbs

A few years later, a committee of the British Parliament evaluated Thomas Edison's lightbulb and concluded that it would be "good enough for our trans-Atlantic friends . . . but unworthy of the attention of practical or scientific men."

Radios

"Radio has no future." Attributed to Lord Kelvin, former president of the Royal Society, ca. 1897.

Trains

"Rail travel at high speed is not possible because passengers, unable to breathe, would die of asphyxia [suffocation]." Dr. Dionysius Lardner (1793–1859), professor at University College London, and author of a book on the steam engine, was one of several doctors who prophesized that the rapid movement of trains would cause death or brain trouble among travelers and vertigo among onlookers.

Cars

Car pioneer Gottlieb Daimler (1834–1900) believed that there would never be more than one million cars worldwide because of the lack of available drivers. Daimler based this prediction on the false assumption that cars would have to be operated by chauffeurs.

Computers

Howard Aiken, who constructed the Mark I computer for IBM in 1943, reminisced: "Originally one thought that if there were a half dozen large computers in this country, hidden away in research laboratories, this would take care of all requirements we had throughout the country." This prediction was based on the false assumption that computers would solve scientific problems only.

3

Defensive Decision Making

Calvin: The more you know, the harder it is to take decisive action.
Hobbes: mmh
Calvin: Once you become informed, you start seeing complexities and shades of gray.
Hobbes: mmh
Calvin: You realize that nothing is as clear and simple as it first appears. Ultimately, knowledge is paralyzing.
Hobbes: mmh
Calvin: Being a man of action, I can't afford to take that risk.
Hobbes: You're ignorant, but at least you act on it.

Risk aversion is closely tied to the anxiety of making errors. If you work in the middle management of a company, your life probably revolves around the fear of doing something wrong and being blamed for it. Such a climate is not a good one for innovation, because originality requires taking risks and making errors along the way. No risks, no errors, no innovation. Risk aversion is already fostered in schools, where children are discouraged from finding solutions to mathematics problems themselves and possibly making errors in the process. Instead, they are told the answer and tested on whether they can memorize and apply the formula. All that counts is learning for the test and making the smallest number of errors. That's not how to nurture great minds.

I use the term "error culture" for a culture in which one can openly admit to errors in order to learn from them and to avoid them in the future. For instance, one of the great assets of American culture is its inclination to engage in trial and error, with little shame in failing. To reassure readers who are embarrassed about making mistakes, here is the story of how even one of the greatest minds could be fooled.

To Err Is Human

Albert Einstein (1879–1955) and Max Wertheimer (1880–1943) were close friends since their days in Berlin, where Einstein was director of the Kaiser Wilhelm Institute for Physics, later renamed the Max Planck Institute for Physics, and Wertheimer one of the founders of Gestalt psychology. Both fled the Nazis in the early 1930s and found themselves in exile in the United States, Einstein in Princeton and Wertheimer in New York. They maintained their friendship by an exchange of letters in which Wertheimer entertained his friend with thought problems.

Wertheimer drew on his expertise in the laws of thinking when he tried to fool Einstein with the following brain teaser:[1]

> *An old clattery auto is to drive a stretch of 2 miles, up and down a hill, /\. Because it is so old, it cannot drive the first mile—the ascent—faster than with an average speed of 15 miles per hour. Question: How fast does it have to drive the second mile—on going down, it can, of course, go faster—in order to obtain an average speed (for the whole distance) of 30 miles an hour?*

Wertheimer's teaser suggests that the answer might be forty-five or sixty miles an hour. But there is no such answer. Even if the old car were able to zoom down the hill as fast as a rocket, it would not achieve an average speed of thirty miles an hour. If you don't figure it out immediately, don't worry; Einstein didn't either. He confessed to having fallen for this problem to his friend: "*Not until calculating* did I notice that there is no time left for the way down!"[2]

Gestalt psychologists' way to solve problems is to reformulate the question until the answer becomes clear. Here's how it works. How long does

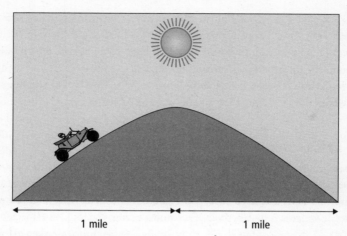

Figure 3-1. Einstein fell for this teaser.

it take the old car to reach the top of the hill? The road up is one mile long. The car travels fifteen miles per hour, so it takes four minutes (one hour divided by fifteen) to reach the top. How long does it take the car to drive up and down the hill, with an average speed of thirty miles per hour? The road up and down is two miles long. Thirty miles per hour translates into two miles per four minutes. Thus, the car needs four minutes to drive the entire distance. But these four minutes were already used up by the time the car reached the top.

There is no disgrace in making an error; nobody is perfect.

A System That Makes No Errors Is Not Intelligent

Gestalt psychologists and their followers use visual illusions to demonstrate how our perception works, including the smart rules of thumb it relies on. When we look around us, we think we perceive the world outside. But we don't. Our brains are not mirrors. They have insufficient information to mirror the world. For instance, the world is three-dimensional, but its image on the retina is only two-dimensional. As a result, we cannot see distance directly but have to make smart guesses based on uncertain cues such as lighting, shading, and perspective. The great physiologist Hermann von Helmholtz called these guesses "unconscious inferences." Without these intelligent guesses we would do badly. Intelligence means going beyond the information given and taking risks.

Look at the checkerboard at the left side of Figure 3-2. The squares you see are black and white. The square marked A, for instance, is black and the square marked B is white. Yet squares A and B are actually the same shade of gray. It's hard to believe, because our eyes see them as two different colors. For a proof, look at the checkerboard on the right side, where the two squares are connected by two vertical stripes of the same shade of gray. These make it clear that both squares are the same color. Another way to prove it is to take a piece of paper and cut two holes into it so you can see only squares A and B. Even if we know better, the illusion remains.

What an impossibly stubborn error! But think for a moment. If our brain did not create this "error," we would see many different shades of gray, not a checkerboard with its black and white squares. But instead of simply measuring the light reflected from each square independently of all the rest, the brain uses context information to infer what is being seen. A cast

Figure 3-2. Checkerboard illusion. Left: Square A looks black, square B white. Right: The connecting vertical stripes reveal that squares A and B are actually the same color. Our brain does not simply measure the light reflected from each square, but uses the neighboring squares to make intelligent inferences. Otherwise we would not see a checkerboard, but only many squares in different colors. Visual illusions are not blunders, but the byproducts of an intelligent system. Reproduced by permission from Edward H. Adelson.

shadow from the object on the right side of the board dims the surface, so that a white square in the shadow can reflect even less light than a black one in full light.

The checkerboard illusion illustrates that intelligence is not the ability to reproduce accurately every degree of light reflected from every square or every piece of information in general. It is the art of making informed guesses. Visual illusions help us to understand how our brains work:

- Our brains have insufficient information about the world.
- Intelligence means going beyond the information given and making informed bets on what's outside.
- By making bets, every intelligent system makes "good" errors.

You may have come across one of the popular books on cognition that feature lists of errors people commit against reason. Typically they draw a direct analogy between visual and cognitive illusions. The argument is that if our perceptual system already commits systematic errors, what can we expect from our reasoning and thinking? Like visual illusions, so their argument goes, cognitive illusions are difficult to overcome. That is why education of the public is doomed to fail and paternalistic strategies to maneuver people into doing the "right" things are the only viable alternative. This argument misses the essence of human intelligence.

The visual system is not good at being a physical light meter, nor should it be. That's not its purpose. It has to go beyond the information given and make bets about what's out there.

Making such "errors" is not a flaw; without them we wouldn't recognize the objects around us. If a system does not make errors, it is not intelligent. Visual illusions in fact demonstrate the success rather than the failure of cognition.

Good Errors

As we have seen, experiencing a visual illusion means making a good error. Good errors are errors that need to be made. Children are known for these. Consider a three-year-old who uses the phrase "I gived" instead of "I gave."

The child cannot know in advance which verbs are regular and which are irregular. Because irregular verbs are rare, the child's best bet is to assume the regular form until proven wrong. Such errors are good, or functional, because if the child decided to play it safe and use only those verbs he has already heard, he would learn at a much slower pace. Learn by failing, or you fail to learn.

Serendipity, the discovery of something one did not intend to discover, is often a product of error. Christopher Columbus wanted to find a sea route to India. He believed he could reach India by ship because he made an error: He grossly underestimated the diameter of the globe. Others knew better and criticized his plan as foolish. They were right. But because of his error, Columbus discovered something else, America. Similarly, some of my own discoveries were never planned, such as the discovery of the "less-is-more effect." Here is the story.

For an experiment, we needed a set of easy questions and a set of hard ones. Because those who took part in the experiment were German, we came up with questions about the population of German cities (which we assumed would be easy) and U.S. cities (hard). We chose the seventy-five largest cities in each country. For instance,

"Which city has a larger population: Detroit or Milwaukee?"
"Which city has a larger population: Bielefeld or Hanover?"

The result blew our minds. Germans didn't do best on questions about German cities, about which they knew lots, but slightly better on American cities, about which they knew little. We'd made an error in assuming that knowing more always leads to better inferences. The experiment was ruined. But this error led us to discover something new, which we called the *recognition heuristic*:[3]

> *If you recognize the name of one city but not that of the other, then infer that the recognized city has the larger population.*

Many Germans had never heard of Milwaukee, and so they correctly concluded that Detroit has the larger population. Because they were familiar with both Bielefeld and Hanover, however, the rule of thumb didn't work for this question. An American who has never heard of Bielefeld will correctly infer that Hanover has more inhabitants, but Germans have a hard time. Similarly, in another study, only 60 percent of Americans correctly answered that Detroit is larger than Milwaukee, while some 90 percent of Germans got it right. The recognition heuristic takes advantage of the wisdom in semi-ignorance. This simple rule doesn't work all the time, only when bigger objects are indeed more widely recognized.

Good errors help us to learn and to discover. A system that makes no errors will learn little and discover even less.

Bad Errors

Educators often think of building young minds that ideally make no errors. This view is an example of a bad error. Intelligence, creativity, and innovation will cease if people are prohibited from making errors. That does not mean that every error is good. The spread of AIDS in Africa was dramatically underestimated by the World Health Organization (WHO), whose computer models assumed that the probability of infection increased with the number of sexual contacts, independent of the number of sexual partners. But ten contacts with one partner lead to a much lower chance of infection than one contact with ten different partners.[4] Steady sources of bad errors are the zero-risk illusion and the turkey illusion. For instance, banks continue to use models such as value-at-risk that assume that all risks are known and can be estimated precisely, even though this illusion of certainty contributed to the financial crisis.

Blunders like these are not only embarrassing in hindsight but can be disastrous. Bad errors are errors that are not functional and should be avoided in the best of everyone's interest.

Positive and Negative Error Cultures

Professions, companies, and groups of individuals have error cultures. On the one end of the spectrum are negative error cultures. People living in such a culture fear to make errors of any kind, good or bad, and, if an error does occur, they do everything to hide it. Such a culture has little chance to learn from errors and discover new opportunities. On the other end of the spectrum are positive error cultures that make errors transparent, encourage good errors, and learn from bad errors to create a safer environment.

Let us compare two professions with opposing error cultures: commercial aviation and medicine. The error culture of Lufthansa's and other international air companies' pilots tends to be a positive one and the reason why flying has become so safe. Rather than providing illusions of certainty, Lufthansa is explicit about how often they risk a plane crash: one in ten million flights. To achieve this extremely low rate of crashes, there are clear-cut safety rules. For instance, the amount of fuel each plane carries is determined by this rule:

The minimum fuel to be carried for each flight consists of:

1. trip fuel to reach the destination,
2. contingency fuel (5 percent of trip fuel) to make up for possible incorrect calculation of trip fuel due to wind prediction errors and the like,
3. alternate fuel to make a go-around at destination and fly to an alternate airport,
4. final reserve for 30 minutes holding above the alternate airport, and
5. extra fuel, decided by the crew, to cope with special factors such as extreme weather.

This safety margin of fuel costs Lufthansa money, because carrying extra weight costs more fuel. On a long haul flight, about 30 percent of the fuel is spent on transporting fuel.

Safety measures are one aspect of an error culture, reporting of actual errors another. Serious errors are reported by those who made them and documented by a special group that talks with the pilots and disseminates the information to the entire community. That enables pilots to learn from the errors of others. Although safety is already extremely high, efforts are made to further reduce the number of accidents, as in the U.S. aviation program System Think, where all participants—pilots, mechanics, air traffic controllers, manufacturers, airlines, and regulators—get together to discuss errors and learn how to make flying even more safe.

Nothing remotely like this exists in hospitals. The error culture in medicine is largely negative; systems of critical incidence reporting are rare. With the threat of litigation looming, hospitals are dominated by defensive medicine, where doctors view patients as potential plaintiffs and where errors are consequently often hidden. National systems of reporting and learning from serious errors, as in aviation, rarely exist. As a result, patient safety in hospitals—unlike passenger safety in planes—is a major problem. The Institute of Medicine estimated that some 44,000 to 98,000 patients are killed every year in U.S. hospitals by preventable medical errors.[5] Note that these are only the documented cases. Let's give the statistics a few faces. Eight-year old Ben Kolb died during minor surgery due to a drug mix-up. Nineteen-year-old Jasmine Grant went into labor with her first child and was mistakenly injected with an epidural anesthetic. Twenty minutes later she went into seizure and could not be revived. *Boston Globe* health reporter Betsy Lehman died from an overdose during chemotherapy. Willie King, a diabetic, had the wrong leg amputated.[6] These errors are common, even at the best U.S. hospitals, and their numbers have been increasing over the years. The WHO reported that nearly one in ten patients is harmed while receiving care in technologically advanced hospitals.[7] Little is known about medical errors in nonhospital settings, where the majority of care is delivered. A negative error culture leads to more errors and less safety, and little interest in effective safety measures. To quote the head of risk management of an international airline: "If we had the safety culture of a hospital, we would crash two planes a day."

Why Do Pilots Use Checklists But Most Doctors Don't?

In the early days of aviation, a pilot could fly a plane without much technology. Checklists were introduced by the U.S. Air Force only after the B-17 bomber proved to be too much of an airplane for any one person to fly. When in 2009 both engines failed after US Airways Flight 1549 took off from LaGuardia, as described above, the pilots went through the engine failure checklist, including restart attempts, while the flight attendants followed through on their protocols and ensured that the passengers adopted a bracing position. Checklists provide a simple, inexpensive tool for improving safety.

In medicine it's a different story. Each year, central venous catheters cause an estimated eighty thousand bloodstream infections and, as a result, up to 28,000 deaths in intensive care units in U.S. hospitals. Patients who survive a line infection spend on average a week longer in intensive care. The total costs of these infections are estimated at $2.3 billion annually. What can be done to save some of these lives? Better drugs to treat infections, better technology? The answer is a better error culture.

In 2001 Peter Pronovost, a critical-care specialist at Johns Hopkins Hospital, developed a simple checklist for ICU doctors to test whether it could reduce line infections.[8] The five steps prevent the introduction of bacteria. Here is the list.

Doctors are supposed to:

1. wash their hands with soap,
2. clean the patient's skin with chlorhexidine antiseptic,
3. put sterile sheets over the entire patient,
4. wear a sterile mask, hat, gown, and gloves, and
5. put a sterile dressing over the catheter site once the line is in.

Every measure on the list was familiar; nothing was new. Pronovost asked the nurses in his ICU to observe whether doctors followed the five steps. The nurses reported that for more than one third of all patients, one or more of the steps were skipped. The line infection rate was 11 percent in the hospital.

Next, he persuaded the hospital administration to authorize nurses to stop doctors if they skipped a step. That revolutionary move upset the hierarchical structure, where typically female nurses are not meant to tell typically male surgeons what to do. After a year of using the checklist, the hospital's line infection rate dropped from 11 percent of patients to zero (!). During the next fifteen months, only two line infections occurred. In this hospital alone, the checklist had prevented forty-three infections and eight deaths—and saved $2 million.

To show that the effect of the checklist was not restricted to his hospital, Pronovost got more than a hundred ICUs in Michigan to cooperate in a large study. Importantly, each ICU was encouraged to develop its own checklist to fit their unique barriers and culture. The participating ICUs had reported a total of 695 catheter-related bloodstream infections annually before the study. Only three months after the introduction of the checklists, most ICUs cut the infection rate to zero. The remaining ICUs were able to cut the rate substantially for the entire eighteen months that the study lasted.[9] This huge life-saving program was implemented without expensive technology and with no extra staff.

Checklists save lives without extra technology and little costs. One might think that by now, many years later, every hospital would use checklists to improve patient safety. But no. Enthusiasm is limited, and checklists remain the exception rather than the rule. Pronovost was asked when checklists would be in the hands of the average doctor or nurse. His resigned response was: "At the current rate, it will never happen." If a new drug were discovered that had a similarly huge effect on reducing infection, it would be trumpeted around the globe and every ICU would have large stacks of the drug, no matter what the cost. In fact, when central-line catheters coated with silver were marketed, hospitals were willing to spend tens of millions on them, even though they reduced infections only marginally.[10]

At some point most of us will find ourselves weak and helpless inside the glassed bay of an ICU. Some of us will get a line infection, and the unlucky ones will die from it. These lives could be saved, but they are not. Patient safety does not appear to be a primary concern for many hospitals. There is something that many patients can do to change this, however:

Ask whether checklists are used; if the answer is no or not forthcoming, choose a different hospital.

Why are checklists used in every cockpit but not in every ICU? Both are largely commercial enterprises, so why is it so much safer in a plane than in a hospital? The answer can be found in their different error cultures. First, the hierarchical structure in hospitals is not fertile ground for checklists, which, as mentioned, might require a female nurse to remind a male surgeon to wash his hands. Second, the consequences affect both parties equally in aviation: If passengers die in a crash, pilots die as well, whereas if patients die, doctors' lives are not endangered. Third, when a plane crashes, there is little point in trying to hide it. The event is reported on the front pages and fewer people will book the airline; when patients die from preventable errors, it is occasionally reported, but rarely finds its way into the headlines and into public consciousness.

What many hospitals don't consider is that a positive error culture could increase the trust of patients, as the following case shows. Matthias Rothmund, a professor of surgery, once made a big error.[11] When one of his patients was checked a few days after a successful tumor operation, the X-ray showed a surgical clamp that had been mistakenly left inside the patient's body. Rothmund immediately informed the patient, removed the clamp, and reported the incident to his insurance, which gave the patient a settlement. For a long time the surgeon was plagued with the thought of his error. Five years later the patient returned to his office with a hernia and said he wanted him to perform the operation. Rothmund was surprised. The patient explained that he trusted Rothmund and his clinic precisely because Rothmund had immediately admitted his error and corrected it.

When Rothmund became president of the German Association of Surgeons, he opened a congress by reporting that 44,000 to 98,000 patients are killed by preventable errors every year in the United States—the figure mentioned on page 51. The news exploded like a bomb. Immediately he was attacked by his peer surgeons for making facts about patient safety public, and, rather than praising him for his openness, the press bashed the entire medical profession for their shoddy work. Zero tolerance for talking about errors produces more errors and less patient safety. At the time when Rothmund forgot the clamp, nobody counted the instruments after an operation. After this accident, he introduced an error culture to his clinic: counting instruments, reporting errors, and openly discussing their causes in order to avoid them in the future.

Defensive Decision Making

Many a committee meeting ends with "We need more data." Everybody nods, breathing a sigh of relief, happy that the decision has been deferred. A week or so later, when the data are in, the group is no further ahead. Everyone's time is wasted on another meeting, on waiting for even more data. The culprit is a negative error culture, in which everyone lacks the courage to make a decision for which they may be punished. Not making a decision or procrastinating in order to avoid responsibility is the most blatant form of defensive decision making. If something goes wrong, somebody else made the decision. But there are more subtle and intelligent ways of avoiding responsibility. Fear of litigation and accountability has developed defensive decision making into an art. It's the modern art of self-defense at the cost of the company, the taxpayer, or the patient.

Hire the Second Best

A friend of mine worked for an international charitable corporation that does much good. Doctors and nurse volunteers provide urgent medical care all over the world to victims of disaster and war. To respond at a moment's notice to urgent emergencies, the organization must assess a crisis quickly and make decisions on people's needs, independent of political interests. Like many charity organizations that are financially independent, the organization lives from donations. To reassure donors who want to be sure that their money is spent as intended and not wasted, the organization hires accounting firms to check and certify its work.

What accounting firm to choose? In one instance, the choice was between a small local firm that asked a reasonable price and was most knowledgeable and a large international firm that charged more money and had less knowledge but a big name. The local firm would send experienced specialists while the large firm would send young fellows who knew comparatively little. The best decision seems obvious: Hire the local company and you get the better expertise for the better price. Yet that did not happen. The organization chose the second-best option, the big name. Why? A nonprofit organization is accountable to its donors. Imagine something going wrong, as it is always bound to do. If donors learned that a firm they'd never heard of had checked the books, alarm bells would go off. But if they had heard of the accounting firm, fewer questions would be asked. This story illustrates a perplexing process:

> *Defensive decision making: A person or group ranks option A as the best for the situation, but chooses an inferior option B to protect itself in case something goes wrong.*

Choosing a second-best option is not stupidity or bad intention. Defensive decisions are imposed by the psychology of the system. In the present case, the psychology was based on a rule of thumb we encountered in the previous chapter:

> *Recognition heuristic: If you recognize the name of one company but not that of the other, then infer that the recognized company provides the better value.*

This simple rule is often a good guide.[12] But it can lead to the dominance of a few firms that grow bigger and bigger and can no longer deliver the best quality. Defensive decision making draws on brand name recognition, but also on anything else that protects the decision maker. The result is a paradoxical social game: The organization protects itself against its donors, wasting part of the donations on inferior services for fear that the donors might cause trouble.

Nonprofit organizations are not the only ones to make self-defensive decisions. Recall the volcanic ash cloud emerging from Iceland in 2010, when it was uncertain whether flying was dangerous. To play it safe, politicians decided that commercial planes could not fly for weeks, knowing that if a plane crashed when flying through the ash cloud, they would be held responsible. When people are killed because they have to take their car instead, the question of blame doesn't even come up.

Someone Must Be at Fault

Peter, a student of mine, once went whale watching on Cape Cod. It was a rough stormy day, and heavy waves hit the boat. When another wave came in, Peter slipped on the wet surface, fell, and hurt himself. Another passenger kindly helped him up. He introduced himself as a lawyer.

> *"Have you been hurt?"*
>
> *"Oh, my ankle hurts. But it will be ok. Thank you," Peter responded gratefully.*
>
> *"Let's sue the owner of the ship. If we lose, you won't have to pay a thing. If we win, we'll split the compensation."*
>
> *Peter was perplexed.*
>
> *"You can't lose on that deal," the lawyer stated, appealing to Peter's common sense.*
>
> *"But it was my fault," Peter stuttered.*
>
> *"Why don't you let a judge find out?" the lawyer continued with impeccable logic.*
>
> *"It really was my fault, not any one else's."*
>
> *Eventually, Peter declined the safe deal. He felt it just wasn't right.*

Not everyone would decline this opportunity. Whale-watching cruises are not the only location where tort lawyers crane their necks and sniff the wind for customers. Well-dressed hunters stroll through hospitals, race after emergency ambulances, and rent billboards for thousands of dollars a month to advertise their services. One might think that such in-depth malpractice surveillance can only be to the benefit of the public, but that's a delusion. It has its price, and a heavy one. In the case of health care, it fundamentally undermines the relationship between doctor and patient, as we shall see below.

Defensive Medicine

If you think your doctor recommends the best care for you, you may be right—and lucky. But a substantial number of doctors feel they have no choice but to order unnecessary tests, drugs, or surgery, even at the risk of hurting the patient. They fear that otherwise, their patients might sue if a disease is overlooked or nothing aggressive is done. They certainly wouldn't recommend those treatments to their spouses and children, who are less of a legal threat. In Switzerland, the rate of hysterectomy in the general population is 16 percent, whereas among doctors' wives and female doctors it is only 10 percent.[13] In the United States, where fear of litigation is higher, about one out of every three American women undergoes a hysterectomy, with numbers varying widely from region to region. The majority of approximately six hundred thousand hysterectomies performed every year in the United States are not clinically indicated. In half of the cases, women have their ovaries removed simultaneously, which is the equivalent of male castration, despite the growing evidence of severe debilitating consequences, including premature death. In total, an estimated 2.5 million unnecessary surgeries are performed on Americans every year.[14] No other country invades the bodies of its citizens so frequently.

There are far too many lawyers in the United States, more per capita than in any other country except Israel, and the number of law students is increasing steadily. But even in countries with less lust for litigation, such as Switzerland, defensive medicine is on the rise. Although only about half of 250 Swiss internists thought that the advantages of PSA screening outweigh its harms in men older than fifty years of age, 75 percent recommended regular PSA screening to these men. Why did they nevertheless recommend it? Many physicians said that they did so for legal reasons—to protect themselves against potential lawsuits, even though there is little danger of litigation in Switzerland.[15]

Now we can define the practice:

Defensive medicine: A doctor orders tests or treatments that are not clinically indicated and might even harm the patient primarily because of fear of litigation.

Many doctors are afraid of lawyers, and some are angry. That's why they like lawyer jokes. Here is a joke that one surgeon told me with a malicious grin:

Question: What do you have if two lawyers are buried up to their necks in sand?

Answer: Not enough sand.

Ninety-three Percent of Doctors Practice Defensive Medicine

In Pennsylvania 824 emergency doctors, radiologists, obstetricians/gynecologists, general surgeons, orthopedic surgeons, and neurosurgeons were asked whether they practice defensive medicine.[16] All six specialties are at high risk of litigation. Ninety-three percent (!) of the doctors reported that they sometimes or often engage in defensive medicine. Since not all will admit to it, even to themselves, this figure may be lower than the actual numbers. What exactly do doctors do to protect themselves against the patient?

Here are the four favorite measures and the number of doctors who resort to them:

Kind of defensive medicine:	Number of doctors (percent):
Order more tests (like imaging) than medically indicated	405 (59)
Prescribe more medication (including antibiotics) than medically indicated	223 (33)
Refer patients to other specialists in unnecessary circumstances	349 (52)
Suggest invasive procedures (like biopsies) to confirm diagnoses	221 (32)

The most frequent unnecessary tests were computed tomographies (CTs), magnetic resonance imaging (MRIs), and X-rays. Almost two thirds of emergency physicians reported doing this, as did half of general surgeons, orthopedic surgeons, and neurosurgeons, and a third of radiologists.

Note that unlike an MRI, an unnecessary CT scan is not simply a waste of money. Radiation doses from CT scans are typically about a hundred times those of a chest X-ray or mammogram, or more.[17] How much is that? Depending on the machine settings and the organ studied, the effective radiation dose for a single CT scan is in the range of 15 millisieverts (mSv) for an adult to 30 mSv for a newborn. The radiation exposure from one CT study involving several scans is about the same as for the average atomic bomb survivor from Hiroshima and Nagasaki who was located one or two miles from ground zero (which was around 40 mSv; range: 5–100 mSv).[18] As a consequence, an estimated 29,000 cancers result from the more than seventy million CT scans performed annually in the United States on children and adults.[19] Kids are more vulnerable to radiation's effects than adults. Their brain tissue grows, their cells divide quickly, and their DNA is more easily damaged. Every year, an estimated *one million U.S. children* have unnecessary CT scans.[20]

In addition, more than a third of doctors reported that they avoid high-risk surgery, delivering infants, and caring for high-risk patients. Avoiding care is called negative defensive medicine, as opposed to positive defensive medicine in the form of excessive care. In each case, good care is thwarted by doctors' collective anxiety.

What to Do?

We live in a health system where doctors do not have the same goals as patients. The doctors are not entirely to blame; after all, the patients are the ones who do the suing and thereby contribute to the relentlessly negative error culture in medicine. Instead of complaining, we need to take more responsibility for our own health and that of our children.

Sign

When my daughter was six we lived in Hyde Park, Chicago. One day, the two of us went for her first visit to the dentist. Let's call him Dr. Push. My daughter had no pain; the only purpose was to get her acquainted with having her teeth checked. In such a situation, the FDA recommends a thorough clinical examination and warns against X-rays: "Radiographic screening for the purpose of detecting disease before clinical examination should not be performed."[21] When I entered the dentist's office I found a small factory: one seat next to another, with Dr. Push scurrying around. When my daughter was finally seated in a chair that was much too high for her, a friendly nurse turned to her:

"We're gonna make a nice X-ray picture of your teeth."

"Sorry, that's a misunderstanding," I intervened. "She has no pains, no symptoms. It's just to get a first examination."

"We do X-rays all the time. Everyone gets an X-ray, so that the doctor can see what's inside." She told me this with a smile but in a firm tone.

"Look, she has no pains, no symptoms. There is no reason for an X-ray."

Her smile froze. War clouds were gathering. "She has to have an X-ray. If you think that's not a good idea, you'll have to explain it to the doctor."

"I would be happy to do so," I responded.

At this she turned around and briskly walked away. After a while, she returned with Dr. Push.

"There's no reason to be afraid," he assured me politely, "it's just an X-ray. I need it so that I can see whether something is wrong with your daughter's teeth."

"True. But she has no pain. I just want you to do a clinical exam. It's not in the interest of a little girl to get X-rays every time she visits a doctor."

"Think for a moment," he said. "If there is something inside her teeth, I can't see it with my bare eyes. I could overlook something. You don't want that, do you?"

I felt the pressure mounting. So I asked him: "Could you please tell me what's known about the potential harms of dental X-rays for children? For instance, thyroid and brain cancer?"

He stared at me blankly.

"Or give me a reference so that I can check the evidence?" I asked.

Dr. Push didn't respond to this either. "You will have to take the responsibility," he threatened, not knowing the evidence.

"I'll take it."

He walked me to his office and handed over a sheet of paper. "Sign here."

Dr. Push grew visibly angry after I asked for evidence he should know but didn't. And I was furious with a man who x-rays children across the board, whether they have dental problems or not, without considering the harms. Yet I shouldn't have been. What really happened was that Dr. Push made me sign in order to protect himself against me. Parents' litigation culture forces him to do so.

Ask Your Doctors What They Would Do, Not What They Recommend

Patients can contribute their own share to better health care by asking for evidence. Patients can also contribute by refusing frivolous lawsuits, like Peter did. And there is a rule of thumb that I personally have found useful.

Around the age of eighty, my mother began to lose her sight in her right eye. A treatment called photodynamic therapy was promoted as a way to stop further progression. I read the few available studies and found the evidence fairly ambiguous: It might help or hurt.

What to do? I located a medical expert who had performed a large number of photodynamic therapies and explained my mother's condition to him.

"What do you recommend?" I asked.

"If you ask me, I think your mother should try the treatment," he explained.

At this moment I realized I had asked the wrong question.

"I have only one mother," I said. "If it were your mother, what would you do?"

"Oh, I wouldn't do it, no, I would tell her to wait," he responded in a flash.

I told my mother, and she declined the treatment. Why would a doctor give one answer when I asked what he recommended, and another answer when I asked what he would do if it were his mother? The doctor knew that his mother wouldn't sue, but I might. Asking about his own mother shifted his perspective. Here is a rule of thumb that is often helpful:

> *Don't ask your doctors what they recommend to you, ask them what they would do if it were their mother, brother, or child.*

But there is a second part to my mother's story that has nothing to do with defensive medicine but with doctors' lack of understanding medical evidence. A few years later she began to lose her sight in her other eye, for the same reason. This time she felt she should take her last chance, and I did not argue with her. After identifying an expert on photodynamic therapy in my mother's hometown, I made the first contact. Here is our phone conversation:

> *"You need to understand that the treatment does not lead to a cure, all it can do is stop further progression of blindness. And you need to understand that the success is not sure, but the probability is 50 percent that the progression will be stopped," the expert said.*
>
> *"We'll take the chance," I confirmed.*
>
> *"I may have to repeat the treatment four to five times, if it doesn't work the first time."*
>
> *"Oh," I said, "did the 50 percent refer to the first treatment or to the entire sequence of four or five?"*
>
> *"To the first, and the same holds again for the second. Again 50 percent."*
>
> *"But that's good news because it means that after five trials, it's almost a sure thing—eventually in more than 90 percent of the patients the progression will be stopped because . . ."*
>
> *"No, no," the expert interrupted me, "after all trials, we still have a probability of 50 percent."*
>
> *"But then the second and subsequent treatments would add nothing, isn't that so?"*
>
> *There was a long pause on the other end of the line. I could almost hear the specialist thinking.*

"Umm . . ." The specialist now saw the problem. "I need to go back and read the journal article."

I too did some research. The specialist had described to me a single-event probability: the 50 percent chance that the progression will be stopped. As we have seen in chapter 1, these are often confusing because the reference class is not specified. It could be all patients who undergo the treatment once, or those who undergo it several times. In this case, the 50 percent applied to patients undergoing it several times. Next, a 50 percent chance of halting the progression of blindness is not informative in itself. It needs to be compared to the chance that the progression stops if nothing is done. The article reported that in 38 percent of patients the process also stops without the treatment.[22] That means that not 50 percent but only 12 percent of patients had a benefit. Then I learned that stopping progression does not mean that it really stops, but is defined as a loss of not more than three lines of visual acuity. Some of these patients who "benefited" according to the study had actually incurred further loss of vision. And then there were possible harms: Some of the patients reported abnormal vision and loss of vision after treatment. Last but not least, in the conflicts of interest section, I found out that the study was financed by the same company that produced the expensive drug used in the treatment and that many of the authors were company employees or paid consultants.

The second part of the story illustrates what a patient should always ask:

- What is the benefit of the treatment?
    - –50 percent of what? (of those who get treated once? or five times?)
    - –How large was the "success" among those who were not treated?
    - –What precisely do you mean when you say "success"?
- What are the harms of the treatment?
- Who financed the study?

I decided not to tell my mother about the specialist's confusion. The end of the story was that I accompanied her to the treatment session, where the specialist was extremely polite to me, and at pains to point out that he'd read the article. My mother hoped so much that it would work. She was unlucky. Very soon after the treatment she went blind. In his records, the specialist listed my mother as a successful treatment.

Procedure over Performance

Fear of blame, criticism, and litigation is the motivation for hiring the second best, making second-best management decisions, and practicing defensive medicine. To avoid blame, people hide behind "safe" procedures. Rely on big names, do what everyone else does, and don't listen to your intuition. Put your faith in tests and fancy technology, even if these are useless or harmful. Among doctors there is a saying: "No one is ever sued for overtreatment." Who wants to risk being sued by patients by standing up for their best interests? Last but not least, financial incentives are aligned with defensive medicine: Health insurers pay doctors and clinics a fortune for overtreatment, but only pennies for taking the time to explain to patients what the treatment alternatives are and their actual benefits and harms.

The emotional fabric of defensive decisions differs from that of risk aversion. It can lead to excessive risk taking. If your intuition says that an investment is overvalued but you join because everyone else invests in it, you may take undue risks. Part of the crowd behavior of financial investors that led to excessive risk taking in the recent financial crisis is a case in point. The problem is not simply risk aversion, but lack of a positive error culture. People need to be encouraged to talk about errors and take the responsibility in order to learn and achieve better overall performance.

Some time ago an experienced headhunter visited me. Using his profound knowledge of the world of business, he had put about a thousand senior managers and CEOs into their positions. Nearly all the time, his selection was based on a gut decision. His world is changing. More and more, experience is replaced by psychometric tests administered by young psychologists who have never seen a company from the inside. I asked him why this change is happening. He said that those who make the hiring decisions fear they will be accountable. If a hire doesn't turn out well and they have to admit that they trusted the intuition of a headhunter, that might count against them. But if they can point to having done psychometric tests that did not detect any problem, then they are on the safe side. Procedure protects. Defensive hiring, like defensive medicine, puts procedure over performance.

4

Why Do We Fear What's Unlikely to Kill Us?

Nothing in life is to be feared. It is only to be understood. Now is the time to understand more, so that we may fear less.

Marie Curie

Only a fool learns from his own mistakes. The wise man learns from the mistakes of others.

Attributed to Otto von Bismarck

Why would we fear being eaten by a shark, but not even think about dying in a car crash on the way to the beach? About ten people worldwide lose their lives every year from shark attacks, while thousands die on the road. Studies document that many people fear what likely never will hurt or kill them, while joyfully engaging in dangerous behavior. Wouldn't we be better off basing our behavior on experience, without passion and temper? But think for a moment. Learning firsthand by trial and error what is harmful and what is not would be truly dangerous. My hypothesis is: In situations where errors have been deadly in human history, we have developed a tendency to avoid learning from experience. Instead, we rely on social learning of what to fear.

Fear is one of the basic emotional circuits in our brain, organized around the amygdala. The amygdala sends more information to the cortex than it receives. This may be why fear influences our thinking more easily than conscious thought can control fear. In dangerous situations, our brain is therefore built to rely more on evolutionary wisdom than on our thinking.[1] This subcortical location shared among mammals suggests that fear has an ancient evolutionary origin. Its function is to make us freeze, flee, or fight in situations of danger. With the exception of intrepid literary characters like Siegfried or Sherlock Holmes, we all experience it. Fear is a protective system that helps us to avoid dangers rather than face them head-on. If an early Homo sapiens, facing a lion, had first tried to calculate the trajectory of its jump in order to decide what to do, he would have been an easy meal (Figure 4-1). Similarly, if trial-and-error learning from personal experience was the only learning mechanism available, animals and humans would long be removed from the gene pool before figuring out what

$$z(x) = x\left(\tan\alpha_0 + \frac{mg}{\beta v_0 \cos\alpha_0} \right) + \frac{m^2 g}{\beta^2} \ln\left(1 - \frac{\beta}{m}\frac{x}{v_0 \cos\alpha_0} \right)$$

Figure 4-1. Fear keeps us from thinking too long in dangerous situations.

predators and situations to avoid. But the objects of fear are not entirely written into our genes; otherwise we could never learn to avoid dangerous new technologies. If neither nurture nor nature, what then?

In this chapter I will describe two ingenious ways we learn to fear things without necessarily experiencing them firsthand: social imitation and biological preparedness. And I will also explain how external control can cause fear to cripple people's ability to deal with uncertainty. Understanding how our unconscious psychology functions can help us take a step toward discarding unnecessary fears as well as fearing the right things.

Social Imitation

Many Europeans are blasé about gathering mushrooms in the forest for dinner; Americans shake their heads at such recklessness. There are more privately owned rifles and handguns in the United States than there are citizens; Europeans would dread the thought that their next-door neighbor might grab a gun when drunk and go looking for trouble. Why do people fear different things? Remarkably, underneath these cultural differences lies a common psychology, one not based on direct personal experience. It certainly wouldn't be advisable to try out every single mushroom, snake, or spider to see which are poisonous. Our psychology protects us from making these deadly errors in uncertain worlds. As the proverb says, only a fool learns from his own mistakes; a wise man learns from the mistakes of others. Underlying this wisdom is an unconscious principle, the *social imitation of fear*:

Fear whatever your social group fears.

This simple principle protects us when personal experience might be lethal. At the same time, it can also make us fear the wrong things. Fearing the wrong things, however, is often less dangerous than making the other error—missing a deadly danger. It's better to experience two false alarms than be killed once.

The strange fears other cultures exhibit are the life-blood of anecdotes told by travelers around the world. But cultures are no longer the isolated units they were before the age of mobility. Thus, differences are never absolute, only average tendencies, and there can be huge differences within a single culture. The stories that follow need to be seen with this caveat.

Christmas Candles

If you've ever spent Christmas Eve in a German town, you likely had a chance to savor the scent of burning candles on a Christmas tree and see their warm light reflected in the shining eyes of joyful children. After all, legend has it that Martin Luther, inspired by a starry Christmas Eve sky, was the first to adorn a tree with candlelight. Germans can hardly imagine anything more traditional and peaceful than wax candles illuminating the branches of their fir trees.

North Americans, in contrast, can go into hysterics at the same sight, with panic-filled visions of the tree—and the rest of the house—bursting into flames. I remember a father in Chicago telling me how dangerous wax candles are and how irresponsibly European parents behave at Christmas. Later on he proudly showed me his Christmas present for his sixteen-year-old son. Under the electrically lit tree he had placed a brand-new 7 mm Winchester Model 70 Coyote Light rifle.

Cultural differences are not entirely without cause. Houses in Germany are almost always built from stone, while houses in the United States are often built from wood, where fire can and has caused more damage. The real damage from Christmas tree lighting, however, is relatively light. About ten Germans die every year around Christmas Day from fire due to inattention when using candles, and a similar number of Americans die from injuries related to electric Christmas lights. These include children swallowing bulbs and adults getting electric shocks and burns from faulty lights.[2] What both cultures share is the conviction that their own tradition is the right thing to do.

Buried Alive

Imagine you lived in the nineteenth century. You were not exactly rich but nor were you poor, so you didn't have to worry about food, clothing, or shelter. What would your greatest nightmare most likely have been? Being buried alive—the same tragedy your friends feared. In those days, this fear was not unfounded. Featured in Edgar Allan Poe's horror story *The Premature Burial*, live burials were not just the product of a fertile literary imagination but actually happened. Before the advent of the electrocardiograph and electroencephalograph, people paralyzed or in a trance were often mistaken for dead.

In the seventeenth century Françoise d'Aubigné, a three-year-old French girl, was pronounced dead at sea and sewn into a sack to be thrown overboard. A sudden meow revealed that her pet cat had crawled into the bag. When the cat was recovered from the sack, the girl was found to be very much alive. She later became the second wife of King Louis XIV and died at age eighty-three.[3] A century later at the public cemetery of Orléans, a servant opened the coffin of a woman to steal her ring. He could not slip it off her finger so decided to cut off the entire finger, the pain of which revived the woman. She scared away the thief, returned home, and eventually outlived her husband.

In fact, until the early 1900s premature burials were discovered weekly, and not all cases were found. Horror stories of claw marks found inside caskets and splinters of wood from the coffin lid embedded underneath the victims' fingernails gave people chills. Before his death George Washington asked to "not let my body be put into a vault in less than two days after I am dead."[4] Frédéric Chopin's last words were, "The earth is suffocating. . . . Swear to make them cut me open, so that I won't be buried alive." Clever inventors saw market opportunities and designed safety coffins with breathing pipes and ropes with which the living dead could ring bells when they awoke in darkness.

Except among miners and submariners, the fear of being buried alive is less rampant nowadays. Yet advances in organ donation have brought an aspect of it back. Some people are afraid to donate their organs because organs are taken from persons who are pronounced dead, but whose bodies are still alive. An eye surgeon told me her story of standing in line behind other doctors from other specialties to remove the eyes of a young man lying on the operation table. His organs had been donated in agreement with his relatives. When the supposedly dead man suddenly sat up, the room quickly emptied. Needless to say, the surgeon did not remove his eyes.

As with Christmas lights, fear of being buried alive has a rational basis, but above that, it is learned by social imitation. And social imitation of fear works even if there is no such rational basis at all.

Ghosts and Unlucky Numbers

Imagine you live in the narrow streets of Nizamuddin, a semi-medieval, semi-contemporary village tucked into the heart of Delhi, India. What would you likely fear? Ghosts and omens, like everyone else. In the streets you might see groups of men texting messages as they watch a ritual goat sacrifice and indoors hear women moaning as they exorcise evil djinns. As one of the women, a twenty-year-old who teaches the Koran, explained:[5] "When you go outside, you never know what evil, *shaitan*, awaits you. You don't want that evil to touch you, to possess you. That's why you wear a burqa."

Like many other forms of superstition, fear of ghosts is learned by social imitation. Ghosts are everywhere; or rather, they were. As a shop owner explained, when electric light came, most of the ghosts went elsewhere.

Educated Westerners are not free of superstition either. In 2008 one third of Americans said they believe in the existence of ghosts.[6] Forty percent of the British believe in haunted houses, like those featured in the stories of Charles Dickens or Stephen King. And quite a few educated citizens are afraid of specific numbers, the same ones their peers fear. When I walked down the aisle of a continental U.S. airlines plane, counting to find my seat, I couldn't find a row 13. The same is true for Air France and KLM. It's a sign of bad luck and these airlines claim that most people don't want to sit there. To be on the safe side, Lufthansa airplanes have neither row 13 nor 17, the unlucky number in Italy. Hotels are superstitious as well. Western hotels sometimes have no thirteenth floor, while many Asian hotels have no fourth floor, the number 4 being considered unlucky in Chinese culture because it sounds like the word "death." In Hong Kong, some high-rises are missing all floor numbers with 4, such as 4, 14, 24, 34, and all of the 40s. That's why Hong Kong elevators are the fastest in the world: They arrive quickly at floor 50.

Genetically Modified Food

Many food anxieties are not based on individual experience but are socially transmitted. Before baking, the delicious Bavarian pretzels are dunked briefly into a mixture of lye (sodium hydroxide) and water. The FDA puts restrictions on the procedure because lye is dangerous. Yet this process is exactly what makes the unique taste and crust of pretzels. In France, raw milk and raw milk cheeses are considered the standard for high quality dairy products, and some of the best Italian cheeses are also made from raw milk. Cheese made from pasteurized milk is considered an insult to good taste by cuisine traditionalists there. The FDA, in contrast, warns of consuming unpasteurized milk and soft cheese, and in Canada the sale of raw milk is forbidden.

One might conclude that Europeans are more risk seeking and North Americans more risk averse in food choice. But when it comes to genetically modified food, the roles are reversed. Europeans as well as Japanese tend to avoid genetically modified food while Americans gobble it up without batting an eyelid. Europeans tend to see genetically modified food as a morally unacceptable gamble against nature, detrimental to taste, and a health risk for society. These fears are not always grounded in facts. A representative survey in all member states of the European Union asked whether the following statement was true:

Ordinary tomatoes do not contain genes, while genetically modified tomatoes do.

True	36 percent
False	41 percent
Don't know	23 percent

Thus, only 41 percent of Europeans understood that ordinary tomatoes also have genes, while the rest believed that nature made them without genes, or did not know.[7] How the majority thinks vegetables reproduce remains a mystery. Part of the fear of genetically modified tomatoes seems to be grounded in basic ignorance about biology.

Radiation

Germans tend to fear radiation, from nuclear power plants to mobile phones to mammograms. So do Austrians, while the French and Americans could care less. In 1972 the Austrians built their first nuclear power plant on the banks of the Danube northwest of Vienna. It took six years to build at the cost of about €1 billion. When it was completed, the Austrians held a referendum whether to use it. A narrow majority of 50.5 percent voted no—mostly young female Austrians with above-average education. The plant, ready to start, was never operated. Then came the Chernobyl nuclear accident, and Austrian spring lettuce and strawberries had to be dumped. This fact reinforced the country's aversion to nuclear power. The plant is still on the riverside, to be visited as the only museum with a one-to-one scale model of a nuclear power plant.

After the 2011 earthquake and subsequent tsunami in Japan, the German media were more occupied with the potential danger of radiation than with the tens of thousands of Japanese who had lost their lives or were desperately searching for their loved ones. In a rush of German angst, sales of Geiger counters and iodine pills went up, and older nuclear power plants were closed down. Protection against a potential meltdown after an unlikely plane crash or terrorist attack became first priority and the politically correct message in the media. Even politicians who months before had asserted that there was no alternative to extending the lifetime of the nuclear plants suddenly agreed on eventually closing down all of the plants. In times of scarcity, Germany might then have to import electricity from neighboring countries—from the nuclear power plants in France and the Czech Republic.

Aside from the dread risk potential of nuclear technology, there may be a historical reason for the German fear of nuclear technology. Germans, like Austrians, live on the very border of what was the Eastern bloc during the Cold War, and would have been hit hard in the event of a nuclear attack.

Americans have comparably little fear of radiation. From the 1920s into the sixties, hip American shoe stores used to offer children the exciting experience of seeing how their feet appeared inside the shoes through a fluoroscopic X-ray device. Radio commercials promised that with X-ray shoe fitters, parents could finally be certain that their children's health was not jeopardized by improperly fitting shoes. The sales gimmick was eventually banned after shoe salespersons developed dermatitis from putting their hands into the X-ray beam. Today, as we have already seen, X-rays and computed tomography are aggressively marketed in U.S. health care to detect diseases early, quickly, and painlessly.

Cultures don't only differ in what they fear but in what they find reassuring. Much of what reassures us is also socially learned.

Reassurance

You're feeling tired, suffer from a headache, and have vague digestive troubles. You decide to consult a doctor. If you visit a doctor in France, a likely diagnosis is that your symptoms have to do with the liver: *une crise de foie*, which translates into a "crisis of the liver." It's a malady from which apparently only the French suffer. Eating and drinking well, so the French believe, is responsible for their national pathology. And if you are French and hear that diagnosis, you most likely feel reassured. Only the liver! Nothing unexpected. An American—like most other people around the globe— would be perturbed to hear that something was wrong with that organ.[8]

If you see a German doctor, a likely diagnosis is that the symptoms have to do with your heart: troubles with your *Kreislauf* (blood circulation), such as low blood pressure. It's a pervasive malady in Germany. That diagnosis is likely to calm down a German. Again, nothing unexpected. Low blood pressure is taken seriously among Germans, something to be treated with medication, while Americans who fear the opposite might think of treating low blood pressure as close to malpractice.

Finally, an American doctor is likely to search for a virus. That would alarm the French and Germans but might reassure American patients. Whereas liver and heart conditions suggest that the cause is within, the American vision is that the body itself is healthy and the enemy comes from without.

If doctors don't know, there is a tendency to attribute the symptoms to whatever cause reassures people: the liver, the circulation, or a virus. Reassurance does not mean that people think the disease is harmless, but that it is nothing extraordinary. French, Germans, and Americans are not the only ones to have a fallback or reassurance category. A British patient, for instance, will likely be diagnosed with a mood disorder or depression.

Medical treatments are also dependent on culture. Germans tend to have a romantic relation to the heart, while Americans tend to regard it as a mechanical pump and literally treat it that way, agreeing to many more coronary bypass operations than Germans and other Europeans do. The Chinese, in contrast, tend to be reluctant to perform any surgery, thinking of bodily health in terms of harmony. The concept of removing a malfunctioning part of the body without attending to its relations to other parts would appear too simple-minded for them to contemplate.[9] All in all, social learning leads to a paradoxical result. In France, Germany, Italy, the United Kingdom, and the United States, doctors' beliefs about diet and health—such as taking vitamin supplements or exercising—more closely resemble those of the general public in their country than of doctors in other countries.[10]

Is Risk Aversion a Question of Culture or Personality?

These stories illustrate some cultural differences in what scares or reassures people. Some might object that it's more a question of personality than culture, whether you're a scaredy cat or fearless lion by nature. In risk research people are sometimes divided into two kinds of personalities: risk seeking and risk averse. But it is misleading to generalize a person as one or the other. The very same person who is averse to the risk of genetically modified corn may be a chain smoker, and another who is terrified of burning wax candles on a Christmas tree may be willing to risk having a gun at home. Social learning is the reason why people aren't generally risk seeking or risk averse. They tend to fear whatever their peers fear, resulting in a patchwork of risks taken and avoided.

Yet social learning is not the only way we learn what to fear or not. The second principle is biological preparedness, which allows us to quickly "learn" to fear situations that were dangerous in our evolutionary history.

Biological Preparedness

Why do children fear snakes and spiders even when poisonous varieties no longer exist in their country? That seems plain foolish. Yet there is a rationale behind their fear. Learning by individual experience whether an animal is deadly would be fatal. Learning by social imitation might also be too slow. Evolution has equipped us with a second learning principle, which is an ingenious combination of nature and nurture. The object of fear is genetically "prepared," but social input is needed to activate the fear.

Learning the Dangers of the Past from Others

Biological preparedness refers to objects and situations that provided threats to the survival of our ancestors, such as spiders, snakes, and darkness. For instance, when a child observes her father shrieking with fear when a spider crawls over his arm, that single exposure can be sufficient to acquire the fear. But when the same child watches her grandmother react with fear toward rifles, motorcycles, and other potentially deadly modern inventions, fear is not as quickly learned. It's easier to make a child anxious about touching a spider than an electrical outlet. Social learning of prepared fear involves this chain:[11]

Prepared object → other human expresses fear of the object → acquire fear.

Unlike learning by trial and error, prepared associations between an object and fear are learned quickly, often in a single trial, and once learned, the emotional reaction is hard to get rid of. Many of the phobias humans readily acquire are biologically prepared associations. These include fears of animals (spiders, reptiles), fears of physical objects or events (wide open spaces, thunder), and fear of other humans (threatening faces, being socially rejected). The prominent role of animals in human phobias is probably due to the evolutionary origin of the fear circuit as a defense against animal predators. Preparedness allows humans to learn what to fear without actually experiencing negative consequences from an encounter.

Preparedness can also be observed in monkeys. Like humans, rhesus monkeys reared in the laboratory show no innate fear toward venomous snakes. But they have a prepared association:

Snaky object → other monkey expresses fear of the snake → acquire fear.

In a series of experiments, monkeys watched videotapes in which another monkey reacted with fear to the presence of a snake.[12] Afterward, the monkeys who viewed the tapes reacted similarly toward snakes and snakelike objects. Yet this works only with prepared objects. When the monkey in the video showed (genuine) fear but the image of the real snake was replaced with one of a brightly colored flower, the monkeys watching the scene did not suddenly become afraid of flowers.

Like dread risk fear, which we encountered in chapter 1, biological preparedness is about learning to fear the dangers of old. Social imitation, in contrast, allows us to learn about new dangers.

What Children Fear

Parents sometimes believe that the arrival of a new baby sibling is an extremely upsetting event for their other children. After all, it means sharing the love and resources provided by parents. For American fourth to sixth graders, however, this event was in fact considered among the least stressful ones, equivalent to giving a class report or seeing a dentist.[13] Do parents know what their children really fear? Studies indicate that parents correctly realize that children fear divorce and Mom's or Dad's death, but are less aware that children feel stressed when their parents fight. Moreover, parents often underestimate the emotional prominence of school life and peer opinions: fear of humiliation, wetting their pants in class, and embarrassment in front of their peers.

Yet there is a caution to such studies. The answers depend on what items researchers and teachers put on the list from which children can pick. A child obviously cannot pick what's not on the list. When a study with 394 Dutch children aged seven to twelve let the children both pick from a list and say freely what they feared, the results differed.[14] Compare the six most-feared situations:

What children pick from a list:	What children say in a free response:
1. Bombing attacks or being invaded	Spiders
2. Being hit by a car or truck	Death
3. Not being able to breathe	War
4. Getting a serious illness	Illness
5. Falling from a high place	The dark
6. Fire or getting burned	Snakes

Half of the most feared events overlap: war, illness, and death. This overlap, however, may be partly due to the fact that children were first given the list and then asked for a free response. The other most feared events don't match: spiders, snakes, and darkness. Fear of spiders and snakes appears particularly astounding because in the Netherlands poisonous spiders and snakes that pose a threat to human life no longer exist. Thus, the children could not learn this fear from personal experience. Is this fear inborn? No. Children's fear of spiders, snakes, and darkness is based on biological preparedness, as mentioned earlier a particularly fast form of social learning. Thus, in order to prevent their children from learning to fear the wrong things, parents who have the fear themselves should do their best not to show it in the presence of their children.

Internal Control Can Help Against Anxiety

Across many cultures, people seem to have become more worried about jobs, safety, and social acceptance. Are we entering an age of anxiety?

Young Americans are said to be growing more depressed from decade to decade. When people of different ages were asked, only up to 2 percent of those born in the early twentieth century reported major depressive disorders, while as many as 20 percent of those born in the middle of the century did.[15] Yet this difference could be more apparent than real. Older people have selective memories and might recollect mainly the rosy days of their own youth. To avoid this possibility, cohort studies compare young people of the same age and follow them over their life course.

Are Young People More Anxious Today?

The MMPI (Minnesota Multiphasic Personality Inventory) is a questionnaire used to assess various mental disorders. It measures depression, hypochondria, hysteria, and other forms of psychopathology. Since the 1930s it has been given to tens of thousands of children and adolescents in the United States, which allows for comparisons over time.

The development is astounding. Between 1938 and 2007 the clinical scores of college students rose steadily, especially in moodiness, restlessness, dissatisfaction, and instability (the so-called F-Scale). The higher the scores, the more these characteristics dominate. Let's take the average score of college students in the 1930s and 40s as the benchmark. In the recent generations, almost all students, ninety-four out of every hundred, scored higher! The same increase in scores was observed for unrealistic positive self-appraisal, over-activity, and low self-control. Across all scales used in the questionnaire, eighty-five of every hundred students had scores above the benchmark: more narcissistic, self-centered, and antisocial, as well as more worried, sad, and dissatisfied. Based on students' own reports, this is the psychological profile of recent generations of young Americans. What was once considered out of balance has become the norm.

What is behind this changing emotional profile? Perhaps modern college makes young people moody and stressed, away from home for the first time and feeling under pressure. But the same changes for the same characteristics have been reported for high school students as well. Also, no differences were found between men and women, or between living locations. Another explanation might be that being depressed or restless is more socially desirable today. While this explains some of the change, the general pattern essentially remains. Or the reason could be economic: The psychological profile might follow the big economic ups and downs, from the Great Depression to today. But the actual increases have little to do with economic changes or with unemployment: Young people's scores increased slowly and steadily, not in waves following economic cycles. Rates of anxiety and depression among children were actually lower during World War II, the Cold War, and the turbulent sixties and seventies than today.

Internal Control: Skills, Not Looks

The best explanation can be found in what young people believe is important in life: in the distinction between internal and external goals. Internal goals include becoming a mature person by strengthening one's skills, competences, and moral values, and living a meaningful life. External goals have to do with material rewards and other people's opinions, including high income, social approval, and good looks. People's goals have shifted steadily since the end of World War II toward more and more extrinsic goals. Annual polls of college freshmen showed that recent generations judged "being well off financially" as more important than "developing a meaningful philosophy of life," while the opposite was true in the sixties and seventies.

With this shift, young people have less control in reaching their goals. As a consequence, young people's emotions and behavior have become increasingly remote-controlled. The *Internal-External Locus of Control Scale* is a questionnaire that measures how much people believe to be in control of their own fate, as opposed to being controlled by others. The questionnaire was given to children aged nine to fourteen from 1960 to 2002. During that time children's belief that they have control over their own destinies substantially declined. In 2002 the average child reported higher external control than 80 percent of their peers in 1960. When children experience little internal control over their lives, they tend to become anxious in the face of uncertainty: I'm doomed; there's no point in trying.

The light at the end of the tunnel is that people who report more internal control tend to fare better in life than those who don't. They play a more active role in their communities, take better care of their health, and get better jobs. We may have no control about whether people find our clothes or skills or appearance attractive. But we do have control over internal goals such as acquiring languages, mastering a musical instrument, or taking responsibility for small children or our grandparents. The shift toward external goals is not a biological fact engraved in stone; it is possible for all of us to refocus on internal goals and shed excessive anxiety about everyday risks and uncertainties.

Part II

Getting Risk Savvy

Solving a problem simply means representing it so as to make the solution transparent.

Herbert A. Simon

A certain elementary training in statistical method is becoming as necessary for everyone living in this world of today as reading and writing.

H. G. Wells[1]

5

Mind Your Money

Make everything as simple as possible, but not simpler.

Attributed to Albert Einstein

Americans are known to be pretty optimistic about their chances for riches. According to a poll, 19 percent of Americans believe that they are in the top 1 percent income group. Another 20 percent believe that they will be there someday.[1] Positive thinking is a good thing when you are young, but it has its downsides. In reality, upward mobility is no longer higher in the United States than in most other Western countries. Large parts of an optimistic American public support tax cuts for the rich from which they will never benefit.

It is easy to laugh at such naïveté. After all, we live in the digital age and can access all the information we want. Or so we think.

In fact, the digital age has changed how we deal with money, using ultra-high-speed computers to predict exchange rates and the stock market, and to employ fancy financial technology that most mortals do not understand. But has all of this really led to better predictions? Recall that the world of investment is largely an uncertain one, and relying on financial theories made for a world of known risk may lead to illusory certainty, what I call the turkey illusion.

Financial Experts: Gods or Chimps?

An asset manager of a major insurance firm once complained to me that his relatives always ask him what stocks to invest in. "I don't know. How could I?" he said. "But they want to believe that I am God." He is an honest man, but others less scrupulous are happy to play along with the delusion of possessing vast powers. At the turn of every year, renowned financial institutions forecast next year's exchange rates and stock prices. Media coverage is guaranteed. After all, everyone wants to know whether the next year will be a good or bad one, and where to put one's money. Nobody expects the predictions to be spot-on, but many assume that they will be somewhere in the ballpark. Most important, large swings up or down should not be missed. How good are these predictions that we hear every year?

Will the Dollar or the Euro Go Up?

Let's begin with exchange rates. Anyone transferring money from the United States to Europe or planning an overseas vacation would be delighted to know the best date for exchanging dollars for euros. Companies who export products overseas and have even more at stake are especially eager to know. To satisfy this desire, banks around the world predict the dollar-euro exchange rate for their customers. Should you rely on what they say? Surely, if the forecasts weren't any good, they wouldn't exist because nobody would pay a cent for them. Checking whether this is true, I did some investigation of the forecasts and of how good they are. In Figure 5-1, I show the end-of-the-year forecasts made by twenty-two international banks for a period of ten years.[2] Let's take a closer look at these forecasts.

In December 2000 the majority of the banks forecasted that by the end of 2001 the dollar and the euro would be about equal in value. This can be seen at the very left of Figure 5-1. Among others, Credit Suisse, Bank of Tokyo-Mitsubishi, Royal Bank of Canada, UBS, and Deutsche Bank all predicted an exchange rate of one to one. Yet the real exchange rate at the end of 2001 was only 0.88 dollars. Every bank overestimated the rate except for Citigroup, which predicted a close 0.85. That was the first and last time in that decade that Citigroup made a lucky forecast. Now consider the predictions for 2002. In compensation for their overestimates the year before, the banks uniformly corrected their predictions downward. Again,

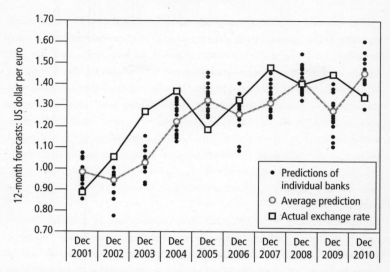

Figure 5-1. Forecasts of dollar-euro exchange rates are worthless. Every December, international banks predict the exchange rate for the end of the following year. Most of the time, the actual rate is outside the entire range of predictions. Yet predictions are not arbitrary: Analysts predict that next year will be like this year. Thus, they are consistently one year behind and miss every up- or downswing. Each point shows the prediction of one of twenty-two international banks, including Bank of America Merrill Lynch, Bank of Tokyo-Mitsubishi, Barclays Investment Bank, Citigroup, Commerzbank, Credit Suisse, Deutsche Bank, HSBC, JPMorgan Chase, Morgan Stanley, and Société Générale.

Based on data from: Consensus Economics, 2001–2010.

these varied by more than twenty cents. But the euro went up; the true exchange rate was 1.05, higher than any of the banks had foreseen. Surprised by the upward move of the euro, the banks corrected their forecasts upward for the following year, 2003. Once again the euro went up in value much faster than imagined, and once again, the actual exchange rate was outside the entire range of estimates. Exactly the same repeated itself in 2004. The swarm of predictions followed the upward trend from the previous year, but once more the real exchange rate was higher than any bank had envisioned.

For the end of 2005 every single bank predicted that the rate would continue to rise, following the same trend as in the year before. But the euro went down and the dollar up. Not a single bank had envisioned that fall. And as in other years, the real exchange rate was outside the entire range of predictions. For the next year, the banks adjusted their predictions downward, again "predicting" last year's trend. The euro went up. This time, at least, some of the banks' estimates happened to be close. In 2007 the euro continued its steep upward climb, and ended higher than all of the banks' estimates. The next year, the predicted and actual rate happened to coincide, for the first and last time. In the final two years, the euro first went up, then down; the bank's average predictions were consistently in the wrong direction.

These forecasts were not made by amateurs, but by a host of handsomely paid financial analysts with fancy mathematical models in their pockets. For instance, JPMorgan Chase, the largest bank in the United States by total assets, misestimated the exchange rate on average by thirteen cents. All of these experts had the same thought: *Next year is like this year.* If you look at the ten years of predictions, they consistently predicted the upward or downward trend of the previous year. In over 90 percent of individual forecasts, the experts followed that rule. You could do that too. The only problem is the dollar-euro exchange rate itself, which does not follow this logic, meaning that every change in a trend will be missed.

Predictions that always work *except when this year is not like last year* provide the false certainty of an airbag that works all the time except when you have a car accident.

Why then do senior managers of major companies still pay for these meaningless predictions? Some might not know because banks don't publish what you see in Figure 5-1. Others are less interested in the actual predictions than in saving their skins. If a company takes losses because of a swing in exchange rates, a manager can say that the banks had predicted otherwise, making the bank, not the manager, accountable. We have seen this already: *defensive decision making,* practiced by individuals who waste time and money to protect themselves at the cost of others, including their companies (chapter 3). Fear of personal responsibility creates a market for worthless products delivered by high-paid experts.

Where Is the Stock Market Going?

Let's begin with the crucial year 2008, the beginning of the subprime crisis. The professional forecasters polled by Bloomberg.com thought it would be a prosperous year; the average prediction was a gain of 11 percent.[3] None expected a loss. By the end of the year, the Standard & Poor index was down 38 percent and much of the world economy lay in ruins. Predictions for the DAX index (German stock index) at the end of 2008 were equally positive. The most optimistic prediction came from the WGZ Bank in Düsseldorf, which expected the DAX to rise from 8,067 points at the end of 2007 to 10,250 points by the end of 2008.[4] Similarly, the Deutsche Bank predicted 8,200 to 8,600 points. The most pessimistic prediction came from the U.S. investment bank Morgan Stanley with 7,770 points. At the end of 2008 the DAX had tumbled to only 4,810 points. Not a single bank had foreseen the crash.

In defense of analysts' skills, one might contend that everyone makes mistakes and that this was likely the only time the stock forecasts failed so dramatically. So let's move a year back in time and see how well thirty banks predicted the closing value of 2007 at the end of 2006. These ranged between 5,800 and close to 8,000 points. Once again, the actual value was outside of the total range, 8,067. The banks' inability to predict has nothing to do with being overly confident or cautious in general. That time round, all thirty banks were too pessimistic, only to be far too optimistic a year later.

Now one could argue that although even big-name banks are dismal at forecasting, there must be some that do better than others. Inevitably, however, some will always do better than others, even if their forecasts are made by throwing dice. One test is to see whether those who are better at predicting the DAX are also better at predicting exchange rates. Figure 5-2 shows the DAX predictions of the best banks two years before the crisis, together with their predictions of the dollar-euro exchange rate. Recall that 2006 was one of the few years where the exchange-rate predictions were not totally off the wall (Figure 5-1). If more than sheer luck was in play, the banks that predicted the DAX best should have also done better at predicting the exchange rate. But there are no signs of any actual skills at work. Credit Suisse, who came out at the top for the DAX, predicted the exchange rate worse than any of the five banks at the bottom of the DAX list.

	DAX (Stocks)	Exchange Rate (Value of Euro in Dollars)
Actual value on December 15, 2006	6588	1.31
The five best forecasts		
Credit Suisse	6100	1.08
Bear Stearns	6060	1.15
ABN AMRO	6000	1.25
Landesbank Rheinland-Pfalz	6000	1.15
WestLB	6000	1.35
The five worst forecasts		
JPMorgan Chase	5000	1.25
Helaba Trust	5100	1.28
Morgan Stanley	5200	1.20
UBS	5300	1.30
Nomura	5400	1.10

Figure 5-2. Illusory certainty of stock and exchange rate forecasts. Forecasts of stocks (DAX) and euro-dollar exchange rates, made at the end of 2005 for the end of 2006. At the time of the forecast, the DAX was about 5,400 and the euro about US $1.18. The bank with the best predictions for stocks, Credit Suisse, made the worst prediction for the exchange rate, and UBS, which made one of the worst forecasts for stocks, made the best prediction for the exchange rate. All in all, the quality of the two forecasts was unrelated, and strikingly poor. The actual stock value was far outside the entire range of forecasts, and the exchange rate underestimated by most banks (see Figure 5-1).

The larger picture is that bank analysts underestimate the volatility of the stock market and of the exchange rate. At fault for one are the mathematical models they use. These treat the highly unpredictable financial market as if its risks were predictable. As a consequence, the forecasts consistently miss large upswings or downswings and only do well if nothing remarkable happens—that is, when last year's trend continues.

Bank analysts and asset managers are in charge of managing the world's money. Can they predict exchange rates and stocks? No. But customers want to believe that they can, and banks do their part to maintain this illusion.

Anyone Can Become a Market Guru

In his novel *Pudd'nhead Wilson* Mark Twain explained the secret of fool-proof predictions.[5] "October. This is one of the peculiarly dangerous months to speculate in stocks in. The others are July, January, September, April, November, May, March, June, December, August and February." A somewhat more subtle method is: *Keep making predictions, but don't keep records.* Roger Babson is credited with correctly predicting the stock market crash of 1929. What is less known is that he had been predicting a crash for years.[6] The trick is to predict a downturn so many times that eventually it is bound to come true, and then forget all earlier forecasting blunders. Elaine Garzarelli from Lehman Brothers became the Roger Babson of the 1987 Black Monday crash. On October 12 she predicted "an imminent collapse in the stock market." Four days later it really did crash. Hyped as the "Guru of Black Monday" by the media, she became one of the highest-paid strategists on Wall Street. But the crash was her last hurrah. Thereafter, her predictions about whether the market would go up or down were right less often than a coin toss. Those who entrusted their money into her hands were painfully disappointed.

The moral of the story is that among the thousands of financial experts there will always be some who get it right. Even a broken clock is right twice a day. But what if someone gets it right several times in a row? Consider 10,000 investment managers whose advice is equal to flipping a coin. After a year, 5,000 can claim to have made money, while the other 5,000 made a loss. Among those who made a win, half of them—2,500—can be expected to land on the winning side again in the second year. Half of these in turn—1,250—can claim that their method worked three years in a row. A simple calculation shows that about ten investment gurus will get it right year after year for ten years in a row. It is hard to resist the temptation to attribute such an impressive result to the guru's unique, deep insights into the market. To use a phrase by Nassim Taleb, if you did so you would be fooled by pure randomness.[7]

Even after having seen the dismal stock and exchange rate predictions in Figures 5-1 and 5-2, you might feel an emotional resistance to the idea that confident professionals are about as good at predicting as the notorious chimpanzee throwing a dart. Two studies suggest that the chimp might well do a better job. In the first study Swedish portfolio managers, brokers, and investment advisers were asked to predict the performance of twenty blue chip stocks.[8] Presented two stocks at a time, they were asked to pick one that would perform better thirty days later. A group of nonexperts were given the same task. Their answers were at chance level; that is, they got it right half of the time. The professionals, however, were worse than chance, picking only 40 percent of the right ones. Repeating the study with other professionals and laypeople produced exactly the same result. How did professionals manage to do a worse job than nonexperts? The professionals seem to have based their predictions on specific information without being aware of its fickleness. Nonetheless, the very same professionals were convinced of their superior powers and that they would make half as many errors as laypeople. And laypeople agreed.

So if you were a professional investor and made worse predictions than your clients, could you still become a financial guru? Assume again ten thousand professional investors who perform at the same level of incompetence as their Swedish peers in the studies. After the first year, we expect that four thousand will get their predictions right, while the other six thousand will fail. In the second year, there are sixteen hundred whose predictions were right twice in a row. After five years, we still expect about one hundred who predicted correctly year after year. And one professional will even manage to have guessed right ten years in a row. All you need is a large batch of incompetent experts and some of them will end up with a fantastic track record.

How to Beat a Nobel Prize Portfolio

I believe in the power of simple rules in the real, messy world. They may not always help, but the first question should nevertheless be: Can we find a simple solution for a complex problem? This question is rarely asked. The reflex is to look for complex solutions first and, if they don't work, to make them even more complex. The same is true in investment. In the wake of financial turmoil that even specialists were not able to predict, simple rules of thumb provide an alternative. Let's take one complex problem that many of us face. Assume you have a chunk of money and want to invest it. You do not want to put all your eggs into one basket and are considering a number of stocks. You want to diversify. But how?

Harry Markowitz won a Nobel Prize in economics for solving this problem. The solution is known as the mean-variance portfolio. The portfolio maximizes the gain (mean) for a given risk or minimizes the risk (variance) for a given return. Many banks rely on this and similar investment methods and warn customers against relying on their intuitions instead.

But when Markowitz made his own investments for his retirement, he did not use his Nobel Prize–winning method. Instead, he employed a simple rule of thumb called 1/N:

Allocate your money equally to each of N funds.

Why did he rely on a hunch instead of crunching the numbers? In an interview, Markowitz said he wanted to avoid regrets: "I thought, 'You know, if the stock market goes way up and I'm not in, I'll feel stupid. And if it goes way down and I'm in it, I'll feel stupid.' So I went 50-50."[9] He did what many investors do: Make it simple. And 1/N is not only simple, it is the purest form of diversification.

How good is this rule of thumb? In a study, it was compared to mean-variance and a dozen other complex investment methods. Seven situations were analyzed, such as investing in ten American industry funds.[10] The mean-variance portfolio made use of ten years of stock data, while 1/N did not need any. What was the result? In six of the seven tests, 1/N scored better than mean-variance in common performance criteria. Moreover, none of the other twelve complex methods was consistently better at predicting the future value of the stocks.

Does this mean that the Nobel Prize–winning method is a sham? No. It is optimal in an ideal world of known risks, but not necessarily in the uncertain world of the stock market, where so much is unknown. To use such a complex formula requires us to estimate a large number of parameters based on past data. Yet as we have seen, ten years is too short a time to get reliable estimates. Say you invested in fifty funds. How many years of stock data would be needed before the mean-variance method finally does better than 1/N? A computer simulation provides the answer: about five hundred years!

That means that in the year 2500, investors can turn from the simple rule to the high-level math of the mean-variance model and hope to win. But this holds only if the same stocks—and the stock market—are still around.

Do our banks understand the limits of optimization in an uncertain world? A few years ago, my Internet bank sent a letter to their customers. It read:

> *A Nobel Prize-Winning Strategy to Success in Investment!*
>
> *Do you know Harry M. Markowitz? No? Then you should: He was awarded the Nobel Prize in economics in 1990. With his portfolio theory, he proved that weighting individual stocks correctly can substantially optimize the gain-risk ratio of a portfolio.*
>
> *So much for theory. The portfolios of most investors, however, look different. Because they are often put together arbitrarily rather than systematically, there is strong need for optimization.*

The letter goes on to explain that the bank uses the mean-variance portfolio, and adds a warning not to rely on intuitive rules. What this bank had not understood is that they'd sent off the letter five hundred years too early.

"I Can Do That Myself!"

Some time ago I gave a keynote at the Morningstar Investment Conference, in which I described in more detail when and why simple rules have an edge over complex strategies.[11] Mean-variance and similar models are good when the risks are perfectly known, such as when they have to "predict" the past. But for predicting the future, they are not necessarily the best; here, simple rules can excel. After the talk, I was invited to a podium with two top financial analysts. The audience, several hundred of the best customers, was curious to hear how they would respond. So was I. The moderator turned to the first analyst:

"You just heard what Professor Gigerenzer argued for: that simple rules can often do better than optimization in an uncertain world. Since you are known for promoting complex investment methods, what do you have to say to that?"

Everyone was waiting to see whose blood would be shed.

"I have to admit," the analyst said, "that I also often rely on 1/N."

I was surprised how quickly this analyst did an about-face when challenged. After the podium, the head of investment of a major international insurance company came up to me and said he would check his company's investments. Three weeks later, he arrived at my office with his assistant.

"I checked our investments beginning 1969. I compared 1/N to our actual investment strategies. We would have made more money if we had used this simple rule of thumb."

But then the real issue came up.

"I have convinced myself that simple is better. But here's my problem. How do I explain this to my customers? They might say, I can do that myself!"

I reassured him that there are plenty of open questions, such as how large N should be, what kind of stocks, when to rebalance, and most important, to figure out when and where 1/N is a successful strategy.

The moral of the story is that in a world of risk that matches with the mathematical assumptions of the mean-variance portfolio, the calculations pay. But in the real world of investment, simple intuitive rules can be smarter. The same holds generally in uncertain worlds.

Less Is More: Einstein's Rule

How can a simple rule of thumb beat a Nobel Prize–winning method? Was that just a fluke? No. There is a mathematical theory that tells us why and when simple is better. It is called the bias-variance dilemma. So that every reader, with or without a background in math, can understand this complex but important explanation, the mathematical details have been omitted.[12] The essence of the theory is captured by an insight attributed to Albert Einstein:

Make everything as simple as possible, but not simpler.

How far we go in simplifying depends on three features. First, the more uncertainty, the more we should make it simple. The less uncertainty, the more complex it should be. The stock market is highly uncertain in the sense that it is extremely unpredictable. That speaks for a simple method like 1/N. Second, the more alternatives, the more we should simplify; the fewer, the more complex it can be. The reason is that complex methods need to estimate risk factors, and more alternatives mean that more factors need to be estimated, which leads to more estimation errors being made. In contrast, 1/N is not affected by more alternatives because it does not need to make estimates from past data. Finally, the more past data there are, the more beneficial for the complex methods. That is why the Markowitz calculations pay off with 500 years of stock data, as described above. The various factors work together: If there are only twenty-five instead of fifty alternatives, then only about 250 years of stock data are needed. In this way, one can begin to understand when less is more, and how much to simplify.

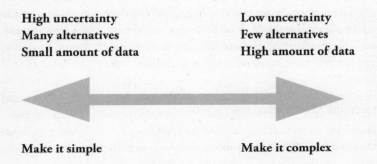

High uncertainty　　　　　　**Low uncertainty**
Many alternatives　　　　　　**Few alternatives**
Small amount of data　　　　**High amount of data**

Make it simple　　　　　　　**Make it complex**

Taking all this into consideration helps to understand a predicament that all forecasters face, what statisticians call the bias-variance dilemma. When we use a particular method to make a prediction, the difference between the prediction and the true outcome (which we cannot know ahead) is called the bias. Bias is unavoidable (except by lucky coincidence) in an uncertain world. But there is a second kind of error, called variance or instability. Unlike 1/N, complex methods use past observations to predict the future. These predictions will depend on the specific sample of observations it uses and may therefore be unstable. This instability (the variability of these predictions around their mean) is called variance. Thus, the more complex the method, the more factors need to be estimated, and the higher the amount of error due to variance. 1/N will always give the same stable recommendation, meaning that it doesn't use any investment data from the past. For that reason, it doesn't suffer from any variance. If the amount of data is very large, such as for five hundred years, the instability is reduced so much that complexity finally pays.

Now it should be clearer when and why complex methods lead to worse predictions: when they suffer from too much variance, under the conditions listed on the left of the table above. Einstein's rule is a general way to realize that less can be more in an uncertain world.

Start Practicing Being Rich

Let's turn our eyes to beautiful Austria. In the golden times of prosperity, when the social system took care of everyone, rich or poor, Austrians did not have to worry about their pensions. In 2003, when the future began to look less rosy, however, Austrians were encouraged to pay into government-subsidized individual pension plans. From Vienna to Salzburg, banks began to advertise these plans. By the end of 2004, 410,000 Austrians (out of about eight million inhabitants) had already enrolled in a plan. After enrollment, people pay a monthly or yearly sum into the plan until they retire. The bank pays a variable interest and the government a premium. No profit is guaranteed, but at the time of retirement everyone gets at least what he or she contributed plus the premium, without correction for inflation.

But the banks didn't spend their advertising budgets on spreading these hard facts. Instead, campaigns focused on wishful thinking. One bank simply told their customers: Start practicing being rich! Billboards across the country proclaimed a big "9 percent." At a time of low interest rates, 9 percent is spectacular, not only in Austria. What a generous social system, where banks and government contribute to citizens' prosperity! But the 9 percent is not an interest rate, it's a premium. The premium is given once a year on the annual amount paid into the pension plan. For example, a person who pays €1,000 annually will receive €90 per year. What the bank contributes is left open; only the sum paid plus the premium is guaranteed. After thirty years, that makes €30,000 plus a €2,700 premium. But that's not what the Austrians looking for a good deal read on the billboards. A study indicated that many who bought the plan believed they would get a 9 percent fixed interest rate.

Are these customers the victims of their wishful thinking or of their advisers? Do bankers explain what 9 percent means in an honest and transparent way?

To answer this question, one of my research associates ran an undercover study. Anne, who was twenty-five at the time, visited ten different banks in the Austrian city of Klagenfurt.[13] In ten one-on-one consultations, she asked each adviser for information concerning the state-subsidized pension plan. All of them recommended signing up for it. She then asked each adviser the crucial question: *Is 9 percent an interest rate?*

Three advisers (1, 3, and 7) wrongly answered yes. After first correctly saying no, adviser 5 changed her mind and also asserted that it was an interest rate (Figure 5-3). Three advisers made the effort to calculate how much more money Anne would make if she entered the pension plan compared to a regular 2 to 3 percent interest rate. Each was at a complete loss when the calculations showed the opposite of what they had thought. The amount of confusion the advisers showed suggests that they were not intentionally lying but simply didn't understand the conditions. Four advisers (2, 4, 9, and 10) answered correctly, but adviser 2 then prophesied a high but illusory interest rate to make the pension plan nonetheless look attractive.

What all advisers had in common was their attempt to persuade Anne into signing up for the plan. Each of them presented it as the only reasonable alternative. The estimated interest rates some of the advisers asserted with confidence, however, were fiction. Many of those who bought into the plan have tried to get out because with almost no interest coming from the banks, they feared ending up with only the money they paid into it together with the modest premium. In this worst case, customers would end up with a total of 109 percent of what they paid into the plan after some thirty years. What that adds up to is a fixed interest rate of less than 1 percent.

Some of the Austrian bank advisers had no idea what they were talking about. But they are not alone. Ignorance about basic finances seems to be an international phenomenon. In one study, American portfolio managers and other investment professionals working for investment companies and major banks or preparing for a career in financial engineering were asked to determine the "volatility" of a certain stock.[14] If the price of a stock moves up and down rapidly, it has a high volatility. If it almost never changes, it has a low volatility. Every stock has a volatility, which is expressed as a number. Only three of eighty-seven respondents were able to provide the correct value for volatility, and most underestimated it.

Back to the Austrian banks. Their "9 percent" billboards and financial advisers exploited the fact that few people ask the essential question: percent of what? As already mentioned in chapter 1, this question is essential to risk literacy. Nine percent is not always more than 1 percent.

The Mother of All Rules of Thumb: Trust

Instead of asking basic questions, many people instead rely on a social rule of thumb to get along with their lives: trust. Trust in politics. Trust in leadership. Trust your doctor. Most bank customers deal with their financial advisers just as they deal with their doctors. First, they establish a relation of trust or distrust, and then they follow the advice of their trusted adviser. Few check whether their advisers actually know what they are talking about. When Italian bank customers were asked what makes them trust their adviser, two thirds first listed their personal relationship, and only one third the adviser's competence.[15] Trust is typically based on

Question: "Is 9% an interest rate?"

Bank 1: Adviser is in his late 40s, explains carefully like a parent.

"Yes, it's all gains. To get the same returns with a savings book you would need 8 percent interest."

Bank 2: Adviser is in her mid-30s.

"No. Premiums are not interest. You get them only for your annual payment. But the average interest for the pension plan is around 6%, compared to 3% for a savings book."

Bank 3: Adviser is in her mid-20s, extremely friendly, insecure, and repeats herself.

"Yes. Premium and interest are the same, except that you get the premium every year." She uses her PC to show how much higher the returns of the pension plan are compared to a 3% savings plan. The result shows the opposite. The client is confused. The advisor looks helpless and calls for an older colleague, who is also surprised that 3% is more than 9%, but confirms that that premium is interest. Embarrassed, both advisers explain to the client: "One shouldn't believe everything the government says."

Bank 4: Adviser is in his early 40s, rather brief and clear.

"No."

Bank 5: Adviser is in her mid-30s, friendly and enthusiastic.

"No, the premium is extra money from the government." She recommends the pension plan, calculates the returns compared to regular insurances. The results confuse both advisor and client. Client asks again whether the premium is interest. This time, the answer is: "Yes, the premium is interest, only from the government."

Figure 5-3. Austrian banks advertised pension plans with a "big 9 percent," which looked like a government-boosted interest rate but was in fact a one-time premium. A young woman went to

Question: "Is 9% an interest rate?"

Bank 6: Adviser is in his mid-30s, not exactly talkative, stares at his documents, avoids eye contact.

"The premium is an annual interest rate from the government. I recommend the pension plan, because with a savings book there is no guarantee—with the pension plan, there is."

Bank 7: Adviser is in her late 30s, appears insecure, turns frequently to her colleague to ask for advice.

"Yes, that's a hard question." Her colleague intervenes. "You get a total of 8.5% [this bank offered 8.5% instead of 9%], which is a fixed interest rate of at least 2.25% from the bank and then the government adds the difference to 8.5%."

Bank 8: Adviser is in his mid-30s, eager, intensive eye contact.

"Premium is interest, but only for the annual payment. Savings is no alternative, because you only get 2.5% interest." To demonstrate the advantage of the pension plan, he calculates its outcome compared to a 2.25% life insurance. The life insurance brings more money. When he sees the result, he calculates again, same result. He appears briefly irritated, but overplays the situation and praises the advantages of the pension plan. The client asks why he advised against the 2.5% savings if 2.25% interest already brings better returns than the pension plan. There is a long pause. "It seems to me, the government-subsidized plan is just an eye-catcher."

Bank 9: Adviser is female, about 30, patronizing.

"No, it's not interest but an annual premium on the annual payment. But the figure is presented in the ads without explanation to attract customers. It's actually misleading."

Bank 10: Adviser is male, early 30s.

"No. Premium is not interest. With a premium, there is no compound interest." The client asks why the ads don't say this. "First, the bank pays for advertisements to deceive and attract customers. And then the bank pays advisors to correct customers' misunderstandings."

ten banks and asked the financial advisors, "Is 9 percent an interest rate?" While the answer is no, quite a number of advisors falsely claimed yes or were confused.

Source: Vitouch et al. (2007).

surface clues, such as whether the adviser listened, smiled, and maintained eye contact. If so, customers generally invested in whatever their adviser recommended and spent the rest of their precious consultation time engaged in small talk. In fact, 40 percent of the Italian customers said that they spend less than one hour per month on their insurance and investments. It's not because they have no time: On average, Italians spend some hundred hours per month sitting in front of their TV screen, watching glitzy but dull shows featuring women called *veline* dressed in heels and not much else. It's because they prefer to rely on a simple investment rule:

Trust your banker.

Like every strategy, simple or complex, trust is neither good nor bad. It all depends on the environment. In this case, trust is a good idea only if your banker:

1. understands the featured financial products, and
2. has no conflicts of interest.

The first condition is about trust in competence, the second about trust in motivation. The story about the pension plans in Austria illustrates that competence is not as widespread as many think. But you won't find out if you simply fall for a friendly smile. You could, however, ask a few questions, as Anne did.

But conflicts of interest may be harder to spot. When customers talk to their bank adviser, many assume that the investment advice they get is in their best interest. In fact, advisers are typically instructed every week to sell those financial products on which the bank earns the highest commission, and they may even get premiums for doing so. Recall that the Austrian advisers all recommended the "9 percent" pension product, whether they understood it or not. The most lucrative product for the bank is most likely not the best one for the customer: Whatever money the bank takes out of the pot will no longer be there for the client. Looking at it from the other angle, if the adviser instead acted in the customer's best interest, the bank might well lose money; that's why altruistic advisers are likely to have a very brief bank career. Conflicts of interest are the rule rather than the exception. They are built into the system, and customers need to understand them. There is no way around basic financial literacy if you don't want to be taken in every time.

Money Mystique

When a speaker uses opaque terms and phrases that no one really understands, there are always a few who are impressed. I know authors who don't even try to write comprehensibly because they believe that otherwise their readers won't find them intelligent. Similarly, many a bank customer falls for fancy financial mystique. While obscure writing won't necessarily drive you into ruin, obscure financial products can. In fact, complex instruments such as credit default swaps were one cause of financial crises. Back in 2003 Warren Buffett already called such financial products "weapons of mass destruction."[16] From homeowners to financial institutions to rating agencies, virtually no one understood, or wanted to understand, their global consequences. Rating agencies rated Lehman highly until the moment it fell apart. The CEO of Morgan Stanley appeared not to realize what was going on, nor did senior bankers around the world.[17] Busy politicians understood even less, and accounting firms didn't get the picture either, or had conflicting interests. Investment advisers marketed certificates aggressively, luring people out of their safe but low-paying savings accounts. Former Federal Reserve Chairman Alan Greenspan, who had praised the increased freedom from regulation before the crash, honestly admitted: "Those of us who have looked to the self-interest of lending institutions to protect shareholders' equity, myself included, are in a state of shocked disbelief."[18]

Thus complex problems such as financial crises are often created, not solved, by complex products. And those who sell these products can count on potential buyers to be impressed, or at least not dare to admit that they don't understand what is offered. Some prospectuses may be a hundred pages long, with lots of fine print. But there is a simple cure to this ailment, although it requires courage to admit to ignorance:

Don't buy financial products you don't understand.

If Americans had used this rule, few would have lost huge parts of their retirement funds. If European bankers had relied on it, they would not have bought the junk, and the financial crisis would not have happened as it did. A top executive once explained to me how for years she was hesitant to admit when she did not understand an investment, for fear of looking stupid. Having learned her lesson, she has now found the courage to protect herself from "financial weapons of mass destruction." When someone offers her an investment option, she responds: "You have fifteen minutes' time to explain how it works. If I still don't understand it, I won't buy it." A simple rule like that can reduce global spread of damage.

Note that this rule is not the same as being risk averse. Putting all our money into a savings account with next-to-no interest or in government bonds may be a sure thing but not much more. A wise investor will still diversify and buy stocks—just not in the complicated, obscure way dreamed up by big banks and Wall Street firms. The point is that transparency helps create a safer world, while complexity can fuel potential disaster.

Safe Investment: Keep It Simple

As mentioned before, the complexity of financial instruments invented in the last decades is one of the reasons why so many people have lost so much money. Some experts in the Ivory Tower of Finance have a vested interest in promoting innovative investment schemes that ordinary people will not understand. Paul Volcker, past Chairman of the Federal Reserve, does not buy the conventional wisdom that "financial innovation" is necessary for a healthy economy. According to him, "the only useful banking innovation was the invention of the ATM."[19]

Clinging to certainty, however, can make people veer to the other extreme and become highly averse to the inevitable risks involved in financial investment. Italian bank customers, in one study, associated risk with predominantly negative terms. Their most common associations with the word "risk" were loss, equities, investment, fear, danger, Argentine bonds, and bankruptcy, in that order.[20] The fact that risks are also chances and opportunities played little role in their minds. These associations reflected their decision making. When their bank adviser offered an investment option to these Italian customers, most asked only two risk-averse questions: Is it safe? Can I withdraw earlier? These questions make little sense: No investment is safe, but some are safer than others. And to withdraw, the only question is how much it will cost.

What are simple, transparent strategies for investing your money? Here are some examples if you want to play it safe.

- One third in stocks, one third in bonds, one third in real estate. This is the 1/N rule that we met before. Here, it means allocating your money equally between stocks, bonds, and real estate.
- Save 20 percent, spend 80 percent. Saving does not mean hiding money under your pillow, but rather investing it in the future.
- Diversify as broadly as you can—far more than experts tell you.[21]

None of these rules is always best, but they provide guidelines and tend to protect you against big losses if you put all your eggs in one basket. Thinking about your money yourself is crucial. As mentioned before, your bank advisers are likely instructed weekly by their managers how many life insurance policies, certificates, and other financial products they have to sell. When the quota for one is satisfied, the next customers—one of whom may be you—are targeted for whatever has not yet fulfilled the business plan, whether you need it or not. This is not your bank advisers' fault— they have little choice if they want to hang on to their job. It is essential to realize that your adviser cannot always recommend what is best for you.

6

Leadership and Intuition

The intuitive mind is a sacred gift and the rational
mind is a faithful servant. We have created a society that
honors the servant and has forgotten the gift.

Attributed to Albert Einstein

The location is a small, elegant lecture room with red armchairs, chandeliers, and a cozy fireplace. I just finished a talk on gut feelings and business, and it's discussion time. The host, a senior executive, stands up.

> "I remember when we, the five members of our bank's board, were immersed in a passionate discussion. Should we go ahead with the planned merger with a global credit group, or better not? It was early in the morning when one of us warned us that he had a bad gut feeling. We asked him to explain what's wrong. He couldn't really say but eventually came up with a few reasons. We destroyed every one, went for the merger, and sailed into disaster."

He paused. The audience, twenty-four entrepreneurs and spouses, the bank's best customers, expectantly waited for the moral of the story.

> "Now," he continued, "I have learned something. If someone has a negative gut feeling, there is no point in asking him why. Because he wouldn't know. We must ask a different question, and not to him. We need to ask ourselves whether he is the one among us who has most experience with the issue. If the answer is yes, then we don't ask further questions and find something else to invest in."

I had given the talk previously to a different group of the bank's customers, and this senior executive recognized what the definition of intuition entails. As defined before, a "gut feeling," or intuition, is a judgment (i) that appears quickly in consciousness, (ii) whose underlying reasons we are not fully aware of, yet (iii) is strong enough to act upon. Having a gut feeling means that one feels what one should do, without being able to explain why. We know more than we can tell. An intuition is neither caprice nor a sixth sense but a form of unconscious intelligence. By definition, the person cannot know the reasons, and may invent some after the fact if you insist. To take intuition seriously means to respect the fact that it is a form of intelligence that a person cannot express in language. Don't ask for reasons if someone with a good track record has a bad gut feeling.

Do Executives Make Gut Decisions?

A few years ago the University of Bielefeld in Germany invited two company owners and two academics to a prestigious gathering organized by the economics and business departments. One of the entrepreneurs had built up a thriving garage-building business and the other a baking machine company. The academics were Reinhard Selten, Germany's only Nobel laureate in economics, and myself. The audience expected a debate between the four of us, theory against practice. But they were in for a surprise. Selten and I recommended scrapping much of the business curriculum and in its place teaching how to make successful decisions in an uncertain world.[1] Against the objections of the faculty, who preferred more mathematically elegant theories, the entrepreneurs defended our proposal to teach what's relevant and useful. Both of them were adamant that what they had learned as MBA students had been of little use. They had amassed their fortunes by trusting their gut feelings, which often worked. But these matters were not talked about during their education, except disparagingly.

To find out how widespread the use of gut feelings in business truly is I have interviewed managers, senior managers, and CEOs in large companies. One of these was a leading international technology services provider. The company had problems with slow decision making, both inside the firm and when dealing with their customers.

With the help of a top executive who had their trust, I asked them how often they rely on gut feelings in professional decisions, whether made alone or as part of a group. Note again, a gut feeling is not caprice or a sixth sense. An executive may be buried under a mountain of information, some of which is contradictory, some of questionable reliability, and some that makes one wonder why it was sent in the first place. But despite the excess of data, there is no algorithm to calculate the best decision. In this situation, an experienced executive may have a feeling of what the best action is—a gut feeling. By definition, the reasons behind this feeling are unconscious. How often did the executives we interviewed trust their gut feelings?

We made sure that the executives were from all levels of the hierarchy, including managers, heads of departments, group executives in charge of a branch of the company, and members of the executive board. Thirty-two answered without having to be asked twice, which signals how important they found the issue. In personal interviews, everyone was provided with the definition of a gut feeling and asked how often they relied on them in important professional decisions.

Not a single one of the executives said that he or she never made gut decisions (Figure 6-1, top). On the other hand, no one professed to make gut decisions all the time. Across all levels in the hierarchy, from managers to the members of the executive boards, the majority responded that they rely on their gut in about 50 percent of the cases. This is a surprisingly high rate. But the very same managers would never admit to it in public.

What keeps executives from following their gut feelings? When asked, three reasons were mentioned again and again:

1. *Rational justification is expected, intuition is not.* As one sixty-year-old senior executive explained: "It's the simple truth that one has to apologize if a decision is not based on 200 percent facts." In the words of another: "We are a high-tech company and our leadership expects numbers and facts." And: "I need to explain a decision after it has been made."

2. *Group decision making conflicts with gut feelings.* Many decisions are made collectively in committees and need to be defended. Executives

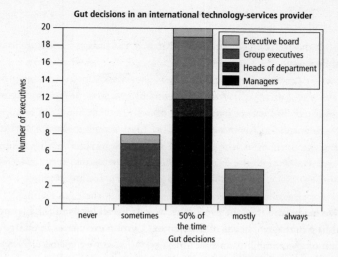

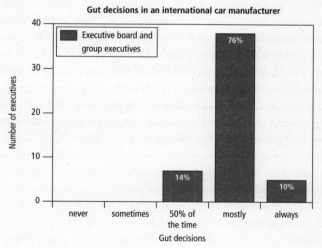

Figure 6-1. How frequently do executives make gut decisions? Based on self-reports of thirty-two executives from a large international technology-services provider (top panel) and fifty top executives from a large international car manufacturer (lower panel). For instance, the majority of the executives from the technology-services provider said that they rely on gut decisions 50 percent of the time. Few of them would publicly admit to doing so. The higher frequency of gut decisions among the car manufacturer is probably due to the fact that its executives were from the two highest levels only, as opposed to from all levels.

often find it difficult to admit, "I have a gut feeling," and convince others to accept it.

3. *The deep anxiety of not having considered all facts.* Some executives reported that fear of overlooking something compels them to continue searching for more facts rather than simply make a decision. Unlike those who feel pressured to provide rational justifications after the fact, these executives wouldn't listen to their inner voice in the first place. As one plainly said, "I lack trust in my feelings."

Is the behavior of these particular executives unusual? In a second study, I asked the fifty top managers and the executive board of a large car manufacturer, which included a high proportion of engineers: "Think of the last ten professional decisions in which you participated. How many of these were gut decisions?" Once again, no one said "never" (Figure 6-1, bottom). Nor did any of them say that they rely on intuition only occasionally. Instead, the majority (76 percent) responded that they do so most of the time. There were even five who said they always make gut decisions. Compared to the responses from the technology services provider, the higher number of gut decisions reported here is probably due to the fact that the executives were exclusively from the two highest levels of management.

My research with managers suggests that the higher up they are in the hierarchy, the greater their reliance on gut feelings. Yet most said that when they have to justify decisions toward third parties, they hide their intuition and look for reasons after the fact. A common complaint is that firms have zero tolerance for making errors, and managers in large firms tend to think that their company doesn't learn from them when they happen. Talking about intuition might be acceptable in personnel selection and in research and development; beyond that it is a taboo topic.

Hide Your Intuition and Hurt Your Company

It is ironic that despite the prevalence of gut decisions in business, up-and-coming managers learn virtually nothing about intuition at their university. Instead, most are taught that there is only one rational way to make decisions, namely good-old decision theory. It asks them to do the impossible: to determine all possible alternatives, all possible consequences, estimate the utility of each consequence, multiply each utility by its probability, and choose the alternative with the highest expected utility. The problem is that the real world of business does not work that way: Good intuitions are needed. Nonetheless, students are likely to learn that intuitive judgments, like visual illusions, are deceptive. And later on, after acting on an intuition in the working world, they feel obliged to hide what they did in a bubble of embarrassed silence.

As we have seen, although about half of professional decisions in large companies are gut decisions, it would probably not go over well if a manager publicly admitted, "I had a hunch." In our society, intuition is suspicious. For that reason, managers typically hide their intuitions, or have even stopped listening to them. I have observed two ways to conceal or avoid gut decisions.

1. *Produce reasons after the fact.* An executive has a gut feeling about an alternative to pursue but fears admitting that it is what it is. So she asks a trusted employee to spend two weeks finding reasons after the fact. With this list in hand, the executive presents the gut decision as if she'd arrived at it by considering all these factors. Rationalization after the fact costs a company time, money, and resources. Another version is to hire a consulting firm. It will deliver a two-hundred-page document analyzing reasons for the gut decision—of course without mentioning that there was ever such a thing in the first place. This procedure costs even more money, time, and attention. Both tactics are ultimately motivated by the leader's fear to accept personal responsibility—which is what a gut decision is all about.

2. *Defensive decision making.* Here, the strategy is to abandon the best option because it cannot be justified if something goes wrong and to favor a second- or third-best option. For example, a senior manager once told me about having a gut feeling to enter a foreign market with a new product but, unable to explain why, went along with

the others and voted against what she felt to be the best opportunity. Again, the idea is to protect oneself, this time by not choosing the best solution for the company. This procedure probably costs a firm more than the strategy of looking for reasons after the fact because of the consequences of second-best courses of action.

Defensive decisions are not a sign of strong leadership and positive error culture. How frequent is defensive decision making? Let's return to the executives from the leading international technology provider whom we met before. I asked the executives how often they chose a second-best option in order to protect themselves, instead of choosing what they believed was the best option. Specifically, the managers were asked: "Consider the last ten important professional decisions in which you participated. How many had a defensive component?"

Seven out of thirty-two managers said they never made a defensive decision (Figure 6-2, top). One of them, a male executive in his fifties, explained: "I believe I have always decided in the best interest of the company. I do well only if the company is doing well. It's my passionate conviction. Even if this company gave me the pink slip, I would still do the same for the next company." That is the type of manager everyone wants to have. But these ideal managers were a minority.

A dozen managers admitted a few defensive decisions, between one and three. One said that these were motivated by fear of blame and of compromising himself by being responsible for an error, which might lead to loss of peer esteem. Others invoked situations with lack of time and incalculable risks. An executive in his early sixties openly admitted that in a few cases he'd simply lacked the courage.

Nearly a third of the managers, however, revealed that about half of their decisions were defensive. One justified his behavior in this way: "I want to be part of the majority, to protect myself from personal attacks. Perhaps I fear my own courage." Another complained that the company provided no incentives for taking risks, only criticism if something went wrong. Several justified their behavior as a means of avoiding conflicts in order to protect themselves and their unit. A member of the executive board admitted that half of his decisions were not in the company's best

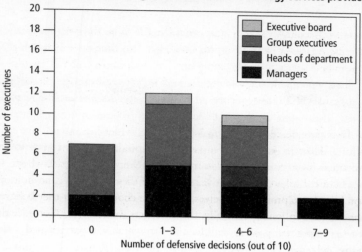

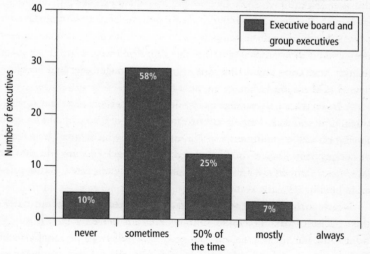

Figure 6-2. Defensive decision making in a large international technology-services company (top panel) and a large international car manufacturer (lower panel). When individuals choose a second-best option to protect themselves if something goes wrong, this is called defensive decision making ("covering your ass"). Defensive decisions protect the individual at the cost of the company or institution. Based on self-reports of thirty-two executives from a large international technology-services provider and fifty-two executives (the two highest levels) from a large international car manufacturer.

interest. According to him, a no-risk mentality reigned in the company, so that he preferred to focus on his own chances and risks and weigh these carefully.

Last but not least, a few even said they would engage in decisions against the best interest of the company in seven to nine out of every ten cases. Those were among the lowest level of managers. One of them explained the spirit of decision making as "better cover your ass."

The defensiveness in this company is symptomatic of what I have found in other large companies. The top executives, including the executive board of the international car manufacturer, reported similar levels of defensive decision making (Figure 6-2, bottom). A majority said that they sometimes did, while only one out of ten reported never having made any defensive decisions at all. Overall, however, these executives reported fewer defensive decisions compared to the technology-services provider, which may again be due to the fact that no lower-level managers from the car manufacturer were asked.

Are Gut Feelings Taboo Everywhere?

Family businesses are one important exception to the rule. In a family- or owner-held company, shares are held by relatively few shareholders, typically by one or a few members of a family, unlike the stocks and other securities of publicly traded companies, which are spread across many investors. Most important, the corporate culture in family businesses is different. They are less anxious about gut feelings; if an error occurs employees are not likely fired on the spot. Rather than being hidden deep down in the desk drawer, errors are talked about more often so that they may be learned from. Plans are made far ahead and good performance is the key, not a formal procedure. The goal is not to maximize gains in the next year, but to develop the company so that it can be handed on to the next generation. Gut decisions are outside the taboo area. Herein lies a big advantage of family businesses: They tend to resemble cockpit culture, while large publicly traded companies generally resemble emergency room culture (chapter 3). The challenge for large companies is to better align the interests of their managers with those of the company, similar to how the interests of a family member are naturally aligned with those of the family business.

Companies could easily break through the taboo and calculate how much revenue they lose through a defensive culture. Reducing defensive decisions would provide an edge of advantage over competitors. To improve its information flow, the leading technology provider used to send questionnaires with a hundred questions to its employees worldwide but didn't really know what to do with the flood of responses. A first measure would be to replace this survey with only two questions: How often do you make defensive decisions? And what do you think could be done to change this? That could be a start for designing a new corporate culture. A second measure, as we will see below, is to make the intuitive rules of experienced leaders explicit and conscious, test these, and use the result to train the less experienced ones.

The Leader's Toolbox

Senior managers routinely need to make decisions or delegate decisions in an instant after brief consultation and under high uncertainty. For their work, classical decision theory is of limited help. In the words of Henry Mintzberg:[2]

> *Managers work at an unrelenting pace; their activities are typically characterized by brevity, variety, fragmentation and discontinuity; and they are strongly oriented to action.*

The rules of thumb that top executives rely on are often unconscious, satisfying the definition of intuition. Inspired by my findings on rules of thumb in the book *Gut Feelings*, the former president of Florida International University, Modesto Maidique, developed an innovative view on the nature of leadership.[3] Every senior manager comes to the job with a personal "adaptive toolbox." This toolbox contains a set of rules of thumb derived from personal experience and values. They are the basis for making decisions about persons, strategies, and investments in a world that puts a premium on efficient use of time.

When Maidique interviewed experienced top managers, some of the rules they intuitively used crossed the border into consciousness. Here are three such rules that some CEOs use to develop and maintain institutions:

- *Hire well and let them do their jobs.*
- *Decentralize operations, decentralize strategy.*
- *Promote from within.*

Although simple, these rules are not arbitrary. They are based on years of experience and each serves a specific goal. For instance, "hire well and let them do their jobs" reflects a vision of an institution where quality control ("hire well") goes together with a climate of trust ("let them do their jobs") needed for cutting-edge innovation. This rule is one of the guiding principles of the Max Planck Institutes, where the first step in hiring a new director is an extensive international search, and the second is to allow the new director the independence and necessary resources to do innovative research. It encourages researchers to take risks and dare to think in new ways. In contrast, funding policies with short-term incentives discourage brilliant researchers from innovative work and push them into producing more of the same.

The decentralization rule serves the goal of making better decisions by benefiting from local knowledge while at the same time increasing responsibility by distributing it. This rule guided the decisions of CEO Marcelo Odebrecht, who was asked by the mayor of Rio de Janeiro to complete the facilities of the 2007 Pan American Games after a previous construction company had failed. In deciding whether to take on such a risky business, he relied on the knowledge of the company's director about the local dynamics, and let the director make the final call. The contract was successfully completed and enhanced the reputation of the company.

Finally, the principle "promote from within" can help to ensure competence and adherence to corporate values. If a department is successful, promoting from within is a valid rule. But if a department is in trouble, specifically because of in-fighting, this is likely not the right solution. Here, someone from outside may be the better choice.

Not every rule works all the time, just as a hammer does not work for all home repairs. This is why every CEO needs to have a wide range of "tools."

Good Leadership

Good leadership consists of a toolbox full of rules of thumb and the intuitive ability to quickly see which rule is appropriate in which context. Here are six rules of thumb that are the result of an interview with Ray Stata, chairman of Analog Devices, in September 2010. He took daring personal risks to move his company into a new field. The rules are different for dealing with people and business strategy.

People:

- First listen, then speak.
- If a person is not honest and trustworthy, the rest doesn't matter.
- Encourage people to take risks and empower them to make decisions and take ownership.

Strategy:

- Innovation drives success.
- You can't play it safe and win. Analysis will not reduce uncertainty.
- When judging a plan, put as much stock in the people as in the plan.

These rules are not limited to business leadership. For instance, "first listen, then speak" is hammered into pilots during their training. In an emergency situation, the captain should not immediately say what he or she believes is the right thing to do, but first ask the other crew members for their opinion. Otherwise, they may be intimidated and hold back their advice.

Like "first listen, then speak," many rules of thumb specify a sequence in time. An analysis of six technology-based ventures showed such temporal rules in the "adaptive toolbox" of each company.[4] One illustrative example is *Follow the pecking order of nations*: Enter one continent at a time. First enter the United States, then use U.S. customers as references to enter

Japan, and finally use Japanese customers as references to the rest of Asia. Companies do not generally start with these simple rules but instead elaborate first and chase too many opportunities before eventually simplifying their portfolio of rules based on their experience.

Business Rules to Avoid

Like any tool, no rule of thumb is always best or worst: It depends on the problem to be solved. Some of the worst decisions stem from rules of thumb that are based on destructive emotions. Here is one:

Seek revenge at any cost.

Early in his career, Warren Buffett made his "$200 billion blunder." He had noticed that a textile company, Berkshire Hathaway, sold off a mill and used the cash to repurchase its stock, which then led to a rise in the value of the stock. When this process repeated itself, Buffett bought a large amount of the company's stock just before the sale of another mill. He shook hands with Seabury Stanton, the CEO, on a deal to tender his stock at $11.50 to make a small short-term profit. Then a letter came from the CEO offering to buy Buffett's shares not at the amount agreed but for 12.5 cents less. Feeling betrayed, Buffett began to buy Berkshire Hathaway stocks until he had the majority control and then fired Stanton. Buffett had his revenge but owned a lousy business that he estimated cost him about $200 billion in lost opportunity. Experience can be a harsh teacher for learning the right rules of thumb.

How to Test Rules of Thumb

Many industries, businesses, and restaurants use simple rules for pricing ("Take the cost of raw food and multiply by three") and for decision making in general ("Don't build a building without a tenant"). How do they know whether and when a rule of thumb is a good one? One way is to test these rules, which is easier the more specific a rule is. Rules of thumb can have different levels of generality:

- *Enter only businesses where you believe you can be the leader.*
- *If a customer has not made a purchase for nine months or longer, classify as inactive.*

The first rule is transportable across many businesses; the second is rather specific. The following study shows how to test how well it predicts which customers will buy from the company in the future.

One Good Reason Can Be Better than Many

Our mailboxes, be they electronic or made of steel, overflow with flyers, brochures, sales catalogues, and credit card offers. For companies who target past and new customers, mass mailings are part of the business plan. At the same time, unfocused advertising campaigns are annoying to people who have no interest in the products and are expensive for companies. Ideally, every company should spend resources on active, loyal customers rather than on those who will not make further purchases. But in a database containing tens or hundreds of thousands of customers, how can active customers be distinguished from inactive ones?

The conventional idea is to solve a complex problem with a complex analysis. One such tool is the Pareto/NBD model featured by marketing experts.[5] For each customer it delivers the probability that he or she is still active—exactly the information companies want. To the dismay of many a marketing expert, however, managers instead often trust simple rules of thumb based on their personal experience. Managers of a major global airline relied on a recency-of-last purchase (hiatus) rule:

If a customer has not made a purchase for nine months or longer, classify him/her as inactive, otherwise as active.

This simple rule focuses on one good reason only: recency of purchase. It is used by frequent flyer programs as well as by apparel retailers. But isn't that a naive rule? It ignores how much the customer bought, the time between purchases, and all the information that complex tools such as Pareto/NBD carefully analyze, as well as fancy calculations. The use of the hiatus rule looks like strong evidence for the story that people decide irrationally because they have limited cognitive capacities and are unable to handle all the information needed to make a good decision. Can one good reason ever come close to using all reasons and impressive calculations?

Two professors of business conducted a clever study designed to demonstrate the superiority of the complex method over the simple rule. They tested how many correct predictions the complex method made compared to the simple rule for the airline, an apparel retailer, and an online CD retailer, CDNow.[6] The result, however, was not what the two professors had been expecting. In two out of three cases the simple rule was faster and required less information, but was nevertheless more accurate. For the global airline, the simple rule predicted 77 percent of customers correctly; the complex method predicted only 74 percent (Figure 6-3). For the apparel retailer, the simple rule was even more effective, 83 compared to 75 percent correct. Finally, for the online CD retailer, both the simple rule and the complex method predicted equally well, 77 percent. Instead of confirming their belief that more information is better, the authors found what I call a *less-is-more effect*.

Less Is More

Is less-is-more a one-off phenomenon? No. Figure 6-4 shows the average result across twenty studies that compared two simple rules with a complex strategy called multiple regression. This strategy is widely used in business forecasting, such as predicting next year's sales; to do so it carefully weighs the importance of each reason. One of the simple rules tested, called tallying, treats all reasons equally, just as 1/N treats all investment alternatives equally. The second, called take-the-best, is a one-good-reason rule (similar to the recency-of-last-purchase rule) that, as its name implies, relies solely on the best reason for making a prediction.[7]

Here we need to keep in mind again the difference between known risks and uncertainty. Known risks correspond to hindsight: We know all the details (such as last year's sales figures) and can explain them after the fact. For "predicting" the past, the complex strategy did the best job in the studies. When it came to the uncertain future (such as next year's sales

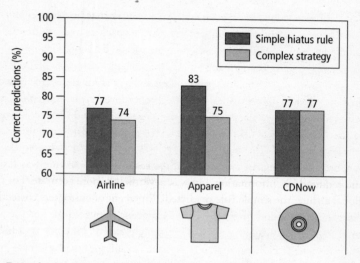

Figure 6-3. Less is more. How to predict which customers will purchase in the future? Managers of three companies rely on a simple rule of thumb (the hiatus rule), while management theorists propose complex strategies (Pareto/NBD model). A test shows that the rule of thumb is better than the complex strategy at predicting which customers purchase in the future, even though it uses only part of the information. This less-is-more effect held for the airline and the apparel retailer, while for the online CD retailer CDNow, both strategies were equally accurate. In uncertain worlds, less is often more.
Source: Wübben and Wangenheim (2008).

figures), however, both of the simple rules made better predictions than the complex method.

There is a world of difference between hindsight and foresight. On the radio, I often hear interviews with stock experts who are asked why Microsoft or some other stock went up yesterday. They always have an explanation. That's hindsight; they already know what happened and can pick some story from their broad range of knowledge that fits the facts. Never are they asked whether Microsoft will go up or down tomorrow. That would be prediction, and prediction involves uncertainty. As various studies have documented, when financial experts are asked to predict the future performance of stocks they tend to perform at chance level or below.

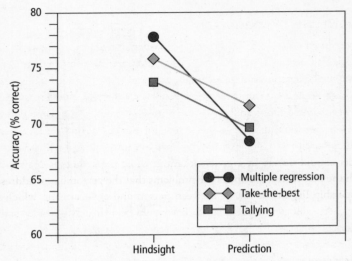

Figure 6-4. Less is more in prediction (uncertainty); more is better in hindsight (known risks). Shown are the average results of twenty studies similar to those in figure 6-3, where high school dropout rates and housing prices, among other variables, were predicted on the basis of cues such as teachers' salaries and students' reading scores. Multiple regression is a complex method that weights and adds all cues, routinely used in the social sciences. Take-the-best is a simple rule of thumb that relies on only the best cue and ignores the rest. Tallying relies on all cues but simply weights them equally. Hindsight means that all data are known and the strategies are fitted to the data. Prediction means that only half of the data are known and the other half are predicted. The complex model excels in explaining the past (hindsight), while both rules of thumb excel in predicting the future.

Source: Czerlinski et al. (1999).

A less-is-more effect occurs when predictions made using a simple rule are better than those using a complex strategy. The reason is not that the simple rule has privileged information. In the twenty studies reported above, the complex strategy had access to all the information the simple rule had and more. In an uncertain world, the reason is that complex strategies are led astray by taking into consideration scores of details, many of which are irrelevant. Remember Einstein's rule in chapter 5?

The Nature of Leadership

What distinguishes an individual as a leader? From Plato to today, the theory that leaders have specific personality traits has been the guiding idea. Intelligence, dominance, persistence, and self-confidence are examples. For Francis Galton these traits were even inherited. More recently it has been argued that leadership is not a sum but a particular constellation of traits. Yet looking at traits alone has not worked well; after all, terms such as "openness" and "extraversion" are too unspecific to tell us what a leader should decide in a given situation. Most important, it deals only with the person and overlooks the problems that the person has to address. Leadership lies in the match between person and environment, which is why there is no single personality that would be a successful leader at all historical times and for all problems to solve.

Another way to pick good leaders is to stop looking for leadership traits and to start identifying people with the ability to use smart rules of thumb. This is a way to describe leadership styles at a very concrete level. Analyzing leaders' adaptive toolboxes provides a new vision for understanding what leadership entails. Their rules are mostly intuitive, meaning that the leader cannot easily explain them—just as we speak our native language without a second thought, but often flounder when asked about grammatical details. True leadership means intuitively understanding what rule will work in what situation.

Common Misconceptions About Intuition

1. *Intuition is the opposite of rationality.* It's not. Intuition is unconscious intelligence based on personal experience and smart rules of thumb. You need both intuition and reasoning to be rational.

2. *Intuition is female.* That has been the doctrine since the Enlightenment. Today, men are also allowed to have intuitions. The key difference is that men are still more hesitant to admit intuition or even listen to their gut.

3. *Intuition is inferior to deliberate thinking.* Deliberate thinking and logic is not generally better than intuition, or vice versa. Logic (or statistics) is best for dealing with known risks, while good intuitions and rules of thumb are indispensable in an uncertain world (Figure 2-3).

4. *Intuition is based on complex unconscious weighing of all evidence.* This thesis has been put forward to explain why intuitive decisions are often excellent. The idea is that if an intelligent process is good, it must function according to the bookkeeping method of weighting everything. But bookkeeping is only best in a world of known risk, not under uncertainty. There is strong evidence that intuitions are based on simple, smart rules that take into account only some of the available information.

7

Fun and Games

If everything on earth were rational,
nothing would happen.

Fyodor Dostoevsky

Let's Make a Deal

The TV game show *Let's Make a Deal* was first aired on NBC in 1963. One of its highlights was the "Big Deal of the Day," in which the host, Monty Hall, showed the contestant three doors. Behind one was the grand prize, a new Cadillac or another luxurious item that elicited screams of joy; behind the others were worthless "zonks" such as goats. *Parade* magazine columnist Marilyn vos Savant, who was listed in *Guinness World Records* as the woman with the highest IQ for five consecutive years, made the "Monty Hall problem" popular. Here, in her own words, is the problem the contestant faces:[1]

> *Suppose you are on a game show, and you're given the choice of three doors. Behind one door is a car, behind the others, goats. You pick a door, say number 1, and the host, who knows what's behind the doors, opens another door, say number 3, which has a goat. He says to you, "Do you want to pick door number 2?" Is it to your advantage to switch your choice of doors?*

Would you switch or stay? If you opt to stay, you are with the crowd. After all, only two doors are left, so chances appear to be equal, and mistakenly switching to a door with a goat could cause endless regret. Marilyn,

Figure 7-1. The Monty Hall Problem. You are a contestant and can pick your prize. Behind one door is a Cadillac, behind the other two are goats. You pick door 1. Now the host, Monty Hall, who knows where the Cadillac is, opens door 3 to show you a goat, and offers you the choice of switching to door 2. Would you switch or stay?

however, advised switching. That caused a storm of some ten thousand letters within one year, close to a thousand of them carrying signatures with PhDs, mostly disagreeing with her. Dr. Robert Sachs, a professor of mathematics at George Mason University, wrote: "You blew it! Let me explain. If one door is shown to be a loser, that information changes the probability of either remaining choice, neither of which has any reason to be more likely, to 1/2." Another writer with a Y-chromosome commented: "You cannot apply feminine logic to odds. The new situation is one of two equal chances." And another, even less charmingly: "You are the goat!" Finally, the dust settled, and almost everyone agreed with Marilyn that probability theory tells us that switching is the best action. Dr. Sachs wrote her a letter of apology, one of the few who had the grace to concede their mistake.

Risk: Switch Doors in the Monty Hall Problem?

Dr. Sachs, like the others, was confused by probabilities. A typical muddled thought is: "There is a one-third probability that the car is behind each of the three doors. One door has been opened, which eliminates it and a third of the probability. Now that the car is behind one of only two doors, the probability needs to be divided equally between the remaining two doors, which is fifty-fifty." This is one of the celebrated "cognitive illusions" that are allegedly engraved in stone in our brains.[2]

To dispel the confusion, however, there is a simple method, the same as explained for HIV testing: Use *natural frequencies*. Let me explain it for the Monty Hall problem. The crucial step is to think of a number of contestants, not just one. Let's take three, who each pick a different door. Assume the car is behind door 2 (Figure 7-2). The first contestant picks door 1. Monty's only option is to open door 3, and he offers the contestant the opportunity to switch. Switching to door 2 wins. The second contestant picks door 3. This time, Monty has to open door 1, and switching to door 2 again wins. Only the third contestant who picks door 2 will lose when switching. Now it is easier to see that switching wins more often than staying, and we can calculate exactly how often: in two out of three cases.[3] This is why Marilyn recommended switching doors.

The Monty Hall problem has been debated at parties, in classrooms, and on the front page of the *New York Times*, keeping people arguing about probabilities. During the game show's long run, millions of dollars may well have been left behind Monty Hall's doors. What I have shown here is that these arguments can be easily resolved by thinking in terms of

switching wins   staying wins   switching wins

Figure 7-2. There is a simple method to working out the Monty Hall Problem. Don't think of yourself alone, but think of three candidates standing in front of the three doors. The candidate who initially chose door 1 wins by switching to door 2 after Monty opens door 3. Similarly, the candidate who initially chose door 3 will also win by switching to door 2. Only the candidate who initially chose door 2 loses by switching. This means that in two of three cases, switching pays.

natural frequencies. The problem is not simply inside the human mind, but in the way the information is framed.

Let me now tell you the second, largely unknown part of the story.

Uncertainty: Is Switching Doors Also Best in the Real Show?

The Monty Hall problem posed by Marilyn and others before her involves a world of risk, not uncertainty. Probability theory provides the best answer only when the rules of the game are certain, when all alternatives, consequences, and probabilities are known or can be calculated. Here is my question: Is switching also the best choice on the real game show?

The crucial issue is whether Monty always offered his guests the chance to switch.[4] (This is not mentioned in Marilyn's original problem, but her omission is not my point.) For instance, if Monty were mischievous by nature, he would make the offer only if contestants picked the door with the grand prize behind it. Switching would then always lead to the goat and NBC could keep the big prize for the next show. Did Monty in fact offer each guest the opportunity to switch?

Barry Nalebuff, one of the first to write about the Monty Hall problem, recalled that he saw Monty offering the option to switch. But he could not recall "whether Monty offered this option all the time and whether or not his making the offer was at all connected to whether you picked the right door." Monty's longtime production assistant Carol Andrews, in contrast, asserted that Monty never afforded contestants an opportunity to switch. Monty Hall himself recalled that he rarely offered the switching option and could not say how often it was accepted. What actually happened may never be resolved. Due to a legal dispute over residual rights, few tapes are in the hands of the public.

The source of uncertainty is not only Monty's and his colleagues' imperfect memory. The real game show revolved around the persona of Monty Hall, and part of his personality was to make spontaneous decisions rather than follow a strict protocol. In other words, the suspense of the game arose from contestants' uncertainty about Monty Hall's motives and actions; this suspense would have been lost if he had followed the same rules in every show. "Where does it say that I have to let you switch every time? I am the master of the show." Monty made it clear that the rules of the Monty Hall problem do not apply to him. "If the host is required to open a door all the time and offer you a switch, then you should take the switch. But if he has the choice whether to allow a switch or not, beware. Caveat emptor. It all depends on his mood."

Is the best decision under risk also the best one on the real show? As Monty himself explained, it can be the worst. After one contestant picked door 1, Monty opened door 3, revealing a goat. While the contestant thought about switching to door 2, Monty pulled out a roll of bills and offered $3,000 in cash not to switch.[5]

> "I'll switch to it," insisted the contestant.
> "Three thousand dollars," Monty Hall repeated, "Cash. Cash money. It could be a car, but it could be a goat. Four thousand."
> The contestant resisted the temptation. "I'll try the door."
> "Forty-five hundred. Forty-seven. Forty-eight. My last offer: Five thousand dollars."
> "Let's open the door." The contestant again rejected the offer.
> "You just ended up with a goat," Monty Hall said, opening the door. And he explained: "Now do you see what happened there? The higher I got, the more you thought that the car was behind door 2. I wanted to con you into switching there, because I knew the car was behind 1. That's the kind of thing I can do when I'm in control of the game."

In the real game, probability theory is not enough. Good intuitions are needed, which can be more challenging than calculations. One way to reduce uncertainty is to rely on rules of thumb. For instance, the "minimax rule" says:

Choose the alternative that avoids the worst outcome.

Ending up with a goat *and* foregoing the money is the worst possible outcome. That can only happen if the contestant switches. For that reason, the rule advises taking the money and sticking with door 1. It's called "minimax" because it aims at minimizing your losses if the maximum loss scenario happens (here, opening the door with a goat). This simple rule would have cut straight through Monty's psychological game and got the contestant the money—and the car to boot.

Intuitive rules are not foolproof, but neither are calculations. A second way to reduce uncertainty is to guess Monty's motivation, which is harder, particularly when nervously standing in the spotlight before TV cameras. It requires putting oneself into his mind. Monty appears to have offered the switch because he knew the contestant had chosen the winning door, and then offered money not to switch in order to insinuate that the car was behind the other door. This psychological reflection leads you to stick with your door, the same choice you would make when using the minimax rule. In fact, Monty himself suggested a version of minimax: "If you can get me to offer you $5,000 not to open the door, take the money and go home."

Thinking of Known Risks Can Get You a Goat in an Uncertain World

The Monty Hall problem illustrates three themes of this book: how to understand risks, how to deal with uncertainty, and—most important—how not to confuse both. Many people misperceive the odds in the Monty Hall problem. Yet there is a simple remedy: to translate the probabilities into natural frequencies to see what the best action is. Natural frequencies are termed "natural" because they reflect the kind of information humans and animals received in history, before the invention of books and probability theory. We can think more easily with them. Equally important is the crucial distinction between the world of risk (the Monty Hall problem) and the world of uncertainty (the actual TV show *Let's Make a Deal*). The best action in the world of risk is not guaranteed to be the best in the real game show. In fact, applying probability theory to uncertain worlds can leave you with a goat—another case of the turkey illusion that risks can be calculated.

Among the thousands of articles written about the Monty Hall problem, the distinction between risk and uncertainty has been virtually ignored.

Street Tricksters

In tourist cities and county fairs you might spot men furtively playing a card game on a street corner, with dollar bills stacked tall on small makeshift tables. The game is simple. There are three cards. One is red on both sides, the second white on both sides, and the third is red on one side and white on the other. The trickster lets you draw one card blindly and places it on the table faceup. Say it's red. Then he offers you a $10 bet: If the hidden side is also red, he wins; if it's white, you do. That seems a fair bet, doesn't it? After all, the card you drew could be either the red-red or the red-white card, so the chance that the other side is red or white seems to be 50:50.

If you are suspicious about being offered a fair deal by a stranger on the street, your intuition is right. To see why the cards are stacked against you, use your brains. Don't try to think in probabilities, but instead draw a natural frequency tree. As always, start with a number of games. To make it simple, consider playing the game six times. This is the top of the tree (Figure 7-3, right). If you draw a card randomly, each of the three cards can be expected to be drawn twice. This is the middle level of the tree. Now look at the bottom level: For each of the two red-red cards, a red side will show faceup; for the two red-white cards, we expect only one red. (The white-white card will of course never show red.) In the three cases where red is faceup, two are with the red-red card, and one with the red-white card. In other words, if you draw a red face, the other side will be red as well two out of three times. That's why the trickster bets on red and makes money. Your chance of winning is not 50:50, but only one in three.[6]

Figure 7-3 (left) illustrates why people get confused when thinking in probabilities about the trickster's offer. Look at the formula and you will see why natural frequencies, in contrast, need little calculation. Once again, the confusion is created by the way the information is communicated. The exact same trees can be drawn for the Monty Hall problem. In the next location we visit, however, the probabilities are hidden in an even more insidious way.

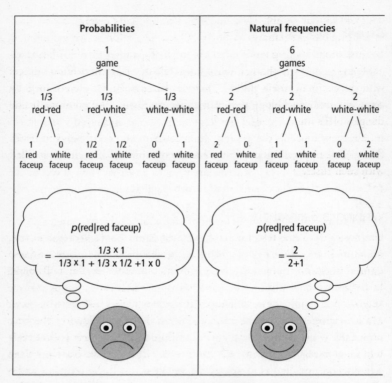

Figure 7-3. Trickster's game. Three cards are in a hat: One is red on both sides, one red on one and white on the other, and one is white on both sides. You blindly draw a card that shows red faceup. The trickster offers you a $10 bet that the other side is also red. Is it a fair bet? Left side: Solving the problem with probabilities is confusing for most people. The probability $p(\text{red}|\text{red faceup})$ is the probability that the card is red facedown given that it is red faceup. The formula is called Bayes' rule. Right side: Natural frequencies help to see that it isn't a fair bet. The chance that the other side is also red is two in three.

How Casinos Deceive You

Every year, Americans spend over $30 billion in commercial casinos, and likely the same sum over again on race tracks, lotteries, and other ways of gambling. That's significantly more than Americans spend on going to the movies. Spending in casinos, however, means losing. And casinos are designed so that gamblers lose money. Why so many people can be lured into losing billions remains a mystery. One explanation is that gambling is not just about making money, but the thrill of gambling itself. A less charitable explanation is that gamblers are reckless, probability-blind addicts who overestimate their skills in games that are largely determined by chance. Most psychological explanations are about shortcomings inside the gambler's mind.

Yet these illusions don't come from nowhere. There are ways to instill false beliefs in people about their chances of winning. The casino is filled with such ruses.

Winning Is Everywhere

Casinos in Las Vegas resort hotels have one or more floors where hundreds, sometimes thousands, of slot machines are arranged back-to-back and row upon row. Entering the doors, you will be bombarded by the loud sound of clanking almost constantly and from every which direction. Metal tokens drop several inches onto a metal tray when players cash out winnings. Many machines amplify the noises to ensure that even the hard of hearing notice the wins.[7] When players win but do not immediately collect their tokens, an escalating stream of beeps fills the air. Each beep corresponds to a credit won, and increases in credit are announced with crescendoing audio effects, often at a faster rate than the actual number of credits won. This imposing sound collage creates the illusion that players have won more than they have.

Sound travels easily between the rows of slot machines on the casino floor. Yet the machines also send visual signals to distant players. In Las Vegas, a siren light sits atop many machines and begins to spin whenever a major jackpot has been hit. Winners are paid out by hand. While they wait for the slot machine attendant to deliver the money, the siren continues to flash and blare. That can go on for half an hour or even longer: Slot machine players regularly complain about how slow attendants are, whether intentionally or not. On busy nights, several large-jackpot winners may be waiting for their booty at the same time, creating the impression that big wins occur more frequently than they actually do. And even when the cacophony of sirens finally ceases, you may find past winners of major jackpots beaming at you from posters on the walls, with oversized publicity checks in their hands.

In the midst of all this commotion to celebrate moments of winning, the losers are lost in silence.

How Slot Machines Fool You

The classical slot machine has three metal hoops, called reels, covered with symbols. A lever is pulled to spin the reels. Each reel has around twenty possible positions where it can come to rest, and each stop has an equal probability of occurring. If a particular pattern of symbols appears in the payoff line, a payout is awarded. An original Liberty Bell slot machine, invented in 1895, can still be admired at the Liberty Belle Saloon and Restaurant in Reno, Nevada. It has only ten stops, and each of its reels is decorated with diamond, spade, and heart symbols, together with images of a cracked liberty bell. A spin resulting in three bells gave the biggest payoff. Later, fruit symbols such as lemons, plums, and cherries appeared on the reels (in Britain they are still called fruit machines). The Liberty Bell paid out 75 percent of the coins thrown into the machine, leaving the "house" a profit of 25 percent.

With twenty stop positions, there would be eight thousand (20^3) possible outcomes, and a jackpot with a unique combination of three symbols can be expected once in eight thousand spins. The players who do not know this information can guess the chance of winning by observing the frequency of wins in a large number of spins and also of the more frequent near misses, when one of the three identical symbols is just above or below the pay line.

Until the 1960s, slot machines worked much as their exterior design suggests. That all changed when electronic slot machines were introduced. The new machines resemble the old ones, but only on the surface. Instead of physically spinning reels, digital random number generators are at work. The spinning reels on display create a false impression about the actual chances of winning. While the reel that the customer sees may have twenty stops, the true, virtual "reel" may have two to ten times as many. Their external design can suggest a one-in-eight-thousand chance of winning, as would have been the case on older machines, but thanks to the microchip designers, the chances are now hundreds or thousands of times lower. This is the reason why electronic machines can offer such large jackpots. To raise undue hopes, the machine is programmed to "show" many near-jackpot misses, although there were actually fewer or none (Figure 7-4). This deceptive design is standard practice.

Why do so many people lose so much money playing slot machines? The answer is not simply that people are probability-blind, or enjoy a tumble on the wheel of fortune more than they enjoy the money they lose, as the typical psychological explanations go. There is more. The casino floor is an assembly of delusions, a theater that makes the players hear and

Figure 7-4. Illusory design. Can you see the foot of the "7" above the right slot? You almost had three sevens! So you think, but you have been misled. What is displayed on electronic slot machines does not mirror the actual result: To increase the illusion of (almost) winning, many more near misses are displayed than actually occur.

see more wins and near-wins than there actually are. As a direct consequence of this illusory experience, players overestimate their own chance of winning.

The casino is often seen as the ideal example of known risks. Yet as the advance of the new slot machine technology shows, lots of inventiveness is put into making actual chances of winning seem more certain than they are, creating another illusion of certainty.

Some Helpful Rules for Leisure-Time Decisions Under Uncertainty

How to Block a Penalty Kick

The Olympic Stadium in Berlin is crowded with seventy-five thousand fans watching the 2006 Soccer World Champion quarterfinal. Argentina is playing Germany. With ten minutes left Argentina tied the score, and after the extra time it's still a draw. Now it's time for the penalty shoot-out, a tense situation where both goalkeepers take turns facing five players from the other team. Shoot-outs are equally nerve-wracking for the fans, who collectively hold their breath before each kick; some can't even bear to look. Yet this shoot-out is unique. The German goalkeeper Jens Lehmann is holding a piece of paper that he looks at before every penalty kick. The Argentinian player facing him might be wondering what's on that sheet. And guessing that it contains information about him, his technique, and his preferred corner. In the end, Lehmann blocked two kicks, eliminating Argentina, and Germany moved on to the semifinals.

The media attributed the victory to the information Lehmann was carrying. My interpretation is different. Studies with expert players in various sports show that their performance decreases when they pay attention to what they are doing or think too long. For instance, when experienced golf players are instructed to pay attention to their swing, their performance decreases.[8] (For beginners the opposite holds: They tend to get better with more thinking, time, and attention.) If expert handball players are given more time to think about the next action, they too decide, on average, on second-best actions. Similarly, when the Argentinian players saw

Lehmann studying his notes, they likely began to consciously ponder what to do, and that helped the Germans. This interpretation is supported by studies on intuition in sports, but also on what we know about the decisive final penalty kick by the Argentinian player Estéban Cambiasso. Taking his time, Lehmann made a show of studying his notes. But unknown to Cambiasso, they actually contained no information about him. Cambiasso made his kick, and Lehmann blocked it.

This scene provides us with a useful guideline for how to win a competition:

If you are highly proficient at a sport, don't think too long about the next move.

If you are a beginner, take your time in deciding what to do.

And, if you want to play it mean:

Make your expert opponents think rather than follow their gut.

The rationale is this: Expertise is a form of unconscious intelligence. The moment one succeeds in making the expert's conscious thought intervene, performance is likely to decrease. As the former German soccer player Gerd Müller, one of the top goal-scorers of all time, once said about intuition in sports, "If you start to think, you are already a goner."

Fast and Frugal Food Choice

You are in a restaurant for the first time ever, and the waiter hands you the menu. Do you study the entire menu? Try to figure out the best option, and nothing less? This strategy is called *maximizing*. In a restaurant where the menu resembles an encyclopedia, this may require stamina.

It's not what I do. I travel lots and after giving a talk typically end up in a restaurant I have never eaten at before. My experience is that it can pay not to open the menu. If it's a good restaurant, I use this rule of thumb:

Ask the waiter: What would you eat here this evening?

I don't ask the waiter what he or she would *recommend*. Then the waiter might begin to think. In a good restaurant, the waiter knows what's going on in the kitchen that evening, and the question also draws on their pride. I have not been disappointed so far, while some of my friends who carefully worked their way through the entire menu have. But no rule works in all situations; I would not rely on it in restaurants on the cheap side. And for some people, it is emotionally unbearable not to see all options and to rely on someone else, even if that person knows better.

Asking a waiter is not the only fast route to ordering a delicious meal. Here are four alternative rules of thumb:

Satisficing: This Northumbrian term means to choose the first option that is satisfactory; that is, "good enough." You need the menu for this rule. First, you pick a category (say, fish). Then you read the first item in this category, and decide whether it is good enough. If yes, you close the menu and order that dish without reading any further. If no, you go on to the second item and proceed in the same way. For instance, if the first item is Citrus Broiled Alaska Salmon but you had salmon yesterday and are up for variety, you pass and move to the second one. It's Blackened Tuna Steak with Mango Salsa, and if that sounds good, you close the menu and order it.

Advice taking: Don't open the menu. Order what the waiter or—in a superior restaurant—a critic recommends. As I mentioned before, the danger is that the waiter ponders too long about what you would like rather than about what's best this evening.

Imitate your peers: Don't open the menu. Find out who at your table has visited this restaurant most often, and order the dish he or she orders. If you are in a foreign country or a restaurant you do not know, this is likely a good strategy.

Habit: Don't open the menu. Order your favorite dish that you always order. This rule applies when you are familiar with the restaurant, know what is good, and don't want to risk disappointment.

If you are a maximizer and try these rules, you will likely feel a creeping anxiety about having overlooked something. Relax, it will fade away after a few positive experiences. Then you can begin to think about the real question: Which rule works best in which situation? Simple rules can supply you with a good choice, protect you from wavering back and forth between alternatives, and save time you can spend talking with your dinner mates. Maximizing, in contrast, can leave you with the dispiriting feeling that you still don't know whether you made the best choice.

How do people actually choose in a restaurant? My colleagues and I asked a representative sample of one thousand German adults (Figure 7-5 top).[9] The largest group reported that they maximize; that is, they go through the menu from the beginning to the end to find the best dish. About a third say that they satisfice. In contrast, few take advice and virtually nobody imitates what their friends and colleagues at the table order. Copying appears to be a taboo among Germans, unlike in more family-oriented countries where it is fine if you order what everyone else is ordering.

Fast and Frugal Shopping

You're setting out to buy a pair of trousers. Some shoppers try to find the best one, and nothing less. They walk into a department store, try on the first pair to see how they fit, and move on to more trousers to find out whether there is something better. After going through the entire selection there, it's time to head to another department store around the corner and check all the trousers there, too. And then there are all the boutiques along the street that might have something better. Shortly before the stores close, they make a purchase, but still can't be sure whether it really was the best buy. There could have been a better deal in the stores in another part of town. Maximizing can be a direct route toward unhappiness: One simply wants too much. Smartphone apps and comparison shopping websites that enable people to find the cheapest price appear to reinforce the desire for the very best deal or the perfect product.

The alternative is satisficing: to go for a product that is *good enough*, not the *best*. After all, in an uncertain world, there is no way to find the best. Even if you got it by accident, you would not know and might still look for something better.

Let's go back into the department store. There, for instance, you might look for a pair of trousers that is black, fits you, and does not cost more than $100. That's an aspiration level. When you find a pair of trousers that meets this aspiration, just buy it and go for a cup of coffee. Don't search for

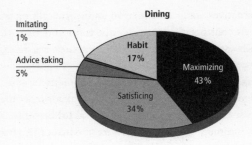

Figure 7-5. Everyday decision making. Top: How do you choose in a restaurant? Maximizing = reading through the entire menu and trying to find the best dish. Satisficing = selecting a category (meat, fish, etc.) and then reading the items until the first dish that is good enough is found. Advice taking = asking the waiter what he or she recommends. Imitating = ordering what your friends order. Habit = ordering what you always order. Bottom: How do you shop for a pair of trousers? Maximizing = going through all items, comparing them carefully, and trying to find the best. Satisficing = buying the first pair of trousers that is good enough. Advice taking = buying what the salesperson or a fashion magazine recommends. Imitating = buying what your friends buy. Habit = always buying the same model or brand. Shown are the responses of a representative sample of one thousand German adults. For instance, 43 percent reported that they maximize all the time, while only 1 percent reported imitating.

any more alternatives. There is no reason for it—you got what you needed. Studies indicate that people who rely on aspiration rules tend to be more optimistic and have higher self-esteem than maximizers. The latter excel in perfectionism, depression, and self-blame.[10]

How many people try to maximize their shopping? In the survey mentioned above, people were asked how they buy a pair of trousers. One out of every five adults, more women than men, said they try to find the best. Singles maximize more than those who are married or live with a partner. The majority, however, tries to find a pair of trousers that is good enough rather than the best. Once again, almost nobody said they would buy the trousers that their friends are wearing (imitating). A few buy what the sales person or fashion magazines recommend, while others buy the model or brand they always buy.

The same rules of thumb apply to many everyday activities. How to decide which TV program to watch this evening? Maximizers use the remote control to run through all TV channels, checking for the best program. Yet because there are commercials on quite a few, they have to run through the channels twice over. And so they spend their evenings flipping back and forth, trying hard to find the best, and may end up not having watched any program at all. The alternative is to use the remote control to find something "good enough" and, once it is found, just watch it. Learning to live with a good-enough choice and the possibility that there is something better out there is necessary in an uncertain world. Food choice, shopping, and watching TV are not the biggest decisions we face. But they can swallow up enormous amounts of time while leaving us restless and dissatisfied. And imagine if everyone tried to maximize in mate or employment choice, to find the perfect job or the perfect partner and nothing less. That would be a recipe for disaster.

8

Getting to the Heart of Romance

Keep your eyes wide open before marriage,
half shut afterward.

Benjamin Franklin

A few years after his historic voyage on the *Beagle*, the twenty-nine-year-old Charles Darwin turned his mind to more domestic matters. Should he get married? Darwin took a pencil and wrote "This is the question" on the top of a scrap of paper. Then he divided it in two columns, like a balance sheet, and listed the reasons for and against marriage.

MARRY

Children—(if it please God)—Constant companion, (& friend in old age) who will feel interested in one, object to be beloved and played with—better than a dog anyhow—Home, and someone to take care of house—Charms of music and female chit-chat. These things good for one's health. Forced to visit and receive relations <u>but terrible loss of time</u>.

My God, it is intolerable to think of spending one's whole life, like a neuter bee, working, working, and nothing after all.—No, no won't do.—Imagine living all one's day solitary in smoky dirty London house.—Only picture to yourself nice soft wife on a sofa with good fire, and books and music perhaps—compare this vision with the dingy reality of Grt Marlboro's St.

NOT MARRY

No children, (no second life) no one to take care for one in old age. . . . Freedom to go where one liked— Choice of Society <u>and little of it</u>. Conversation of clever men at clubs—Not forced to visit relatives, and to bend in every trifle—to have the expense and anxiety of children—perhaps quarreling. <u>Loss of time</u>—cannot read in the evenings— fatness and idleness—anxiety and responsibility—less money for books etc—if many children forced to gain one's bread.—(But then it is very bad for one's health to work so much)

Perhaps my wife won't like London; then the sentence is banishment and degradation with indolent idle fool.

Darwin concluded that he should marry, and wrote "Marry–Marry–Marry Q.E.D." under the left column.[1] Aware of the consequences for his personal freedom, he added on the reverse side the insight "There is many a happy slave." The following year, Darwin married his cousin Emma Wedgwood and eventually had ten children. How did Darwin decide to marry, based on the reasons he envisioned—constant companion, better than a dog, no children, fatness and idleness? He did not tell us.

Maximizing or Rules of Thumb?

There are two ways Darwin might have arrived at his conclusion: maximizing and rules of thumb. Maximizing here means to estimate how much each of the pros of marriage is worth (the utility), estimate the probabilities that these will actually occur with the person in question, multiply the probability of each reason by its utility, and add all these numbers up. Repeat the same procedure using the cons for the alternative "not marry." Finally, choose the alternative with the highest expected utility. This method is also known as the maximization of subjective expected utility and taught worldwide at universities as the very nature of rational choice. It is based on the ideal that we know or can estimate the risks. Benjamin Franklin featured a version of this bookkeeping method for marriage decisions, as we will see in a moment.

In an uncertain world, however, where the weights and probabilities are not knowable, the entire calculation may be built on sand. The alternative is to use rules of thumb that are likely to lead to a good decision. One class of rules of thumb is *one-reason decision making*:

Find the most important reason and ignore the rest.

Here, the decision is based solely on one reason—no calculation is performed. In fact, the passage immediately before Darwin's "Q.E.D." can be read to suggest that there was only one decisive reason, that of having a constant companion: "Imagine living all one's day solitary in smoky dirty London house.—Only picture to yourself nice soft wife on a sofa . . ."

Research has shown that people often base decisions on one good reason only. Moreover, such decisions can be better than when trying to consider all reasons.[2] Combining different reasons would require converting all reasons into a common currency. Darwin would have had to estimate how many conversations with clever friends have the same utility as ten children, or how many hours of obligatory visits to relatives-in-law can be traded against soft moments on the sofa. Trade-offs are a property of numbers, not necessarily of the human psyche. In fact, making trade-offs is sometimes seen as immoral. True love, friendship, military honors, and PhDs are considered priceless and therefore incommensurable with items for sale.

Relying on one good reason is not the only rule of thumb that Darwin might have used. Social rules of thumb are an alternative, such as social imitation:

Marry when most of your peers have gotten married.

After all, Darwin was already twenty-nine, an age when most of his peers were likely to have found a wife. It has been observed that imitation is driven by social pressure to marry, which increases with the number of married peers in one's social network and with age.[3] If Darwin had been guided by social imitation, however, he would not have had to write down the pros and cons in the first place.

Whom to Marry?

Benjamin Franklin once advised his nephew on how to make rational decisions about marriage:[4]

April 8, 1779

If you doubt, set down all the Reasons, pro and con, in opposite Columns on a Sheet of Paper, and when you have considered them two or three Days, perform an Operation similar to that in some questions of Algebra; observe what Reasons or Motives in each Column are equal in weight, one to one, one to two, two to three, or the like, and when you have struck out from both Sides all the Equalities, you will see in which column remains the Balance. . . . This kind of Moral Algebra I have often practiced in important and dubious Concerns, and tho' it cannot be mathematically exact, I have found it extreamly useful. By the way, if you do not learn it, I apprehend you will never be married.

I am ever your affectionate Uncle,
B. FRANKLIN

Franklin, one of the founding fathers of the United States, was a prolific inventor, author, artist, and statesman, and also outspoken about marriage. He had two children with his wife, Deborah, and one illegitimate son. As mentioned above, Franklin's bookkeeping method is taught today as the method of maximizing expected utility, also called rational choice. The last sentence of his letter indicates how seriously Franklin took it. Did you choose your partner that way? I've asked friends of mine who teach this method how they made their choice—assuming that they actually had one. Out of them all, only one decision theorist said that he'd applied Franklin's method:

"Did you make the calculation when you chose your wife?" I asked.

"Do you think I went to a disco, got drunk, and hooked on a random encounter? No, I did the calculation," he responded, frowning at my question.

"Could you explain how?" I probed.

"I sat down and listed all alternatives."

I thought it would be impolite to ask how many.

"Then I began to think about all important consequences," he continued.

"Such as . . . ?"

"Whether there will still be affection after the honeymoon; whether she will listen to me after being married."

"And . . . ?"

"Whether she will let me work in peace. And take care of the children. And all the other important things. Then I estimated for each woman the probability that these outcomes will occur. And the utility of each outcome for me."

"Hmm . . . ?"

"And multiplied the probabilities by the utilities and calculated the woman with the highest expected utility. Then I proposed to her."

"What did she say?"

"She accepted! We're now married."

"What did she say to calculated romance?"

"I never told her."

It's easy to be amused by his accounting method. Yet online dating sites use the same type of algorithms for matching partners, weighting hundreds of personality characteristics for the perfect date. Although such services glorify the power of math to get you dates, there is no evidence that their algorithms lead to romantic relations that are superior to traditional ways of finding partners and lead to kissing fewer frogs.[5] In fact, I recently met my calculating friend and found out that he is now divorced.

The point of this story is not that Franklin's bookkeeping method is of no use. My point is that it is designed for a world of known risks, not for a world of uncertainty, and as consequence, most experts do not practice what they preach. The problem is that the method is often taught as if it were relevant for all real-world decisions. Yet actual choices of partners are mostly made in a different way. Not by calculation, but by a gut feeling. And sometimes that feeling is based on an unconscious rule of thumb. Here is one:

Try to get the partner that your peers desire.

This simple strategy needs no analysis of pros and cons. Once again, it's social imitation. And it may do well, if only because it can lead to a social domino effect, more or less guaranteeing that your friends will also like the person and admire you for being successful.

When Benjamin Franklin was still young, he proposed what he called a "paradoxical" rule of thumb for choosing a lover:[6]

In your amours you should prefer old women to young ones.

Franklin was not short of inventing reasons for justifying this rule. According to him, older women were more experienced and discreet, their conversation was more improving, there was no hazard of children, and last but not least, he expected them to be grateful.

The Mating Game

Franklin's bookkeeping method takes for granted that the candidates are all known. Except for closed, small communities this is rarely the case; we usually meet new people in a temporal sequence. For that reason, it's impossible to know who might come along after we've settled on a partner. But waiting forever can put off others, who might go ahead and marry someone else before there's an opportunity to come back and reconsider. Thus, the question is when to make a proposal? The classical version of this question is the so-called Dowry Problem:

> *Sultan Saladin searches for a new wise man as his adviser. To test a candidate, the sultan offers him the woman with the largest dowry in his sultanate as his wife, provided he can pick her out of a group of one hundred beautiful women. If he can't, he will be fed to the beasts. The women enter the room, one by one, in a random order. When the first woman enters, the wise man can ask about her dowry and must immediately decide whether or not to choose her. If not, the next woman enters, and so on, until he chooses one. The wise man doesn't know the range of dowries and can't return to a woman he rejected. What strategy gives him the best chance of selecting the woman with the largest dowry?*

One might pity the wise man because his hope to fame and fortune is doomed. After all, the chance of picking the best appears to be only one in one hundred. Yet with a bit of intelligence, he can do better with this strategy:

> *37 percent rule: Let the first thirty-seven women pass and remember the highest dowry so far. Then choose the first woman with a higher dowry than that.*

This rule increases the chance of winning from one in one hundred to about one in three. That's not certain, but the wise man now has a much stronger chance of ending up with a wife and a job.

Satisficing

The 37 percent rule is mathematically elegant because the number of options one lets pass is equal to N/e, where N is the number of alternatives (in our example, one hundred), and $e \approx 2.718$ is the base of the natural logarithm system. When people were given the dowry problem (also known as the secretary problem) to solve, however, most made their choice long before candidate 37 appeared.[7] Should we conclude that people are impatient and choose a marriage partner too soon?

I don't think that follows. People's minds are tuned to the uncertainty of the real-world mating game, which differs in important aspects from the dowry problem, where there is one right choice and the chances of finding it can be calculated. We can't just ask everyone straight out for his or her "mate value"; there is high uncertainty about what you get, and you may only find out years later. Some look for psychological strengths such as intelligence and humor, others for physical cues such as male jaw size and female waist-to-hip ratio.[8] Ultimately, the success of a relationship will depend on both partners' behavior. How perfect your partner is will depend on how perfect you are. Thus instead of dreaming of the ideal partner, you should simply look for someone who is "good enough" (and be kind to that person).

Interestingly, when applying the dowry problem to an uncertain world where the best hope is to find a good-enough partner, uncertainty actually helps. It's not necessary to investigate 37 percent of all partners. About 10 percent is sufficient, while going for the "optimal" 37 percent rule leads to worse results and takes more time. Rules of thumb that lead to a shorter search for partners are consistent with the actual patterns of mate choice observed by demographers.[9] As is often the case, less can be more in an uncertain world.

Whatever the percentage is, we have again encountered a general rule for making good decisions of this kind: *satisficing*.

1. *Set your aspiration level.*
2. *Choose the first alternative that meets your aspiration level and then stop searching.*

This strategy can help you find a spouse, a house, or other important things. Unless the aspiration level is too high, it will lead to fast decisions. If it proves to be too high, it can be lowered, step by step.

There is one drawback to all these methods, be it bookkeeping or on-line sites or satisficing: none prevents us from dropping a partner once a more desirable one comes around the corner. But leaving partners repeatedly is not good for building families with healthy children. Evolution has equipped us with a specific emotion to prevent that, romantic love. It keeps us committed and blind to the one who comes around the corner. We can add a third step to satisficing that says: Fall in love. Love is a gut feeling, an inner voice that we mostly cannot explain.

Throw a Coin but Don't Look at the Result

Some people, however, have lost the ability to listen to their inner voice. The voice continues to speak but can no longer be heard. A friend of mine once had two girlfriends—one too many. Ominous clouds of trouble were gathering on the horizon. Still he could not make up his mind. Finally, he recalled what he had learned as a student: Franklin's bookkeeping method. He sat down and wrote the names of both women on a balance sheet, then drew a line between them. Then he thought of all the reasons for and against each, weighed them, and made the calculation. When he saw the result, something unexpected happened: An inner voice told him that it was not right. His heart had already decided for the other woman.

If you are having difficulties hearing your inner voice, there is a much faster method: Just throw a coin. While it is spinning, you will likely feel which side should *not* come up. That's your inner voice. You don't have to make any complicated calculations to hear it. And you don't have to bother looking whether heads or tails came up.

Psychological deafness can be the result of a one-sided education in "rational" argumentation. I have seen quite a few cases where people tried to be level-headed and weigh all pros and cons they could think of. But while writing the numbers down, they felt that the answer was not coming out right and simply changed the numbers to make the result fit their intuition.

Intuitions About the Right Romantic Partner

Men have featured in my anecdotes on mate choice simply because theirs was the privilege to choose over the past centuries. Even in the Western world today "popping the question" is often left to the male partner. In a historical context this one-sidedness is curious, given the traditional belief that women have better intuitions about romance. From Kant to Darwin, many otherwise intelligent men believed that women are attuned to their hearts rather than to the heavier responsibilities of earning a livelihood. Today, we should expect this viewpoint to have vanished along with petticoats. But has it? We asked one thousand Germans and one thousand Spaniards, age eighteen and older: "Who has better intuitions about the right romantic partner: men, women, or neither?" This question was asked in personal interviews with a representative sample in each country. Even in the twenty-first century, astounding stereotypes are alive (Figure 8-1).[10] Two thirds of German females believed that women have better intuitions and only a quarter thought that there is no difference, while less than one tenth trusted men's intuitions more. In Spain, it was virtually the same, number for number. Surely males have greater confidence in their own intuitions? But only slightly more thought so. In general, males in both countries agreed that women's intuitions were better, and most did not consider themselves very good at finding the right romantic partner.

Such uniform stereotypes are especially startling given the differences between the two countries. Since World War II, gender equality has been an important issue in Germany, whereas until the end of the Franco regime in the mid-1970s the role of women in Spain was largely confined to hearth and home. None of this appears to matter for the stereotype of

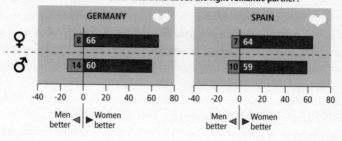

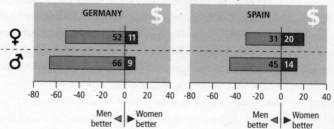

Figure 8-1. Stereotypes about men's and women's intuition have not changed much. Both females and males believe that women have better intuitions about the right romantic partner, and men better intuitions in stock picking. Surprisingly, this stereotype is the same for old and young. For instance, 66 (60) percent of females (males) in Germany believe that women have better intuitions about the right romantic partner, while few (8 and 14 percent) believe that men do better. The remaining 26 percent believe that there is no difference.

Source: Face-to-face interviews with one thousand Germans and one thousand Spaniards, from Gigerenzer, Galesic, et al. (2013).

female intuition. The biggest surprise was that twenty-year-olds shared it with fifty-year-olds.

When it came to the "practicalities" of life, which have traditionally been seen as incompatible with women's intuition, the stereotypes now swung in the other direction. We asked the same Germans and Spaniards about one aspect of this, financial investment: "Who has better intuitions for buying stocks?" Two thirds of the German males said that men were better; less than one tenth believed that women were. In this case, the Spanish had more balanced opinions. Even so, male superiority in buying stocks remained the dominant conviction in both countries. And once again, young and old thought alike.

When asked about other intellectual and professional tasks, such as scientific discovery, the Germans and Spanish also believed that men's intuitions were best. And when it came to other personal intuitions, such as understanding other people's intentions, these were again considered to be women's domain.

Dr. G. Stanley Hall, the first president of the American Psychological Association, claimed in 1904 that these stereotypes reflect the actual natures of men and women.[11] There is, however, little evidence for this. Men do have on average more knowledge about investment, which makes them more confident, expect better returns, and trade more often than females. But at the end of the day, do men actually make more money with stocks than women? The available studies show that there is no difference; if anything, women earned slightly more.[12] Although women have less knowledge about the stock market, they take fewer undue risks and rely on successful simple heuristics such as "buy what you know" and "invest equally."

I find it surprising that these gender stereotypes about intuitions in romance and finance are still alive and kicking. If the saying is true that everyday theories mirror the psychological theories of the past century, we will have to live with these stereotypes far into the twenty-first century.

Parents' Dilemma

From an evolutionary perspective, the ultimate goal of romance is children. Love for one's children is fairly stable across parents' lives, while one in two to three marriages end in divorce, depending on the country. With more than one child, parents face the question: how to distribute their love and time? It is a crucial question. The belief that one's parents favored a brother or sister is a potential cause of much sibling rivalry, a theme that fuels not only many of Shakespeare's plays, from *Richard III* to *King Lear*, but also psychoanalytic explanations of emotional disorders.

The classical answer to how parents should allocate their time and resources, once again, is maximizing.[13] Parents should favor those children who will generate greater wealth as adults, together with those who will support them in old age. Yet parents cannot foresee the future and calculate which child will produce higher utility per unit of investment. Parents and children live in an uncertain world, where success depends on talent, environment, luck, and many other factors that are hard to predict. In this situation many parents rely on a simple rule:

Distribute your time equally over your children.

This is the same rule, $1/N$, that was more successful than Nobel Prize–winning portfolios in stock investments (chapter 5). And it works for children too. A father of two girls told me about reading a bedtime story to his younger daughter while the older one clocked the time with a stopwatch, just to be sure her sister wasn't getting a bigger share of his time. Such a rule is simple because it does not require much calculation. At the same time it satisfies parents' egalitarian values.

Or so one might think. Surprisingly, the hours of care siblings received by age eighteen in U.S. families differed strikingly, and in a systematic way (Figure 8-2). All in all, parents spent the least time with middle children. Is this because the other siblings are more demanding? Or are middle children more self-reliant? Why would parents otherwise treat them unequally? In fact, parents may follow the $1/N$ rule to a T, but the outcome depends on the number of children. Let's take a family with two children, where the parents divide their care time equally per day or week. After eighteen years, the total care time each child receives during childhood will be the same, which is shown in Figure 8-2 by the black squares.[14] In another family with three children the parents also distribute their time equally. For this family, eighteen years of treating their children equally will unintentionally lead to inequality: Because middle-born children never have any time on their own and always have to share their parents' time and attention, in the long run they receive a smaller share than their siblings who were born before and after them (unless of course they are the only ones not to leave the nest).

Thus, the middle child will end up with less time than the oldest and the youngest, which is what happened in the U.S. families shown in Figure 8-2. Moreover, the advantage for the oldest and youngest is the greater the more years the siblings are born apart. The same happens in families with four children.

Parental investment is an example of how the same rule of thumb can produce both an equal and an unequal distribution of resources—and

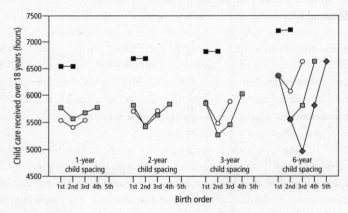

Figure 8-2. Parents spend more time with their firstborns and last-borns than with middle-borns. Why? Paradoxically, parents who try to allocate care time every day or week equally to all children (the 1/N rule) produce the complex pattern of inequality shown here. In two-child families, both siblings end up with equal time from their parents at age eighteen (black squares). In families with three (white circles), four (gray squares), and five children (gray diamonds) however, the middle-borns get less total time. Their disadvantage increases the further the siblings are spaced apart, as shown by the average child spacing. For instance, the 2-year spacing included periods from 1.5 to 2.5 years.

Source: 1,296 families in Syracuse,
New York, in Lindert (1977) and Hertwig et al. (2002).

thus a more or less just outcome. It depends on the circumstances: here, the number of children and the number of years between them.

Explaining behavior in terms of rules of thumb is different from traditional psychological explanations. Most of the time, observed behavior is attributed to preferences, traits, and other internal dispositions. Look again at the pattern of parental investment in Figure 8-2. Observing that parents spend more time with their firstborns and last-borns, one might conclude that parents are fonder of these rather than of middle-borns. After all, firstborns tend to be more mature and identify more strongly with their parents, while the last-borns are the cutest. Yet looking at the rules of thumb people use provides a better understanding of what is going on. The simple 1/N rule predicts the entire complex pattern, leaving no need to come up with a story after the fact. Parents try hard to be just, but now we understand why it's sometimes impossible.

Communicating the Risks of Romance

To become savvy about romance and its aftermath, you need to consider more than the consequences of the strategies you use to pick a partner and maintain a contented family. Risk communication can also play an important role.

Condoms

Not everyone looking for romance is a parent or wants to be. The eighteenth-century Italian adventurer and womanizer Giacomo Casanova is reported to have used "assurance caps" to prevent impregnating his mistresses. Sigmund Freud, the founder of psychoanalysis, opposed condoms because they cut down on sexual pleasure and their failure rates were too high. In order to decide which contraceptive method to use, if any at all, it would be prudent to know how reliable today's condoms are.

On its website the Centers for Disease Control and Prevention (CDC) had publicized that "condoms are 85-98% effective at preventing pregnancy," that is, 2–15 percent ineffective. As we have seen with probabilities of rain in the first chapter, transparent communication clearly specifies the reference class to which the probability refers. On this government website, no reference class was specified. A woman contemplating the use of condoms might think:

1. She will get pregnant 2–15 percent of the times she has sex.
2. 2–15 percent of women relying on condoms get pregnant in the first year of using them.
3. 2–15 percent of condoms are defective, or
4. 2–15 percent of men don't know how to use a condom safely.

There is no way for a woman to know. Women who interpret the statement in terms of alternative number 1 would conclude that sex once a week almost certainly leads to pregnancy, thus making the condom useless. Those who think in terms of alternative number 3 might instead believe the solution is to check every condom carefully before using it, while alternative number 4 leads to the conclusion that the best strategy is to choose the right man who can handle it properly. Mirta Galesic and I pointed out this ambiguity in the *British Medical Journal*.[15] After becoming aware of the potential misunderstanding, the CDC improved its website and made clear that the effectiveness of condoms refers to the number of women out of a hundred who will have an unplanned pregnancy in the first year of using them (alternative 2). If experts don't specify the reference class clearly, people will intuitively think of one and act on it.

Sexual Problems

A friend of mine, a psychiatrist, used to prescribe antidepressants to patients with mild depression. He always took care to explain potential side effects, including loss of sexual interest and impotence: "If you take the medication, you have a 30 to 50 percent chance of developing a sexual problem." Many patients were nervous and unwilling to take the drug. Finally he recognized the problem and changed his line: "Of ten patients to whom I prescribe the drug, three to five report a sexual problem." Now some patients were less apprehensive about taking it. Why is that?

In his original explanation the psychiatrist had thought about his patients as the reference class and assumed that they'd done the same. But when patients were asked, it became clear that they were focused on something else: Many thought that something would go awry in 30 to 50 percent of their sexual encounters. If you tend to look at the sunny side of life, "three to five patients out of ten" doesn't make you nervous, because you think those are the others. But even the greatest optimists are in trouble if the number refers to their own sexual encounters. As a consequence, willingness to use the drug was reduced. Only when the psychiatrist stopped talking about a single-event probability and switched to a frequency statement, which automatically specifies a reference class, was the confusion ironed out.

Inspired by my friend's story, we asked older adults with different levels of numeracy what a "30 to 50 percent chance of developing a sexual problem" meant.[16] If misunderstanding the question is due to people's intelligence, then having high or low numeracy should make all the difference. In contrast, if the problem is due to how risk is communicated, then numeracy should make only a small difference.

What does it mean that a patient has a "30 to 50 percent chance of developing a sexual problem"?	Low numeracy	High numeracy
1. 30 to 50 percent of patients taking the drug will have sexual problems.	33%	38%
2. Patients taking the drug will have a problem in 30 to 50 percent of their sexual encounters.	33%	33%
3. Patients taking the drug will find sexual intercourse to be 30 to 50 percent less enjoyable than usual.	21%	10%
4. Something else	13%	19%

Only one third of the people with low numeracy and a few percentage points more of those with higher numeracy understood that the 30 to 50 percent chance meant (1). When we asked younger adults the same question, more than two thirds chose (1), but there was again little difference between those with low and high numeracy. The upshot is that numeracy—the ability to think with numbers—made next to no difference. It is less a problem of people's intelligence than of experts who don't know how to communicate what they mean.

9

What Doctors Need to Know

Medicine today resembles the church in the
sixteenth century. What we need is a reformation.
Few doctors are trained to judge and evaluate a
scientific study. I myself chose to be trained as a
surgeon to avoid two things: statistics and psychology.
Now I realize that both are indispensable.

Guenther Jonitz, president of the Berlin
Chamber of Physicians

Your mother or sister took a routine mammography screening for breast cancer. She got a positive result and is scared stiff, fearing the worst. But what does a positive result really mean? The surprising answer is that most likely she does not have breast cancer. Mammography produces lots of false alarms. In this chapter, I will explain an intuitive method that helps patients and doctors to understand test results. Although it is so simple that even fourth graders can learn it, few doctors and patients are familiar with it. Let's begin with a look behind the scenes why doctors learn all kinds of things except understanding risks.

Why Luxury Hotels Dislike Their Stars

Since the fall of the Wall, Berlin has been changing at breathtaking speed. The only constant is the daily avalanche of tourists pouring through the streets on foot, perched on Segways, and behind the wheels of Trabis.[1] Entertainment is big; the city hosts three opera houses and one of the world's finest symphony orchestras. For those who can afford it, there are twenty-one five-star hotels. I should have said, there were. In 2008 something unexpected happened. Over the course of a few days, six hotels' stars vanished into thin air. Was this due to annoyed customer complaints on the Internet? Reports of cockroaches scuttling underneath king-sized beds? Or guests electrocuted in the bathtubs? None of this. The hotels did not lose their stars; they simply got rid of them. Some returned one star, others all five, renaming themselves "exclusive city hotels." All of them are still in business, with the same excellent service, the same prices, the same great locations. The Hilton at the Gendarmenmarkt, for instance, still offers its spectacular view of one of the most beautiful squares in Europe. Only the stars are gone.

Each of the hotels had the same reason for dumping their stars.

For many years fancy hotels have hosted continuing medical education (CME) conferences, which doctors are required to attend in order to renew their license. All over the world, the pharmaceutical industry organizes such events. To attract doctors, a dream hotel in an attractive location is chosen and the industry pays the bill, sometimes even including spouses. In the United States alone, the industry spends more than $1 billion annually to support CME.[2] Golf clubs and other goodies await participants at their destination. I have met happy doctors and nurses who sang their praises about being flown to Hawaii, hotel on the beach, all expenses paid. Once back home, they tend to prescribe the company's drugs to their patients, if only to return the favor. Returning favors, however, is not what health care should be about. Many doctors appear to swallow the bait. Among Californian doctors, although virtually no one (1 percent) believed that presents influenced what they prescribed to patients, one third of the very same doctors believed that these did influence other doctors' prescriptions.[3]

After years of opulence government agencies became concerned that doctors were being bribed by this practice. In Germany, the industry reacted quickly to prevent a corruption investigation and founded an organization called Voluntary Self-Regulation for the Pharmaceutical Industry (FSA). This organization issued guidelines that CME should no longer be conducted in luxury hotels, but in other hotels adequate for the purpose.

At this news six of the Berlin hotels panicked and dropped their stars. CME had become too good a business. Similarly, in the United States, the Loews hotel Lake Las Vegas removed the "resort" from its name to avoid putting off pharmaceutical groups, and other hotels followed suit. I spoke to the head of the Voluntary Self-Regulation, and he explained that at issue was not the number of stars, but unnecessary luxury, such as spas that are not vital for CME. Some hotels, however, wrongly thought the number of stars was what counts, and decided to play it safe.

You might ask, why is CME not conducted by medical organizations? Good question. In fact, a few organizations do offer their own courses, but can't compete with the financial resources the industry has at its disposal. Not surprisingly, most doctors prefer the beach and golf clubs to simple classrooms with frugal meals and no partners included. Paying for their own further education would solve these problems but doesn't seem to be a welcome option. Some medical associations have tried to make CME independent of commercial interests, so that doctors are given unbiased evidence. Few have succeeded. As a result millions of doctors worldwide know what the industry wants them to know.

Helping Doctors Understand Test Results

"The lecture hall is on the second floor," the woman at the reception desk told me. I looked around the impressive entrance hall of one of those post-five-star hotels in Berlin. The organizer of the CME greeted me, and we walked to the lecture hall. It was crowded with 160 physicians, most in their forties and fifties, who were attending four training sessions on this beautiful spring day. I entered a large lecture room equipped with the newest technology. In the next seventy-five minutes, I was going to teach the doctors how to better understand risks and uncertainties as part of their CME. For the doctors and the sponsoring pharmaceutical company, this was their first course ever on the topic. I was impressed that the industry would support a course on risk communication when even most medical schools neglect to teach it.

After stepping up to the podium I began with an unrelated issue, the story recounted in the first chapter of this book of how a TV news speaker was confused about probabilities of rain. There was laughter, which put the doctors at ease for what was coming.

A piece of new legislation was the reason why I, rather than someone from the pharmaceutical company, was on the podium. The industry is no longer allowed to use CME for promoting its own products. When deliberating about which independent speakers to hire, the pharmaceutical company did something clever: They asked physicians what they would like to learn. At the top of the wish list was the art of risk communication. And so I ended up teaching a number of sessions. This proved to be a most valuable way to spend my time; I have rarely had audiences so eager to learn.

That day, I had 160 gynecologists in the room. Once they relaxed, I got down to the real issues: hormone replacement therapy, Pap smears, HPV, breast cancer screening, and other treatments and tests they are confronted with on a daily basis. I began with a question:

> A 50-year-old woman, no symptoms, participates in routine mammography screening. She tests positive, is alarmed, and wants to know from you whether she has breast cancer for certain or what the chances are. Apart from the screening results, you know nothing else about this woman. How many women who test positive actually have breast cancer? What is the best answer?

> 1. 9 in 10
> 2. 8 in 10
> 3. 1 in 10
> 4. 1 in 100

Most of the doctors looked unsure and cast their eyes downward. I reassured them. "Don't look down, look around you. The others don't seem to know either." There was a collective sigh of relief. I continued:

> I will now give you the relevant information to answer the question about the chance of cancer after a positive test. First, I'll present it in the way that is customary in medicine, in probabilities.

> • The probability that a woman has breast cancer is 1 percent (prevalence).
> • If a woman has breast cancer, the probability that she tests positive is 90 percent (sensitivity).

- *If a woman does not have breast cancer, the probability that she nevertheless tests positive is 9 percent (false alarm rate).*

A woman tests positive. She wants to know whether that means that she has breast cancer for sure or what the chances are. What do you tell her?

The best answer is one in ten. That is, out of ten women who test positive in screening, one has cancer. The other nine women receive *false alarms.* Yet the 160 gynecologists' answers, monitored by an interactive voting system offering the four choices above, were all over the map (Figure 9-1, top). Thirty doctors would tell the woman that her chance of having cancer is minimal, only one in one hundred, after a positive test (right side). Others—the majority—believed that eight or nine out of every ten women who test positive would have cancer (left side). Imagine what unnecessary fear and panic these physicians cause. Only 21 percent of doctors would correctly inform women, which is less than you would expect by chance (that would be 25 percent, because there were four alternatives to choose from). If patients knew about this diversity of opinions they would be rightly alarmed; the doctors themselves were deeply concerned about it.

After letting this sit, I explained that there is a simple method to improve comprehension: to translate probabilities into natural frequencies:

- Ten out of every 1,000 women are expected to have breast cancer.
- Of these 10 women with breast cancer, 9 test positive.
- Of the 990 without breast cancer, 89 nevertheless test positive.

Now it is easy to see that some ninety-eight (eighty-nine + nine) are expected to test positive, of whom only nine actually have cancer. This is close to one out of ten. One can make it even simpler with one hundred women and a bit of rounding off:

- One out of every 100 women has breast cancer.
- This woman with breast cancer is likely to test positive.
- Of the 99 without breast cancer, 9 nevertheless test positive.

Doctors before training

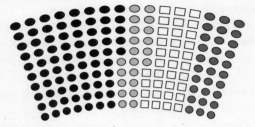

Doctors after training

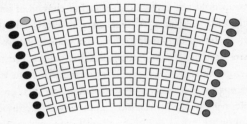

● 9 in 10   ◔ 8 in 10   □ 1 in 10   ● 1 in 100
   women   women   women   women
                              (Best estimate)

Figure 9-1. Most gynecologists don't understand what a positive mammogram means. Top: At the beginning of a continuing medical education (CME) session, I asked 160 gynecologists what they would tell a fifty-year-old woman with a positive screening mammogram about her chances of having breast cancer. Almost half (47 percent) of the doctors believed that her chance is nine in ten, 13 percent that it is eight in ten, 21 percent believed that it is one in ten, and 19 percent that it is one in one hundred! If patients knew this divergence in opinions, they would be rightly alarmed. Bottom: After learning in a seventy-five-minute CME session how to think in natural frequencies, 87 percent of the doctors could find the best answer themselves: one in ten. That is, out of every ten women who test positive in screening, only one has breast cancer; the other nine are falsely alarmed.

Thus, we expect a total of ten women who test positive. Only one of them has cancer.

After doctors learned how to translate confusing probabilities into natural frequencies, 87 percent were able to figure out themselves that the best estimate was one in ten (Figure 9-1, bottom). There were also a few "hopeless causes" who still believed that most women with positive tests would have cancer (left side). But even they would have seen the light if we'd had more time.

Doctors often think that everyone else understands probabilities while they are among the few with a missing math gene. This is why teaching them in a group is so important, to show that they are not alone and no longer have to hide. They realize that there is often a simple solution to what appears to be a complex problem. They also learn to see through other confusing statistics, such as relative risks. Many a participant left the session a more confident doctor. After my first CME lecture, a representative of the industry approached me: "Very helpful," he commented, "but we will of course go on using relative risks for advertising benefits." "I can't stop you from doing that," I said, "but I will continue to teach doctors to see through that trick. And I respect your company for supporting a risk literacy course for doctors."

Despite being rated by the doctors as the one from which they learned most, the course was discontinued after two years. The education of physicians is too important to be left to the medical industry.

Fear

Altogether I have taught about one thousand doctors in their CME. Based on this, my estimate is that about 80 percent of doctors do not understand what a positive test means, even in their own specialties. They are in no position to counsel their patients adequately, nor can they critically evaluate a medical journal article in their own field.

A few years ago, after holding an evening lecture at the annual conference of a large medical society, I had dinner with the presidents and officials of various national health associations. Next to me sat a woman I admire greatly. She was president of a medical society and had succeeded in promoting excellent women as heads of departments against the resistance of her male peers. A woman of courage. After telling me tales of male chauvinism, she said:

> *"Can I ask you something about your lecture?"*
>
> *"Please go ahead."*
>
> *"You mentioned that when ten women test positive in mammography screening, only one actually has cancer. Is that really true?"*
>
> *"You can look that up in medical journals."* I was surprised that she never had.
>
> *"You know,"* she continued, *"I have a Swedish doctor in my group who also said the same thing as you, but we never believed her."*
>
> *"Why didn't you check yourself?"*
>
> *"I can't explain it,"* she answered, *"I think I just believed in the technology."* And then her voice lowered: *"I myself had a positive mammogram many years ago. I was shocked and devastated. I thought I would die. Then the biopsy showed that there was no cancer, it was just a false alarm. But after that shock, I get very anxious before each mammogram. It's a cycle of fearing the worst and relaxing after the result, and then the same thing year after year."*

Lack of risk literacy has taken its toxic toll on this woman's emotional life. Healthy women age fifty to seventy who participate in mammography screening regularly can expect a false alarm sooner or later, just as frequent flyers do when screened at airports. Roughly one out of every three women ends up getting a false positive result at some point. Someone needs to tell them that a suspicious result likely means that there is something wrong with the test, not with their bodies. If other women react like the medical society president, then millions endure cycles of fear in their lives. In fact, for months after a false alarm, women frequently experience anxiety, unhappiness, sleeping problems, and a negative impact on sexuality.[4]

Patients assume that their doctor knows the medical evidence. And some lucky patients are right. Yet gynecologists are not the only professionals who often misunderstand what a test result means. Similar ignorance has been found in other specialties, in the United States, Europe, and Australia.[5]

Doctors are not always aware, or do not admit, that they do not understand health statistics. In one Australian study of fifty doctors, only thirteen said they could explain what the "positive predictive value" is (the probability of a disease given a positive test). And when asked to do so, only one succeeded.[6]

Everyone Can Understand Test Results

How Natural Frequencies Work

We have already seen that natural frequencies help us to understand what a positive HIV test means and that it is better to switch in the Monty Hall problem. But how is this possible? Let's look more closely at the two ways to communicate information about breast cancer screening that I presented to the doctors in the CME. The first one, which confuses many people, uses *conditional probabilities*. Explanations of conditional probabilities, such as the sensitivity and the false-positive rate, can be found in Figure 9-2. For instance, sensitivity is the probability of getting a positive test if the person has the disease, written as p(test positive|disease). Such a

Test Result	Disease	
	Yes	No
Positive	(a) sensitivity	(b) false-positive rate
Negative	(c) false-negative rate	(d) specificity

Figure 9-2. A test can have four outcomes: (1) The result is positive and the patient has the disease. (2) The test is positive but the patient does not have the disease. (3) The test is negative but the patient has the disease. (4) The test is negative and the patient does not have the disease. The rates with which these four results occur are called (a) sensitivity (or true-positive rate), (b) false-positive rate, (c) false-negative rate, and (d) specificity (true-negative rate). The two errors that every test can make are shaded.

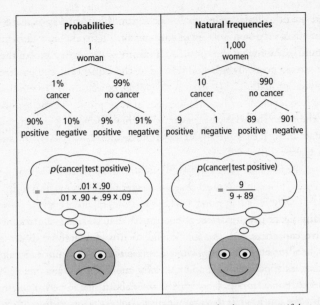

Figure 9-3. What is the probability that a woman has breast cancer if she tests positive in mammography screening? If the information is presented in probabilities, most doctors and patients are confused (unhappy face), but if it is presented in natural frequencies, most see the correct answer (happy face). Only nine out of ninety-eight women who test positive actually have breast cancer, which is roughly one in ten. The four numbers at the bottom of the right tree are the four natural frequencies. The four numbers at the bottom of the left tree are called conditional probabilities (see Figure 9-2).

probability is called conditional because it is not a simple probability of an event A occurring, but one of A if B. To make sense of conditional probabilities, we need to make complicated calculations that most of us find confusing (as shown by the unhappy face on the left of Figure 9-3). The formula is called Bayes' rule, named after the English dissenting minister Thomas Bayes (c. 1702–1761), who is thought to have discovered it.[7]

As we have seen, a simpler way to communicate the same information is with natural frequencies. To represent a problem in natural frequencies, you begin with a number of people (here, one thousand women), who are divided into those with and without the condition (breast cancer); these are again broken down into two groups according to the new information (test result). The four numbers at the bottom of the right tree are the four natural frequencies. The four numbers at the bottom of the left tree are conditional probabilities (Figure 9-2). Unlike conditional probabilities (or relative frequencies), natural frequencies always add up to the number on top of the tree. The secret to them is that they do most of the calculation for you, making it easier to understand the results (as shown by the smiling face in Figure 9-3).

Tools for Thinking

For many years psychologists have argued that because of their limited cognitive capacities people are doomed to misunderstand problems like the probability of a disease given a positive test.[8] This failure is taken as justification for paternalistic policymaking mentioned in chapter 1: Better keep people away from important decisions about risk, whether medical or political. We don't need more paternalism, however; we need to teach people tools for thinking.

In the mid-1990s, psychologist Ulrich Hoffrage and I demonstrated for the first time that the problem is not simply inside people's minds but in the way information is communicated: When the same problems are given in natural frequencies, people more readily understand them. Since that discovery my researchers and I have trained not just doctors but also judges, patients, and others to learn this simple method. Schools in several countries now include natural frequency trees in their textbooks, helping children to understand how to think about risk. In some classes, children learn to use hands-on versions of natural frequencies, brightly colored tinker cubes.[9] Today, major medical organizations such as the Cochrane Collaboration, the International Patient Decision Aid Standards Collaboration, and the Medicine and Healthcare Products Regulatory Agency (the UK's equivalent to the Food and Drug Administration) recommend using natural frequencies.

If everyone followed this recommendation rather than treating others as if they were incurably risk illiterate, many people would benefit from less needless anxiety about false medical test results as well as from a better basis to make informed medical decisions.

Prenatal Screening

Imagine you are thirty-five and pregnant. In many countries doctors advise all women thirty-five and over to attend screening for Down syndrome. Down syndrome, or trisomy 21, is the most frequent clinically important chromosome aberration at birth. Children born with this syndrome have forty-seven chromosomes instead of the usual forty-six, resulting in some impairment of mental ability and physical growth, and a particular set of facial characteristics. For women over thirty-five, the joy of being pregnant is tempered by anxiety about this or other birth defects. The risk of a child having Down syndrome, however, does not jump suddenly at thirty-five, but increases with the mother's age. That is why this age limit makes little clinical sense. The question to ask is, how big is the risk at each age? For thirty-year-olds, the risk of delivering a baby with Down syndrome is about one in one thousand, varying across countries. If the mother is thirty-five, the risk increases to about three in one thousand, and for a forty-year-old, to about ten in one thousand.

For many pregnant women prenatal screening is an extremely stressful situation. Two tests are offered, a first-trimester blood test used for screening and, if the result is positive, a second invasive test such as amniocentesis or chorionic villus sampling (CVS). The first-trimester test includes a sonogram that can detect the excess skin on the necks of fetuses with Down syndrome and tests for serum markers. It can be done between the eleventh and fourteenth week.[10] If the test is positive, women need to decide whether to undergo an invasive test such as amniocentesis, which leads to a miscarriage in about one in two hundred women. For a woman in her late thirties, this risk is about the same as the risk of having a baby with Down syndrome.

It's therefore crucial to understand what a positive first-trimester test means. A British study found that some pregnant women and obstetricians believed it means that Down syndrome is absolutely certain, or close to certain.[11] Once again the illusion of certainty is attached to a medical technology. But no test is absolutely certain. Each and every one makes errors. First, the sensitivity of a first-trimester screening is about 90 percent, meaning that the test detects 90 percent of babies with Down syndrome and misses the rest. Second, the false positive rate is about 5 percent, meaning that the test correctly identifies 95 percent of babies without Down syndrome and errs on the remaining 5 percent.[12] Now we can find out what a positive test means for a forty-year-old woman:

- About 1 percent of babies have Down syndrome.
- If the baby has Down syndrome, there is a 90 percent chance that the test result will be positive.
- If the baby is unaffected, there is still a 5 percent chance that the test result will be positive.

A pregnant woman has been tested and the result is positive. What is the chance that her baby actually has Down syndrome?

In a British study, twenty-one obstetricians were given this information and asked what the answer is. Only one could answer the question correctly. Most thought the chance was very high, 90 to 100 percent, or very low, close to zero. In the same study, midwives, pregnant women, and the partners accompanying them to the appointment were also given the information.[13] None of the midwives, only one out of twenty-two women, and only three out of twenty companions could figure out what the chance of a baby with Down syndrome was.

Once again the problem is simpler if we just replace the confusing percentages with natural frequencies. We expect that:

- About 10 out of every 1,000 babies have Down syndrome.
- Of these 10 babies with Down syndrome, 9 will get a positive test result.
- Of the remaining 990 unaffected babies, about 50 will still have a positive test result.

How many pregnant women with a positive result actually have a baby with Down syndrome?

With natural frequencies, the answer is easier to figure out. Out of every one thousand women age forty, we expect that fifty-nine babies (nine + fifty) receive a positive test result and that only nine of these have a baby with Down syndrome. The other fifty women are falsely alarmed (Figure 9-4). In other words, only one out of every six or seven women with a positive result actually has a baby with Down syndrome. Thus, the chance is like rolling a "six" on a dice. Even if the test is positive, the baby most likely does not have Down syndrome.

When the twenty-one British obstetricians were given the same information in natural frequencies, thirteen (compared to only one previously)

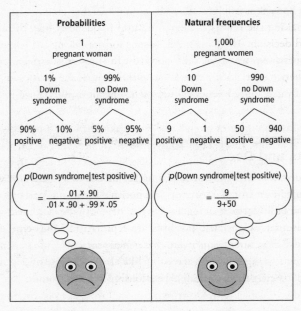

Figure 9-4. What is the probability that a forty-year-old pregnant woman has a baby with Down syndrome if she tests positive in the first-trimester test? If the information is presented in probabilities, most doctors and patients are confused (unhappy face); if it is presented in natural frequencies, most see the correct answer (happy face). Only nine out of fifty-nine women who test positive actually have a baby with Down syndrome, which is roughly one out of every six or seven.

understood what the test result meant. A bit of rounding off might help those who still did not get it. To simplify, take one hundred pregnant women (instead of one thousand). We expect one to have a baby with Down syndrome, who will likely test positive. Of the remaining ninety-nine women, we expect five more to test positive, which results in a chance of one in six of having a baby with Down syndrome.

The younger a pregnant woman is, the less likely the chances. If she is thirty-five rather than forty years old, her baby's chance of having Down syndrome after a positive test is only about one in twenty. That means the baby most likely does not have it. The tree also helps to understand that a negative test result is not certain either; about one out of every ten cases of Down syndrome is overlooked.

By making the numbers clearer, natural frequencies help to make an informed decision. There are good reasons for not taking the test: when a woman is young, when she does not want to risk a miscarriage, or when she would not abort a baby with Down syndrome. If she decides for prenatal screening, she needs to know what a test result means.

New Genetic Technology Requires Risk-Savvy Parents and Doctors

Future advances in newborn screening for biochemical genetic disorders may result in an immense increase in positive identifications but also in even more false alarms. For instance, when newborns are screened for metabolic disorders, eight false positives are reported for each true positive identified.[14] Few parents are aware that genetic screening tests are not certain. Parents who go through screening like an anxious rite of passage may end up damaging their emotional relationship with their child.

Dysfunctional Parent-Child Relations

In a study in Boston, parents of children who had a false alarm for one of twenty biochemical disorders were compared with parents of children with normal newborn screening results.[15] Mothers of false-alarm children reported more worry about their children's future, rated themselves as less healthy, and more frequently stated that their child required extra parental care. But that was not all.

A false alarm means that after the initial stress from perceived bad news, the infant's good health was confirmed in a repeat screening. Nevertheless, mothers of false-positive babies more frequently reported having difficult children, and a dysfunctional relationship with them. Fathers reported the same negative feelings, albeit with less intensity. And half of all children screened for biochemical genetic disorders showed disturbed behavior four years after their parents received the false-positive result. When children sense that parents think there might be something wrong with them, this may become a self-fulfilling prophecy.

If parents had been better informed about the errors the test makes, the amount of stress they endured while waiting for the repeat screening could have been reduced. In other words, risk literacy could have moderated emotional reactions to stress that harmed these parents' relation to their child. Yet most of the doctors were not trained to understand tests for genetic disorders in the first place and were in no position to inform parents correctly. The age of women giving birth is increasing in many countries, along with the chances of children having Down syndrome. Although large amounts of resources are being invested in improving prenatal diagnosis, little to nothing is invested in making doctors and patients competent in understanding these tests.

Designer Babies

A baby is born. A sample of blood is taken with a heel prick to screen for genetic disorders. This procedure has become routine in the United States and other countries, often without asking parents for consent or telling them that their baby's DNA will be stored by the clinic or government. Why not screen the baby before it's born? Advances in genetic technology allow embryos to be screened for hundreds of genetic risk factors, including Down syndrome, breast cancer, and sickle-cell anemia, using nothing but a blood sample from the mother. Parents who desire the ideal baby, and nothing less, will go for that. Already companies are offering services from pre-implantation diagnoses to direct-to-consumer genetic testing.

Genetic technology will impact our emotions and values. Some parents see genetic optimization as a great possibility and a basic right; others are morally appalled by the thought of designer babies. One thing we can be sure of is that genetic screening will lead to more abortions. Moreover, if parents decide against screening because they don't want to know and end up having a not-so-perfect baby (or one with devastating birth defects), they may be severely criticized by friends and family or even strangers on the street: You could have found out, why didn't you prevent it? In the future, optimization may start even earlier than prenatal screening. Why not have both partners' DNA tested before pregnancy? Or even better, have a test handy before the first date?

The ethical turmoil arising from genetic screening has attracted much attention. What's not in the spotlight is that most doctors and patients will not understand the results of this both fascinating and controversial technology. If most doctors already misunderstand the chance of Down syndrome after a positive test, what can we expect when they evaluate the results of hundreds of tests? If doctors err on the side of too much certainty, as with mammography and first-trimester tests, they will tend to "see" genetic diseases that the baby doesn't have. And if parents do not learn to think for themselves, using natural frequencies, they might abort babies who are perfectly healthy.

Medical Schools Fail

Some psychologists argue that doctors, just like ordinary folks, fall prey to the same persistent cognitive illusions. If that were true, natural frequencies would not help. But they do. The explanation is not simply inside doctors' minds, in some neural quirk or shabby mental software. Don't simply blame the doctors.

The major cause is the unbelievable failure of medical schools to provide efficient training in risk literacy. Medical progress has become associated with better technologies, not with better doctors who understand these technologies. Medical students have to memorize tons of facts about common and rare diseases. What they rarely learn is statistical thinking and critical evaluation of scientific articles in their own field. Learning is geared toward performance in the final exam, which shows little correlation with clinical experience.[16] With a portion of self-irony, medical professors tell this joke:

> *Two students, one from biology, one from medicine, are asked to learn the telephone book by heart. The biology student asks, why? The medical student asks, by when?*

So who is going to change this? The moral responsibility is with the medical schools. When I give talks on the subject to medical societies, the typical answer is that nobody has an interest in making doctors risk literate. Changing a university is like cleaning up an old cemetery. Every professor wants to pack as much of his or her specialty into the curriculum and into medical students' minds, and there is simply no place for anything else. Too crowded, period. Fortunately, some are making room for change. A few medical departments have begun to teach methods of risk communication, such as natural frequencies, and devised their curriculum. Most medical schools, however, do not even recognize the problem. After all, medical students are taught biostatistics. Yet a glance at Figure 9-1 reveals how inefficient these courses are.

During a talk to the Austrian Chamber of Physicians, I once explained the problem of doctors who don't understand evidence. In the discussion afterward, a man in the audience raised his hand. He introduced himself as a professor at the Medical University of Vienna. The problem with innumerate doctors, he said, may be a problem in New York or London, but not in Vienna. He himself teaches biostatistics and takes care that every medical student understands numbers. Positively surprised, I congratulated him. Then a young woman raised her hand. She identified herself as a former student of the professor. "I attended his course on biostatistics, and I can assure you, we didn't understand a thing."

Medical schools should act soon, before patients become aware that their doctors do not understand the tests and treatments they are advised to undergo. Whereas defensive medicine jeopardizes trust in doctors' motives, here it is trust in their competence that is at stake.

First Priority Is Shareholders, Not Patients

I recently gave a talk on how to improve health care to the thirty top managers of a leading international health technology provider and a similar number of politicians, heads of health insurances, and deans of medical schools. The event was not open to the public. I pointed out the widespread lack of risk literacy among patients and doctors; the routine misinformation in health brochures, ads, and other media; and the disturbing fact that medical schools still don't teach their students how to understand health statistics. In my conclusion, I pleaded for a health care system that promotes informed patients and doctors.

After my talk, a panel discussion with the CEO and a moderator was arranged. I asked the CEO whether his (immensely profitable) company would consider it an ethical responsibility to do something about this key problem. The CEO made it clear that his first responsibility is with the shareholders, not patients or doctors. I responded that the banks had also thought so before the subprime crisis. At some point in the future, patients will notice how often they are being misled instead of informed, just as bank customers eventually did. When this happens, the health industry may lose the trust of the public, as happened to the banking industry. Surprised by this analogy, the CEO took a short breath before hastily dismissing that possibility.

Rather than thinking about how to solve the problem, the dean of a medical school denied that medical students don't learn statistical thinking. When I asked him directly whether he was sure that graduates from his department are able to read and evaluate an article in a medical journal, he hesitated, eventually muttering angrily that some may and some may not. I offered to test his students and to help develop a curriculum ensuring that every young doctor finally understands medical evidence. Although that cooled down the heated debate, the dean never took up my offer. The rest of the panel discussion was about business plans, which really captured the emotions of the health insurers and politicians present. Risk-literate doctors and patients are not part of the business.

The SIC Syndrome

Are patients aware that many doctors do not understand the results of their tests? And are patients aware that doctors practice defensive medicine, as shown in chapter 3? As far as I have seen, rarely. For instance, a study on defensive medicine in Spain reported that most doctors chose different treatments for their patients than for themselves.[17] Perhaps doctors misjudged patients' treatment preferences? No. Doctors predicted patients' treatment preferences very accurately, but nevertheless chose second-best treatments that protected them from litigation. Unaware of this, patients mistakenly believed that their doctor would have chosen the very same treatment in their place.

The doctor-patient relationship depends on personal bonding and trust. The more patients become aware of doctors' innumeracy and defensive decision making, the more trust will be eroded. Parents will begin to question the motives behind their doctor recommending an MRI or CT scan for their child, and women will begin to second-guess why they should have a C-section. As patients realize that more testing and treatment is not always better, they may stop listening to doctors entirely and rely instead on dubious Internet gossip. Health care does not deserve this fate.

Altogether, three time bombs are ticking away in current health care systems that threaten to undermine trust. Physicians don't do the best for their patients because they:

1. practice defensive medicine (Self-defense),
2. do not understand health statistics (Innumeracy), or
3. pursue profit instead of virtue (Conflicts of interest).

Let's call this the SIC syndrome of our health system. These conditions often work together to produce bad care. Innumeracy is the least known problem of the three. Conflicts of interest engendered by the changing orientation of medicine from virtue to profit have become an international phenomenon. In Western countries, for instance, it is legal for physicians to receive "bribes" in the form of cash by pharmaceutical companies for every new patient they put on their drugs. In China, where most hospitals are government-owned and base salaries are quite low, physicians can enlarge their income substantially by selling drugs and imaging techniques. If they don't, they lose money. These extra bonuses can be higher than their base salaries.[18] Patients need to be aware that the SIC syndrome leads to too much "care."

About ten million U.S. women have had unnecessary Pap smears screening for cervical cancer—unnecessary because, having already undergone complete hysterectomies, these women no longer had a cervix.[19] Unnecessary Pap tests cause no harm to the patient, but in terms of the health system, they waste millions of dollars that could have been used to more benefit elsewhere. And these procedures waste doctors' time and attention. As early as 1996 the U.S. Preventive Services Task Force noted that routine Pap smears are unnecessary for these women, yet few listened. Fifteen years later these unnecessary Pap tests were still in the top-five list of what not to do.[20] Why do so many doctors ignore the recommendations of medical societies? The answer is the fee-for-service system, in which doctors are paid for every test they conduct. Those responsible doctors who don't do unnecessary tests lose money—the C in the syndrome, caused by a system with false incentives.

Less Is (Often) More in Health Care

Just as in finance, complex technologies are not always better and safer in health care. One reason for their overuse in the medical world is conflicts of interest—the C in the SIC syndrome described above. Actions that increase the flow of income, such as imaging and surgery, are encouraged. For instance, some doctors perform dramatically more bypass surgery than any others, even on patients who don't need it. In one case the surgeon's peers defended his actions by saying, "Oh, he's got four kids in college."[21] When his kids graduate, will he stop pulling out the scalpel so readily? In some for-profit hospitals, administrators set a quota of hysterectomies, knee surgeries, and other operations that surgeons are expected to perform every week, no matter which patients turn up. And there are nonmonetary conflicts that lead to overtreatment, such as when doctors need to have performed a particular number of surgeries in order to qualify as a specialist. A second reason for the overuse of technology in health care is that many doctors recommend unnecessary and possibly harmful treatments and tests to patients in order to protect themselves from being sued—the S in the SIC syndrome. Both conflicts of interest and defensive medicine lead to the same result: Rather than doing what is best for the patient, doctors waste their time on unnecessary tests and treatments—even when simpler and more effective ones are available.

Bedside Exam or MRI?

Dizziness, nausea, and vomiting are among the symptoms of what is called acute vestibular syndrome. In rare cases it results from a dangerous brain stem or cerebellar stroke. When a patient enters emergency care with these symptoms, doctors need to get the diagnosis right. How can they find out whether the patient had a stroke? One popular way is to do an MRI (magnetic resonance imaging) at admission. An MRI machine uses a powerful magnetic field and pulses of radio wave energy to generate two- or three-dimensional images of organs inside the body. Patients need to take off all or most of their clothes, put on a gown, and the part of their body under investigation is placed or strapped inside the machine. This procedure makes some people nervous or feel claustrophobic. If contrast material is needed to achieve better-quality pictures, an intravenous (IV) line is inserted into the arm. The entire process may take between fifteen and ninety minutes and typically costs over $1,000.

The alternative is a bedside examination—what skilled doctors were doing long before the invention of MRI. It requires a trained doctor. The HINTS examination consists of three tests, and can be performed in one minute. There is no waiting time, no discomfort, no IV line. It is called HINTS because it consists of tests for Head Impulse, Nystagmus, and a Test of Skew. For instance, in the head impulse test, the patient stares at the examiner's nose. The examiner rapidly moves the patient's head ten to twenty degrees to the side. A normal response to the rapid head movement is an equal and opposite eye movement that enables the eyes to remain fixed on the target. An abnormal response occurs when patients are unable to keep their eyes focused on the examiner's nose during the movement, meaning that they have to shift their gaze when the head movement has ended.

In a study of 101 high-risk patients with acute vestibular syndrome, diagnosis was made with both an MRI and with the HINTS examination.[22] While MRI missed strokes in 8 out of 76 patients, the HINTS examination caught all correctly and missed none. The bedside examination caused one false alarm among the 25 without stroke, which is clearly the less harmful error. This simple examination was decidedly better than expensive imaging technology at detecting a dangerous stroke.

What about CT scans? These miss considerably more strokes than MRIs, lead to more misdiagnoses, and potentially harm the patient because of the radiation. A simple bedside exam can increase patient safety and at the same time save time and money. Last but not least, it can be used anywhere in the world, including developing countries. Less is more.

Ottawa Ankle Rules

A man injures an ankle while jogging. He is hurried to the emergency department of the nearest hospital. It could be a fracture. To find out, most patients with ankle sprains undergo X-rays, even though only one out of seven actually has a fracture; the others receive unnecessary doses of radiation.[23] Is there an alternative to indiscriminately x-raying everyone? A team of doctors at the Ottawa Hospital developed a set of simple rules to test for fractures of the ankle: the *Ottawa ankle rules*. This procedure tests the ability to walk four steps (Figure 9-5). If there is no pain in the malleolar zone (the zone above the mid-foot), no X-ray is required. Otherwise, the question is whether there is bone tenderness at the lateral malleolus, either at the posterior edge or tip. If yes, an X-ray is required. If not, the same question is asked with respect to the medial malleolus. Again, if there is bone tenderness, an X-ray is required. Otherwise, the final question is: Is there inability to bear weight for four steps? If yes, an X-ray is required, otherwise not.

This rule is fast and frugal. It is fast because it requires the patient to

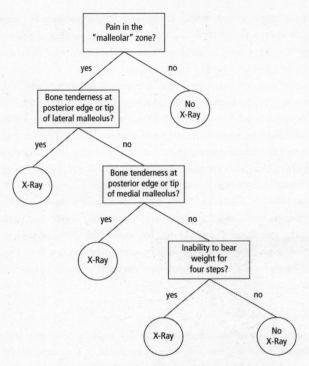

Figure 9-5. Simple rules for safer health care. If a patient has sprained an ankle, the Ottawa ankle rules allow the doctor to determine whether the patient needs an X-ray. The test is fast and frugal: The patient walks four steps, and a sequence of four questions at most are asked about pain and bone tenderness. The rule belongs to the class of fast-and-frugal trees and correctly detects fractures and helps avoid unnecessary X-rays.

walk only four steps, and it is frugal because the decision may already be made after the first or second question. It is an example of a large class of simple rules that are called fast-and-frugal trees.[24] Such a tree is not a complete tree with all possible information branches, but one that allows a decision after each question or test. Here, it enables the doctor to quickly exclude fractures and send only those patients for an X-ray who need one.

How effective is this fast examination? A review of thirty-two studies showed that the ankle rules correctly detected fractures in more than 98 percent of all cases. It is highly successful in avoiding unnecessary radiation for patients. Like the bedside examination, it can be applied everywhere in the world, independent of whether high-tech is available or not. And like the bedside examination, it is based on the experience of skilled physicians.

Given these facts, how many emergency physicians use the ankle rule instead of indiscriminate x-raying? Fewer than one third of U.S. physicians report using it, compared to more than 70 percent of Canadian physicians.[25] The fact that more Americans are indiscriminately x-rayed is not because their doctors are less aware of the simple rules than their Canadian colleagues. Here is a letter to the *Western Journal of Medicine* that a Californian doctor wrote in response to a Canadian article promoting the ankle rules:[26]

> *In our community, this is folly. Anyone who has been in practice for a while knows that the reason we take these x-rays is legal, not medical. . . . We live in a nation whose legal system serves by and large, to paraphrase a famous attorney, "a nation of attorneys, by attorneys, and for attorneys" and that has established a legal system whereby lawyers get a share of any action, necessary or not. Anyone who shows up at an emergency department with an ankle complaint darned well better get x-rays, or the physicians will pay if they don't have them taken.*
>
> *Anyway, what's all the fuss? A $50,000 fluoroscan machine [a video x-ray] can give a reading in a twinkling. It costs $30,000 to process any single claim, whether anything comes of it or not, according to our malpractice carrier. My advice: Buy a fluoroscan, photograph all symptomatic ankles, take x-rays of them all, and have them documented.*

U.S. malpractice litigation has led to medical practice that is not in the best interest of the patient. Defensive medicine and financial interests work hand in hand: Radiology has become one of the highest-earning professions, together with the profession radiologists fear most, malpractice law. Yet more diagnosis is not always better, and new expensive technology is not always better. In its place, simple clinical rules based on physical exams and patient history can substantially reduce radiology and increase patient safety. Other examples include NEXUS, the Canadian cervical spine rule, and the Canadian CT Head rule. Machines physically separate doctors from patients. This is not to say that technology can't help, but a good doctor should always examine the patient by sight and touch. Otherwise, the art of healing gets lost in the noise of high-tech, profit-driven medicine.

If It Ain't Broke, Don't Fix It

In the past, people went to a doctor when they were sick, and doctors did not encourage the healthy to seek care. Now people seek care when they are well, and doctors encourage healthy people to be diagnosed and eventually treated. What should one do?

1. Go for regular health check-ups, or
2. Visit a doctor only when it really hurts and then go straightaway.

Doctors subject to the SIC syndrome will definitely insist that you come for regular check-ups even if you feel healthy. They will have your blood pressure taken and cholesterol checked, may do cancer screening, or may even use advanced technologies such as magnetic resonance imaging. Just to be sure. If the doctors are syndrome-free and well informed, they will provide you with the evidence: Sixteen studies with a total of 180,000 adults (under 65 years of age) investigated whether regular check-ups decrease cancer mortality, cardiovascular mortality, or total mortality. The answer is no three times over.[27] Nor did check-ups reduce morbidity; that is, suffering from symptoms. The only effect found was that the number of new diagnoses among those who went for check-ups increased, making healthy people worry and leading to further diagnoses and treatments without noticeable benefit. But as always in life, there is no foolproof strategy: Not visiting a doctor when you're not feeling palpably sick carries the risk of overlooking something that could be cured early. It's up to you to decide which strategy is best for you.

Free Access to Information

Patients and doctors could make better decisions if they were better informed. But those who search for the relevant information find it hard to access or understand. As will be shown in the next chapter, patients and doctors are routinely misled by relative risks, double-tonguing, and other tricks. There are also other barriers that need to be overcome. Here are some services we need.

- *Free access to the Cochrane Library.* The Cochrane Library (www.the cochranelibrary.com) is one of the best resources for the results of medical research. It is nonprofit and summarizes what we know about treatment of thousands of medical conditions. Residents of many countries, including Australia, Ireland, Norway, Spain, Sweden, and the UK, have free Internet access to the library, sponsored by their health organizations or governments. Residents of the United States, Canada, and Germany don't; they can read only the abstracts. Their governments have not been willing to spend the small amount of about one cent per citizen per year. Informed citizens don't appear to be a spending priority. As a serious consequence many doctors in private practice also have no access to the information they would need.
- *Free access to medical records.* In many countries, patients have no access to their own medical records. Traditionally, the records belong to the hospitals and the practitioners. Access to one's medical history should be a basic right in a democracy. We need an "information revolution" to allow patients to view their medical records.
- *Free access to medical journals.* We have repeatedly seen that doctors often do not know the relevant medical evidence. One reason is that many doctors have no free access to the top medical journals. I am not just talking about developing countries. Publishing companies such as Elsevier and Springer block access to their medical and other scientific journals. A doctor, medical student, or patient who wants to look up a new study on the Internet will find a price tag next to the abstract. Without paying some $30 to $40 per article, or working within an institution

that has paid the publisher an exorbitant fee, individuals have no access. There is a movement among scientists and universities to boycott those publishers who prevent scientific information from being distributed in this way. After all, the authors of these articles, the reviewers, and the editors all typically work for free to produce the articles, and the research is often publicly funded. In the digital age, publishers of scientific journals add little but take the copyright, and charge libraries outrageous subscription fees. They do not even allow the authors to disseminate their own new research quickly by posting it on their websites. This system needs to be stopped, and the copyright needs to go to the editors, scientific organizations, or others who want to disseminate evidence rather than make a fortune out of public money.

Besides these services that are still closed to many of us, there are others that are open but not widely known. Sources for reliable information about health include:

- U.S. Preventive Services Task Force, www.ahrq.gov/CLINIC/uspstfix .htm
- Agency for Healthcare Research and Quality, www.ahrq.gov
- Dartmouth Atlas of Health Care, which shows the wild variability in how doctors treat patients, www.dartmouthatlas.org
- Bandolier Oxford, www.medicine.ox.ac.uk/bandolier/
- Foundation for Informed Medical Decision Making, www.informed medicaldecisions.org
- Harding Center for Risk Literacy, Max Planck Institute for Human Development: www.harding-center.com
- A useful watchdog group that rates what's good and bad in health journalism: www.healthnewsreview.org

10

Health Care: No Decision About Me Without Me

If you haven't had a mammogram, you need more
than your breasts examined.

American Cancer Society, 1980s campaign poster

We want the principle of "shared decision making"
to become the norm: no decision about me without me.

Department of Health, UK

While running for president of the United States, former New
York City mayor Rudy Giuliani said in a 2007 campaign advertisement:[1]

*I had prostate cancer, 5, 6 years ago. My chance of surviving prostate
cancer—and thank God, I was cured of it—in the United States?
Eighty-two percent. My chance of surviving prostate cancer in England?
Only 44 percent under socialized medicine.*

For Giuliani, this meant that he was lucky to be living in New York
and not in York, since his chances of surviving prostate cancer appeared to
be twice as high. That was big news. It was also a big mistake. Despite the
impressive difference in survival rates, the percentage of men who died of

prostate cancer was about the same in the United States and the UK.[2] How can survival be so different when mortality is the same?

The answer is that when it comes to screening, differences in survival rates don't tell us anything about differences in mortality rates. In fact, over the past fifty years, changes in five-year survival for the most common solid tumors had no connection with changes in mortality.[3] There are two reasons.

How Rudy Giuliani Was Misled

The first reason is called *lead time bias*. Imagine two groups of men with invasive prostate cancer. The first consists of men in Britain, where screening for prostate-specific antigens (PSA) is not routinely used and most cancer is diagnosed by symptoms. The second group is made up of men in the United States, where routine use of the test began in the late 1980s and spread rapidly, despite the lack of evidence that it saves lives.

In the British group, prostate cancer is detected by symptoms, say at age sixty-seven (Figure 10-1 top). All of these men die at age seventy. Everyone survived only three years, so the five-year survival is 0 percent. In the U.S. group, prostate cancer is detected early by PSA tests, say at age sixty, but they too die at age seventy (Figure 10-1 bottom). According to the statistics, everyone in that group survived ten years and thus their five-year survival rate is 100 percent. The survival rate has improved dramatically, although nothing has changed about the time of death: Whether diagnosed at age sixty-seven or at age sixty, all patients die at age seventy. Survival rates are inflated by setting the time of diagnosis earlier. Contrary to what many people have been told, there is no evidence that early detection and subsequent treatment of prostate cancer prolongs or saves lives.

The second reason why survival rates tell us nothing about living longer is *overdiagnosis bias*. Overdiagnosis happens when doctors detect abnormalities that will not cause symptoms or early death. For instance, a patient might correctly be diagnosed with cancer but because the cancer develops so slowly, the patient would never have noticed it in his lifetime.

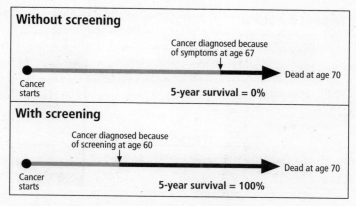

Figure 10-1. Lead time bias. There are two groups of men who all die of prostate cancer at age seventy. The men in the top panel do not participate in prostate cancer screening, and their cancers are detected at age sixty-seven. For them, the five-year survival rate is zero. The men in the bottom panel participate in screening, and their cancers are detected earlier, at age sixty. For them, the five-year survival rate is 100 percent. In screening, increases of survival rates do not mean that lives are saved or prolonged, causing such statistics to be misleading.

Source: Gigerenzer, Gaissmaier, Kurz-Milke, Schwartz, and Woloshin, 2007.

These cancers are called slow-growing or nonprogressive cancers.[4] PSA screening detects both progressive and nonprogressive cancers but, like most other cancer screening tests, cannot tell the difference between them. Figure 10-2 (top) shows 1,000 British men with progressive cancer who do not undergo screening. After five years, 440 are still alive, which results in a survival rate of 44 percent. Figure 10-2 (bottom) shows 1,000 Americans who participate in PSA screening and have progressive cancer. The test, however, also finds 2,000 people with nonprogressive cancers—meaning that they will not die from them. By adding these 2,000 to the 440 who survived progressive cancer, the survival rate leaps to 81 percent. Even though the survival rate increases dramatically, the number of men who die remains exactly the same.

Talking about survival can be useful for surgery or other medical

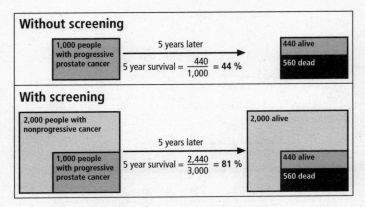

Figure 10-2. Overdiagnosis bias. Top panel: These men do not participate in screening and their survival rate is 44 percent. Bottom panel: Screening detects not only men with progressive cancer but also many more with nonprogressive cancer, which by definition does not lead to death. These inflate the survival rate from 44 to 81 percent.

Source: Gigerenzer, Gaissmaier, et al., 2007.

treatments (where there is no possibility of setting the time of diagnosis earlier or of overdiagnosing patients), but in the context of screening it is always a misleading message. Misunderstanding what survival means has unnecessarily turned many people into patients and transformed healthy lives into troubled ones. Many a man whose nonprogressive cancer is detected undergoes unnecessary and harmful surgery or radiation treatment. Up to five in a thousand men die within one month of surgery and about ten times as many have serious complications.[5] The number of men who spend the rest of their lives wearing diapers is legion. Many have been misled to believe that incontinence is the price they had to pay for survival, and that survival means living longer.

More Men Die with Prostate Cancer Than from It

Prostate cancer is not a deadly strike out of the blue. In fact, it is highly common. Consider a group of five American men in their fifties. One of

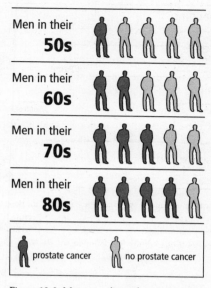

Men in their
50s

Men in their
60s

Men in their
70s

Men in their
80s

prostate cancer   no prostate cancer

Figure 10-3: More men die *with* prostate cancer than *from* it. Autopsy studies indicate that about one in every five American men in their fifties has some form of prostate cancer. When these men are in their sixties, another one has it. The older men get, the more likely they have it. A man in his eighties who does not have prostate cancer is the exception rather than the rule. But only about 3 percent of men die from it. (These numbers are rough estimates and vary between countries and ethnic groups.) Prostate cancer is a frequent condition; most men will not notice any symptoms because their cancers grow slowly or not at all.

them is likely to have some form of prostate cancer (Figure 10-3).[6] When these men are in their sixties and seventies, two or three are expected to have prostate cancer, and when they are in their eighties, four of the five will. Almost every man lucky enough to live a long life will eventually get it. Yet most will never notice because the cancer grows only slowly or not at all. Fortunately, the lifetime risk of dying from prostate cancer is only about 3 percent. More men die *with* prostate cancer than *from* it.

Giuliani is not the only politician who failed to appreciate the difference between survival rates and mortality rates. A report by the UK Office for National Statistics noted that five-year survival for colon cancer was 60 percent in the United States compared to 35 percent in Britain. Experts dubbed this finding "disgraceful" and called for government spending on cancer treatment to be doubled. In response, then Prime Minister Tony Blair set a target to increase survival rates by 20 percent over the next ten years: "We don't match other countries in its prevention, diagnosis and treatment."[7] Despite these large differences in five-year survival, the mortality rate for colon cancer in Britain was about the same as the rate in the United States. Higher survival does not mean longer life or a better health system. Nevertheless, Giuliani himself appears to be absolutely convinced that his prostate operation saved his life, as do other U.S. politicians, including John Kerry. In the late 1990s, Congress initiated a postal stamp featuring "Prostate Cancer Awareness," which promoted "annual checkups and tests." Giuliani and the U.S. Postal Service were obviously of one mind. To this day, celebrities recount in advertisements their personal stories about how early detection saved their lives.

Is there a way to reach people with the facts? There is. It's a simple tool called the icon box.

Screening for Prostate Cancer

An icon box brings transparency into health care. It can be used to communicate facts about screening, drugs, or any other treatment. The alternative treatments are placed directly next to each other in columns and both benefits and harms are shown. Most important, no misleading statistics such as survival rates and relative risks are allowed to enter the box. All information is given in plain frequencies. The aim is not to tell people what to do, but to provide the main facts so that everyone can make an informed decision. An icon box brings light into the darkness of persuasion and is an antidote to paternalism.

Let's contrast Giuliani's statement with an icon box for prostate cancer. The box summarizes the results from all medical studies using the best evidence from randomized trials.[8] In these trials, about half of the men were randomly assigned to a group who were screened for prostate cancer with PSA testing and digital rectal exam, the other half to the control group (no screening). If a cancer was detected in the first group by screening or in the control group by symptoms, then the patients typically underwent cancer treatment. The box shows what happened to the men after ten years.

What's the Benefit?

Let's begin with the positive aspect, the benefit. First, is there any evidence that early detection reduces the number of deaths from prostate cancer? The answer is no: There was no difference in the number of men who died of prostate cancer, no matter whether men went for screening or not. Second, is there evidence that detecting cancer at an early stage reduces the total number of deaths from any cause whatsoever? Again no. In the course of ten years, a fifth of the men who did not undergo screening died, as did a fifth of those who faithfully went for screening. Simply stated, there is no evidence that early detection saves lives; it reduced neither prostate cancer mortality nor total mortality.

The studies vary slightly in their estimates of the benefit (or lack thereof). The most optimistic estimate stems from a European study that reported a reduction of prostate cancer mortality of approximately one death in every one thousand men.[9] This study is included in the icon box. Once again, no difference in total mortality was found.

Why then do many men, like Giuliani, believe that early detection saved their lives? They are likely among the two out of every hundred men in Figure 10-4 (right side) who have nonprogressive cancer; that is, a form of cancer that would never have caused symptoms. After surgery or radiation therapy, every one of these men might think that their lives were saved by the test. But without the test and treatment they would in fact also be alive—and in better health.

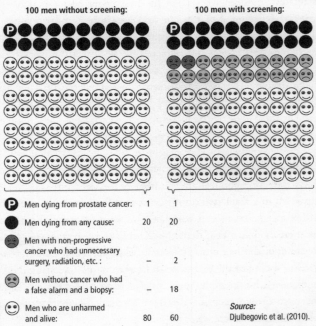

Prostate Cancer Early Detection

by PSA screening and digital rectal examination.
Numbers are for men aged 50 years and older, not participating vs. participating in screening for 10 years.

○○○ HARDING CENTER FOR
○○○ **RISK LITERACY**
○○●

100 men without screening:

100 men with screening:

		Men dying from prostate cancer:	1	1
●		Men dying from any cause:	20	20
		Men with non-progressive cancer who had unnecessary surgery, radiation, etc. :	–	2
		Men without cancer who had a false alarm and a biopsy:	–	18
		Men who are unharmed and alive:	80	60

Source:
Djulbegovic et al. (2010).

Figure 10-4. Icon box illustrating the benefits (or lack thereof) and harms of prostate cancer screening with PSA test and digital rectal examination. One hundred men aged fifty and older don't participate in screening (left) and the same number do (right). After ten years, some twenty had died in each group, one of them from prostate cancer. No life was saved by taking PSA tests, but about twenty men in the screening group were harmed (right panel, second group). Two had unnecessary surgery or radiation, which can lead to incontinence and impotence. Eighteen had false-positive test results, unnecessary biopsies, and were worried about having cancer. An icon box provides information in a transparent way—that is, without using relative risks, five-year survival rates, or other misleading statistics. To simplify, the number of men who died from prostate cancer is rounded from about 0.8 to one in one hundred. The bottom line: Prostate cancer screening has no proven mortality reduction, only proven harm. Based on about two hundred thousand men in the screening group and as many in the control group.

What's the Harm?

The icon box also shows the harms that occurred to men who went for screening. There are two kinds of harms: for men without prostate cancer and for men with prostate cancer that is nonprogressive. When a man without cancer repeatedly has a high PSA level, doctors typically do a biopsy. But unlike a mammogram, a PSA test does not tell the doctor where to insert the needle. As a result, men are often subjected to the nightmare of multiple needle biopsies in search of a tumor that is not there in the first place. These false alarms occur frequently because many men without cancer have high PSA levels.[10] Out of one hundred men who participated in screening, about eighteen experienced one or more false alarms with biopsy.

Men with nonprogressive prostate cancer suffered even more. If a biopsy showed any signs of cancer, most were pushed into unnecessary treatments, such as prostatectomy and radiation therapy. As the icon box shows, out of every one hundred men who underwent screening, two were treated unnecessarily. Giuliani, as mentioned above, is possibly one of them. Between 20 and 70 percent of men who had no problems before treatment ended up incontinent or impotent for the rest of their lives.[11] Altogether, twenty men are harmed by unnecessary biopsies, surgery, or radiation. For these unfortunate men, early detection actually lowered the quality of their lives, without extending its length.

A Word of Warning from the Man Who Discovered PSA

After a talk I gave to a health organization, a man approached me and introduced himself as the CEO of a bank management institution. "The story you told is my story. My doctor always advised me not to take PSA tests, and so did my father's doctor. But then there was a substitute doctor and he did a PSA test, cancer was detected, and then what happened was exactly what you said. Now I'm sixty, and I'm running to the bathroom all the time." An icon box can save you from incontinence and impotence.

We are told again and again that if you find prostate cancer early, your life might be saved. A plausible story, but it's on shaky ground. The result is the "Great Prostate Mistake," as Richard J. Ablin, the man who discovered the prostate specific antigen (PSA), has called it. He condemned PSA screening and the business made with his discovery:[12]

Testing should absolutely not be deployed to screen the entire population of men over the age of 50, the outcome pushed by those who stand to profit. I never dreamed that my discovery four decades ago would lead to such a profit-driven public health disaster. The medical community must confront reality and stop the inappropriate use of PSA screening. Doing so would save billions of dollars and rescue millions of men from unnecessary, debilitating treatments.

PSA tests may be useful for diagnostic purposes, such as after surgery, but not for screening. Because there is no evidence that lives are saved and strong evidence that some men are harmed, the National Cancer Institute explicitly recommend that men without any symptoms not be screened routinely, and its website (www.cancer.gov) states that men should consider benefits and harms before making a decision. Similarly, the U.S. Preventive Services Task Force recommends against routine PSA tests or digital rectal exams.

Even so, many hospitals and doctors adopt a policy of automatic screening or persuade men into screening. They do this for three familiar reasons, the SIC syndrome: Many doctors and clinics protect themselves against patients who might sue by recommending screening (the S for self-defense). Others do not know the medical evidence (the I for innumeracy). Out of a random sample of twenty Berlin urologists, only two knew the benefits and harms of PSA screening.[13] And the profit that can be made is substantial (the C for conflicts of interest). In the United States alone, some $3 billion are spent every year on performing the test and follow-ups; if the entire U.S. male population were screened, the first year would cost taxpayers $12 to $28 billion. For comparison, a WHO expert panel concluded that getting rid of measles worldwide would cost only half as much.[14]

Prostate cancer screening is a prime example of how time and money are wasted in health care. Doctors could use the time for helping instead of harming patients. The billions wasted could be used for saving lives instead.

When I presented the icon box on PSA screening during a talk at the annual conference of private health insurers, the head of one company approached me afterward. "You are spoiling our business plan," he said, decidedly annoyed. "To get an edge over the state-run health insurance plans, we pay for PSA tests. Now you show evidence that it's for no good." Why don't they offer their clients something that helps rather than hurts them?

Let me say it clearly: A doctor who advises men to undergo PSA testing without explaining the actual benefits and harms is not a good doctor.

Let's have a closer look at two of the reasons why this game persists: doctors' flawed understanding of health statistics and money-driven conflicts of interest.

Do Doctors Understand Survival Rates?

Do doctors understand survival rates, or are they fooled just like Rudy Giuliani? As far as I can tell, no study ever asked this question. For that reason some of my colleagues and I conducted a national sample of 412 physicians in the United States.[15] These doctors practiced family medicine, general medicine, and internal medicine. Most of them had ten to twenty years' experience. The first question was:

Which of the following prove that a screening test "saves lives" from cancer?

1. More cancers are detected in screened populations than in unscreened populations. (47 percent)
2. Screen-detected cancers have better five-year survival rates than cancers detected because of symptoms. (76 percent)
3. Mortality rates are lower among screened persons than unscreened persons in a randomized trial. (81 percent)

What do you think? Almost half (47 percent) of the doctors mistakenly believed that detecting more cancers proves that the test saves lives (1). What they didn't consider is that all screening tests of any value on the market will detect cancers. And, as the icon box for prostate cancer screening demonstrates, early detection is not always a godsend for patients. Although a few kinds of cancer screening, such as Pap smears, can save lives, most save none and harm large numbers of people; some can even have fatal results. Within one month after lung cancer surgery, 5 percent of patients are no longer alive. That does not stop advertising campaigns for lung cancer screening, such as with spiral CTs. The point is not that spiral CTs are no good. In fact, they are too good. They are so accurate that they detect about as many lung cancers in nonsmokers as in smokers![16] In other words, they detect nonprogressive cancers in nonsmokers—abnormalities that, technically speaking, are cancer but do not lead to symptoms. Detecting more cancers is not proof that lives are saved. Every doctor should know this elementary fact.

Like Rudy Giuliani, three quarters of the doctors falsely believed that higher five-year survival rates proves that lives are saved (2). The majority (81 percent) also correctly believed that lower mortality rates are proof (3). But if most doctors believe that both survival and mortality rates prove the same thing, there must be some confusion. We tested this in our next question.

A result can be phrased either as a survival or a mortality rate. Will this influence what doctors recommend to patients? Doctors were asked:

Imagine that a 55-year-old healthy patient asks you about a screening for Cancer X. Please answer the following question based on data for patients age 50 to 69, which come from a large trial of U.S. adults that lasted about 10 years.

	Without screening test	**With screening test**
five-year survival rate	68 percent	99 percent

Would you recommend this screening test to your patient?

The majority of physicians (nearly 70 percent) said that they would definitely recommend the test to their patients. Later, doctors were asked the same question about screening for Cancer Z, which was in fact the same as Cancer X. But now the information was provided in mortality rates:

	Without screening test	**With screening test**
Mortality rate	2 deaths per 1,000 people	1.6 deaths per 1,000 people

This time, only 23 percent said they would recommend the test (Figure 10-5). It was disturbing to see that the majority of doctors in the United States can be easily persuaded by survival rates.

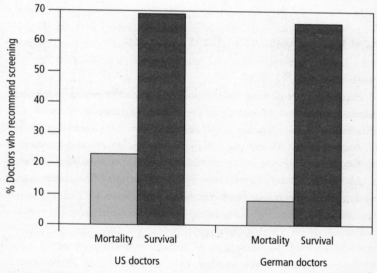

Figure 10-5. Do doctors understand five-year survival rates? Most do not. If the information is presented in terms of mortality rates, very few doctors recommend screening to their patients. If the same information is presented in terms of misleading survival rates, most recommend screening. Based on a national sample of 412 U.S. doctors and 65 German doctors.

Source: Wegwarth et al. (2011, 2012).

Are doctors in Germany any better? When we asked sixty-five German internal medicine physicians, they too could be easily manipulated into recommending screening.[17] We also asked these physicians to explain what lead time bias is (see Figure 10-1). Only two of the sixty-five could do it. And when we asked them about overdiagnosis (see Figure 10-2), not a single one could explain it.

All in all, most of the doctors in Germany and the United States drew wrong conclusions from survival rates. In addition, almost half of the U.S. doctors falsely believed that detecting more cancers proves that lives are saved. Under the influence of their confusion, they would recommend screening to patients. To change this to the better, icon boxes should be standard when doctors talk with patients about medical procedures.

How Prestigious Institutions Fool You

Speaking Double-Tongue

As long as nobody notices, institutions can twist information to influence doctors and patients. What would you do to win over patients? One trick is shown in Figure 10-6. See if you can catch it before continuing on. The ad is for M. D. Anderson, one of the most prestigious cancer centers in the United States. According to the ad, survival has steadily increased at the clinic over the years in comparison to the much lower nationwide rates. The Center claims: "As national mortality rates for prostate cancer fluctuated between 1960 and 1990, five-year survival rates for prostate cancer among M. D. Anderson patients continued to improve." This increase in survival is presented as an "overall increase in longevity." And there we have it: Survival is equated with living longer, and the increase in survival rates is compared to nationwide *mortality* rates. Unlike us, many of the ad's readers who have never heard of lead time bias and overdiagnosis will be fooled into believing that the center has made considerable progress in the war against cancer. This commonly used trick, *double-tonguing*, means reporting survival rates to make one's own success look

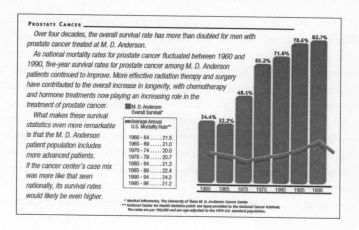

PROSTATE CANCER

Over four decades, the overall survival rate has more than doubled for men with prostate cancer treated at M. D. Anderson.

As national mortality rates for prostate cancer fluctuated between 1960 and 1990, five-year survival rates for prostate cancer among M. D. Anderson patients continued to improve. More effective radiation therapy and surgery have contributed to the overall increase in longevity, with chemotherapy and hormone treatments now playing an increasing role in the treatment of prostate cancer.

What makes these survival statistics even more remarkable is that the M. D. Anderson patient population includes more advanced patients. If the cancer center's case mix was more like that seen nationally, its survival rates would likely be even higher.

■ M. D. Anderson Overall Survival*
▬ Average Annual U.S. Mortality Rate**

1960 - 64	21.5
1965 - 69	21.0
1970 - 74	20.0
1975 - 79	20.7
1980 - 84	21.3
1985 - 89	22.4
1990 - 94	24.2
1995 - 98	21.2

34.4% 32.2% 48.1% 65.2% 71.6% 78.6% 82.7%

1960 1965 1970 1975 1980 1985 1990

* Medical Informatics, The University of Texas M. D. Anderson Cancer Center
** National Center for Health Statistics public use tapes provided to the National Cancer Institute. The rates are per 100,000 and are age-adjusted to the 1970 U.S. standard population.

Figure 10-6. Double-tongue advertisement for prostate cancer screening. The ad compares the survival rates at M. D. Anderson, one of the most respected U.S. cancer centers, with the mortality rates in the United States. The statistically uninformed reader, who may not notice the difference, is led to conclude that the center has made considerable progress in treating patients.

amazing, and then reporting mortality rates to make others' success look small or nil.

Conflicts of Interest

Why is the public being so blatantly deceived? I think there are two quite different groups to blame. The first consists of true believers in screening who don't want to see the scientific evidence or don't understand it. The second group is commercially motivated and has a business plan that puts patients at risk for unnecessary treatments. These two groups often cohabit peacefully: If the one avoids the evidence, the other has a better conscience about its business plan. One scheme is to offer screening at sharply reduced costs or even for free in order to make it a "loss leader." It's the same strategy supermarkets and other stores use: pricing an item well below cost in order to attract customers and stimulate more profitable sales later. In the words of oncologist

Dr. Otis Brawley, now chief medical officer of the American Cancer Society, in his former position as director of the Georgia Cancer Center at Emory:[18]

> *We at Emory have figured out that if we screen 1,000 men at the North Lake Mall this coming Saturday, we could bill Medicare and insurance companies for $4.9 million in health care costs [for biopsies, tests, prostatectomies, etc.]. But the real money comes later—from the medical care the wife will get in the next three years because Emory cares about her man, and from the money we get when he comes to Emory's emergency room when he gets chest pain because we screened him three years ago. . . .*
>
> *We don't screen anymore at Emory, once I became head of Cancer Control. It bothered me, though, that my P.R. and money people could tell me how much money we would make off screening, but nobody could tell me if we could save one life. As a matter of fact, we could have estimated how many men we would render impotent . . . but we didn't. It's a huge ethical issue.*

We need more directors like Dr. Brawley. But we also need more risk-savvy patients. A clinic that offers PSA tests to uninformed men without providing an icon box can only win. If the test result is negative, the patient is reassured. If the test result is positive, the patient is grateful that the clinic detected the cancer early, even if he soon ends up incontinent. As Dr. Brawley noted, profiting from uninformed patients is unethical. Medicine should not be a money game.

Screening for Breast Cancer

I have chosen prostate cancer screening to demonstrate the incredible mass of misinformed patients and doctors. It is unfortunately the rule rather than the exception. Most people have equally inflated beliefs about the effectiveness of other cancer screening, drugs, and treatments. The tricks are always the same: survival, relative risks, double-tonguing, and others. In each case icon boxes can work to get patients' heightened expectations back on solid ground. Consider breast cancer screening. In the good old days of male chauvinism, the American Cancer Society could simply say:[19]

> *"If you haven't had a mammogram, you need more than your breasts examined."*

Today, that's fortunately no longer acceptable. But although society has stopped making overt jokes about female brains, the paternalist attitude toward women hasn't changed much. Many women complain to me about the emotional pressure they get from their doctors. "You aren't getting screened? Be sensible and think of your children." And across all Western countries, women are still often treated like children: told what to do, but not given the facts needed for an informed decision. A delicate pink health leaflet by the Arkansas Foundation for Medical Care explains:[20]

> *Why should I have a mammogram? Because you're a woman.*

After this deeply informative answer, women get zero information in the rest of this leaflet about benefits and harms that would let them make up their own minds. Instead they are told to tell every other woman to do what they were told to do: "That's why you should ask your mothers, sisters, daughters, grandmothers, aunts, and friends to have mammograms, too."

How can women be empowered to make an informed decision? A fact box is one means.[21] Unlike the icon box for prostate cancer screening, it uses numbers instead of icons. These are all stated as simple frequencies, with no relative risks or misleading five-year survival rates. The fact box is based on the evidence from available randomized trials, here with women age fifty and older who were divided at random into two groups: One group was screened for breast cancer regularly, the other was not screened. The box shows what happened to the women after ten years.

What's the Benefit?

Let's first look at the positive side, the potential benefits. There are two questions a woman might ask: First, is there evidence that mammography

Breast Cancer Early Detection
by mammography screening

◯◯◯ HARDING CENTER FOR
◯◯◯ **RISK LITERACY**
◯◯●

Numbers for women aged 50 years or older who participated in screening for 10 years on average.

	1,000 women without screening	1,000 women with screening
Benefits		
How many women died from breast cancer?	5	4*
How many women died from all types of cancer?	21	21
Harms		
How many women without cancer experienced false alarms, biopsies or psychological distress?	–	100
How many women with non-progressive cancer had unnecessary treatments, such as complete or partial breast removal?	–	5

* This means that about 4 out of 1,000 women (50+ years of age) with screening died from breast cancer within 10 years – one less than without screening.

Source: Gøtzsche, PC, Nielsen, M (2011). *Cochrane database of systematic reviews* (1): CD001877.
Where no data for women above 50 years of age are available, numbers refer to women above 40 years of age.

Figure 10-7. Fact box for breast cancer screening with mammography, based on the available studies with hundreds of thousands of women fifty and older. For every one thousand women who participated in screening, one less died from breast cancer within ten years. But there was no difference between the two groups in terms of how many died of cancer in general, including breast cancer. Among those who went for screening, about a hundred were falsely alarmed and five had unnecessary treatments, such as lumpectomy and mastectomy.

screening reduces my chance of dying from *breast cancer*? The answer is yes. Out of every one thousand women who did not participate in screening, about five died of breast cancer, while this number was four for those who participated. In statistical terms that is an absolute risk reduction of one in one thousand.[22] But if you find this information in a newspaper or brochure, it is almost always presented as a "20 percent risk reduction" or more. Second, is there evidence that mammography screening reduces my chance of dying from *any kind of cancer*, including breast cancer? The answer is no. The studies showed that of every thousand women who participated in screening, about twenty-one died of any kind of cancer, and the number was the same for women who did not participate.

In plain words, there is no evidence that mammography saves lives. One less woman in a thousand dies with the diagnosis breast cancer, but one more dies with another cancer diagnosis. Some women die with two or three different cancers, where it's not always clear which of these caused death. That is why the total cancer mortality (including breast cancer) is the more reliable Figure. That's the number you will have a hard time finding. After all, what would women say if they learned that they had been asked for years to attend mammography screening without proof that it saves lives?

What's the Harm?

Now let's look at the harms. First, women who do not have breast cancer can experience false alarms and unnecessary biopsies. This happened to about a hundred out of every thousand women who participated in screening. Legions of women have suffered from this procedure and the related anxieties. After false alarms, many of them worried for months, developing sleeping problems and changed relationships with family and friends. Second, women who do have breast cancer, but a nonprogressive or slowly growing form that they would never have noticed during their lifetimes, often undergo lumpectomy, mastectomy, toxic chemotherapy, or other interventions that have no benefit for them, leading only to a lower quality of life. This happened to about five women out of a thousand who participated in screening. Apart from temporary harms such as baldness, nausea, and anemia, more serious consequences of chemotherapy can include long-term fatigue, premature menopause, and heart damage.

The fact box on mammography screening allows women to make informed decisions based on their personal values. When I showed the box to a gynecologist, he stopped his paternalistic treatment of women and began to use it. He told me that a third of his patients looked at the facts and said "no way," another third said "not now, but let's discuss this again in five years," and the others decided to participate in screening. While the fact box clearly shows that there is no good reason to push women into screening, my point is exactly not to replace the old paternalistic message with a new one by telling women not to go to screening. Every woman *who wants to make her own decision* should get the facts she needs—without being told what to do.

The fact box is not like a package insert that lists all possible side effects in miniscule print just to protect the company from being sued. It is simple and transparent. There are other potential harms the fact box does not list because there is no reliable evidence for them. For instance, a few women might get cancer from the X-rays; crude estimates are between one and five in ten thousand. And many women also experience pain from the squeezing of their breasts while being x-rayed.

How to Make Patients Smart

Does John Q Public understand a fact box? Lisa Schwartz and Steve Woloshin from Dartmouth Medical School have developed fact boxes for drugs, screening, and other treatments. They showed that these boxes dramatically increase understanding.[23] For instance, less than 10 percent of people correctly understood the absolute risk reduction of a statin, but with the help of a fact box this jumped to over 70 percent. Fact boxes improve consumers' knowledge of benefits and side effects, and result in better choices of drugs. They can also fight the daily barrage of medical news and advertisements faced by both doctors and patients. Schwartz and Woloshin then presented the results of several fact box studies to the FDA's Risk Communication Advisory Committee, which voted unanimously that the FDA should adopt the fact box as a standard.[24] But the recommendation was nonbinding. Eventually, after the *New York Times* covered the presentation, two senators submitted a bill to Congress calling on the FDA to adopt fact boxes for drugs. The bill was incorporated into the health care reform bill signed into law in 2010. Wonderful, we might think; it's about time. Unfortunately, the bill does not clarify two basic issues: who writes the fact boxes and where the boxes should appear. This is why we still have no fact boxes in package inserts or drug ads.

Who and where? The answer appears obvious. Regulatory agencies such as the FDA should write the fact boxes, since they have the data and have already written a report on every drug they approve. This fact box should then be part of inserts and ads. And they should be available in every doctor's waiting room. Then patients would finally have easy access to clean information.

Infantilizing Women

The writer Barbara Ehrenreich expressed her unhappiness about the infantilizing breast-cancer industry with its pink ribbons, teddy bears, and relentless cheerfulness.[25] Has feminism been replaced by the pink-ribbon breast-cancer cult? she asked. When First Lady Laura Bush traveled to Saudi Arabia in 2007, what vital issue did she take up with the locals? Not women's right to drive, vote, or leave the house without a man, but "breast cancer awareness." In 2010, when the U.S. Preventive Services Task Force dared to recommend that regular screening mammography not start until age fifty, all hell broke loose. The belief in the benefits of screening is so firmly entrenched that few women are willing to consider the medical evidence that suggests otherwise. And when they do ask, many are taken in with just four tricks. You will recognize these by now.

Trick #1: Don't mention that mammography screening doesn't reduce the chance of dying from cancer. Only talk about the reduction in dying from breast cancer.

Trick #2: Tell women that screening reduces breast cancer mortality by 20 percent or more. Don't reveal that this is the same as an absolute risk reduction of one in one thousand, which would sound less impressive.

Trick #3: Tell women about increased survival. For instance, "If you participate in screening and breast cancer is detected, your survival rate is 98 percent." Don't mention mortality.

Trick #4: Don't tell women about unnecessary surgery, biopsies, and other harms from overtreatment. If you are asked, play these down.

These four tricks have been highly successful in shaping many women's attitude toward mammography screening. Trick #1 is ubiquitous. Hardly a health brochure dispenses with it. Trick #2 is used in the majority of brochures worldwide.[26] Most websites use it too, although at least one out of five does provide information in transparent absolute numbers. Tricks #3 and #4 can be found in many magazines, leaflets, and websites all across the world, as the following three examples illustrate.

Tricking Women in Three Languages

In the Spanish edition of *Newsweek*, Julio Frenk, former minister of health of Mexico and currently dean of the Harvard School of Public Health, and his wife, Felicia Knaul, economist and author of a book on breast cancer, wrote:

> *Only early detection prevents women from dying of breast cancer. In rich countries, where screening is common, detection is early, so treatment is more effective. The probability of five-year survival after early-state diagnosis is 98 percent.*[27]

This number is impressive. But as I explained before, high survival rates don't tell us anything about whether or not lives are saved. It is painful to see Trick #3 used by the dean of the Harvard School of Public Health, who should know better. The proper Figure would be an absolute risk reduction of one in one thousand, as shown in the fact box.

Susan G. Komen for the Cure is one of the largest, best funded, and most trusted breast cancer organizations in the United States. Its logo is—take a guess—a pink ribbon. Komen has in fact dominated the pink ribbon marketplace, pairing, for instance, with M&M's to sell pink-coated candies high in sugar and fat and with the fast food restaurant chain KFC to promote fried and grilled chicken sold in pink branded buckets, both foods possibly causing obesity and cancer.[28] It has invested about $2 billion for breast cancer research education and advocacy, with some one hundred thousand volunteers working worldwide. One of its recommendations is that all women from the age of forty onward get a yearly mammogram. In a promotion, Komen shows the face of a woman next to a vertical red arrow on which is written: "What's key to surviving breast cancer? You." The arrow points to what women should do: "GET SCREENED NOW." Under the arrow, the text says:

LESS TALK. MORE ACTION. Early detection saves lives. The 5-year survival rate for breast cancer when caught early is 98%. When it's not? 23%.

That again was Trick #3. The promotion provides no other information about benefits or harms.

Let me end on a positive note. Can we do anything about the tricks played on patients? Yes. One bargaining chip is reputation. For years, I have argued that biased reporting in health pamphlets is a major cause of the bulk of misinformed patients and doctors. Such pamphlets are distributed by trusted organizations around the world. One of these was the Deutsche Krebshilfe, the largest German cancer care organization, which receives about €100 million a year in donations. One of its pamphlets combined Tricks #2 and #3:[29]

Women whose tumor has been detected in an early stage have a 5-year survival rate of over 98 percent after the operation. Studies showed that among women age 50 to 69, mammography screening reduces mortality from breast cancer by up to 30 percent.

Here, the reduction from five to four in every one thousand women, typically presented as 20 percent, is generously rounded up to 30 percent. In interviews and public lectures, I noted that the Krebshilfe risked losing its credibility (and, implicitly, its funding) for its misleading pamphlets. Eventually, the organization's head of public relations flew from Bonn to Berlin to ask whether I had a personal vendetta against the organization. I said, "Not at all. On the contrary, I'd be happy to help rewrite your pamphlets so that everyone can understand the evidence." It turned out that she was not aware of the tricks used in its many cancer brochures. I took my time to explain what transparent facts look like. The organization agreed to my proposal, and with the help of my colleague Odette Weg-warth there is now an entirely new generation of pamphlets for various cancers. All misleading relative risks and five-year survival rates have been axed and replaced by absolute numbers. For the first time, the potential harms of screening are mentioned, including how often they occur. This laudable move will rightly secure the organization the trust of the public.

Not everyone has the opportunity to give public lectures, but we can all put pressure on health organizations, daily newspapers, and others that provide misleading information. Thanks to the Internet it's easy to voice complaints publicly, but an old-fashioned letter to the editor works just as well. Once people make clear that they can no longer be fooled, those interested in retaining their credibility will have to get their act together and provide trick-free information.

What Do Men and Women Know?

How does this biased information policy affect the public? To find out, we asked over ten thousand men and women in nine European countries: Austria, France, Germany, Italy, the Netherlands, Poland, Spain, the UK, and the European part of Russia.[30] Men were asked about the benefit of prostate cancer screening and women about that of breast cancer screening. In every country, most men and women overestimated the benefit vastly or didn't know (the dark parts in Figure 10-8). The British came up last: 99 percent of British men overestimated the benefit vastly or did not know. In fact, a fifth of them believed that 200 of every 1,000 men would be saved (!). Their huge miscalculation is likely due to a widely publicized study on screening that was touted around the globe as having found a "20 percent mortality reduction" from prostate cancer (Trick #2). Yet this impressive 20 percent was nothing but a reduction from 3.7 to 3.0 in every 1,000 men.[31] Quite a number of British men seem to have fallen into the trap. Are more British women informed? Yes, almost four times more! In absolute numbers, however, that's not even 4 percent of the British women. In fact, a fourth of all British women believed that 200 of every 1,000 women would be saved (!). Their huge miscalculation is likely due to the fact that the absolute risk reduction—from 5 to 4 in 1,000 women—has been presented to them as a "20 percent mortality reduction" from breast cancer (again Trick #2). Few women knew that the best answer is around 1 in 1,000. Once more, the same relative-risk trick that was played on British women in the contraceptive pill scare (covered in chapter 1) was successful. Then it generated great fear; this time, undue hopes.

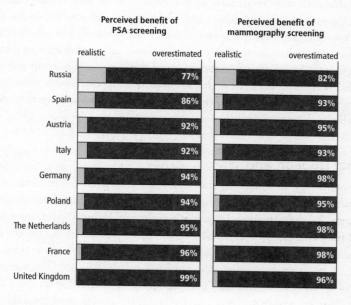

Figure 10-8. The vast majority of Europeans overestimate the benefit of prostate cancer screening and breast cancer screening. In face-to-face interviews with more than ten thousand citizens in nine countries, men were asked: "One thousand men age fifty and older from the general population participate every two years in screening for prostate cancer with PSA tests. After ten years, the benefit is measured. Please estimate how many fewer men die from prostate cancer in the group who participate in screening compared to men who do not participate in screening." The response alternatives were zero, one, ten, fifty, one hundred, or two hundred in one thousand, and "don't know." Women were asked the same question for mammography screening. Numbers show the percentage of men (women) who overestimate the reduction in prostate cancer (breast cancer) mortality. The major reason appears to be the systematic misinformation of the public (examples in the text). Russians do best, not because they get more information, but probably because they get less misleading information.

Source: Gigerenzer et al. (2009).

Across all European countries, only 11 percent of men and 8 percent of women had a realistic idea of the benefits. The country that did best was Russia: 23 (18) percent of Russian men (women) got it right. The reason is probably not that Russians get more information, but that they get less misleading information.

Did those who more often consulted their GPs, health pamphlets, or the Internet for medical information make better estimates? Not at all. The Internet did not help; it offers easy access to an overabundance of misleading health information, often funded by those with commercial interests. Frequent consultation of doctors and pamphlets also failed to improve understanding and was even slightly associated with people's overestimating the benefit. Thus, few Europeans are in a position to make an informed choice about breast and prostate cancer screening.

I don't know of a similar study in North America or Asia, but I would be surprised if people elsewhere were better informed. In fact, a national telephone survey of U.S. adults reported that the majority were "extremely confident" in their decision about prostate, colorectal, and breast screening, believed they were well informed, but could not correctly answer a single knowledge question.[32] People have a moral right to be informed in a transparent way, but they aren't.

Facts and fiction about cancer screening

Note that screening is for people without symptoms.

1. If I participate in screening, I will reduce my chance of getting cancer. *No, screening is not prevention. Just as accident insurance does not reduce the chance of an accident, screening does not reduce incidence; it can only detect cancers that are already there.*

2. A positive test means that I have cancer. *No, most people with positive mammograms, PSA tests, or fecal occult blood tests do not have cancer.*

3. If the test is negative, I can be sure that I don't have cancer. *You can be more confident, but not sure. Misses happen; no test is perfect.*

4. If I get cancer, I will die from it. *Cancer is not necessarily a death sentence. Most men with prostate cancer don't die from it—they might not even notice it and die with the cancer, not of it. But pancreatic cancer kills most in a short time.*

5. Early detection saved my life because after treatment, I am still alive. *This conclusion may or may not be true. It is not for those who have been "overdiagnosed." Tests can detect tiny tumors that are nonprogressive and would have never affected your health. As a consequence, people suffer from needless appointments, needless tests, and needless drugs and surgery.*

6. Isn't the fact that mortality rates decline over the years proof that screening works? *No, the proof is in randomized trials (see icon and fact boxes). For instance, the mortality rates for stomach cancer have declined since the 1930s in Western countries without any screening. The reason is probably the invention of refrigeration and other improved methods of food preservation.*

7. Why is total mortality (or total cancer mortality) more relevant to understanding the benefit than cancer-specific mortality? *First, some patients have multiple cancers, and it is difficult to determine which of them caused death. Second, surgery following screening can kill as many as it cures, or more. These unlucky patients are included in the total mortality rate, but not in the cancer-specific rate. Third, consider the seemingly paradoxical fact that cigarette smoking reduces breast-cancer*

mortality by one in one thousand women (the same effect as for mammography screening).[33] The reason is that smoking kills earlier so that some women don't live long enough to get breast cancer. Here, smoking appears to reduce breast cancer mortality but in fact increases total mortality.

8. Wouldn't I be best off by screening for all cancers? *No, you wouldn't, because some lead to more harm than gain. For instance, the U.S. Preventive Services Task Force explicitly recommends against screening for cancers of the prostate, lungs, pancreas, ovaries, bladder, and thyroid. Pap smear screening for cervical cancer, in contrast, appears to save lives; this has not yet been tested in a randomized trial.*

9. What can I do against cancer? *Because about half of cancers are due to behavior, prevention has much more potential than early detection. Avoid smoking, obesity, poor diet, and excessive alcohol consumption, and increase physical activity such as walking for three to five hours a week. Lifestyle change also has benefits for health in general.*

Fight Cancer with Prevention, Not Screening

Prevention is not the same as early detection (screening), although the terms are often mixed up. Some screening programs misleadingly advertise themselves as cancer prevention. Accordingly, more than half of German women (56 percent) wrongly believe that screening prevents cancer.[34] Early detection means detecting a cancer that is already there, while prevention means reducing the chance that cancer will occur.

As the facts show, the war against cancer is not won by early detection. The best defense is prevention and developing better therapy.

Cancer is caused by cells that do not behave as they should. Every person has thirty billion cells that are the offspring of one egg cell. Every second, five million cells divide themselves in your body, and if there are too many incorrect divisions, cancer results. Is cancer human destiny? The war on cancer is being fought with three weapons: early detection, drugs, and prevention.

Cancer Drugs

Since President Nixon declared the war on cancer, billions have been invested into the development of drugs. Nearly every month, the exciting discovery of a new wonder drug is proclaimed by the media. There are a few effective treatments, such as for cancer of the testicle, but in general, the results have been disappointing. These drugs are typically reported to prolong life by a few weeks or months. Yet even that brief an extension is not always the case. Take Avastin, the world's best-selling cancer medicine, with sales of $6 billion in 2010. It is used for the treatment of advanced cancers of the colon, breast, lung, and kidney, among others. An analysis of sixteen trials with more than ten thousand people showed that when Avastin was added to chemotherapy, *more* people died than when receiving chemotherapy alone.[35] Thus, not only did the drug fail to prolong lives of hopeful patients for a few weeks or months, it in fact shortened them. Given the huge amount of money at stake for the pharmaceutical industry (Avastin treatment costs up to $57,000 per year for one patient), we are fed false hopes and expensive drugs that can do us more harm than good. And their side effects can dramatically decrease the quality of the last months or years of one's life.

Equally alarming, an analysis of fifty-three "landmark" publications in top journals on cancer drugs revealed that the positive effects of most (forty-seven) studies could not be replicated.[36] In one case, the scientists who tried to replicate an effect over and over again without any success contacted the study's lead researcher, who admitted having done the experiment six times and getting the result only once. But he put that one result into the paper because it made for a good story. Publishing only the positive result fosters exciting but shoddy science. The reason for this violation of scientific honesty is a system with the wrong incentives: Publishing in prestigious journals pays, whether or not the results are correct. Replication does not.

Drugs have also been developed for prevention, with limited success beyond the triumphant marketing headlines. Consider tamoxifen for preventing breast cancer. Sometime back a full-page advertisement appeared in mass magazines and reached about forty-one million readers on its first appearance. The headline, stretched over the back of a young woman in a lacy bra, reads: "If you care about breast cancer, care more about being a 1.7 than a 36B" (Figure 10-9).[37] But what exactly does 1.7 mean? You might think it's high risk, and if you are at high risk, then you should take tamoxifen (Nolvadex). What it actually means is a 1.7 percent chance of being diagnosed as having breast cancer in the next five years; in other words, a 98.3 percent chance of not developing breast cancer. The eye-catching bra distracts from the two questions one should ask: What are the benefits and what are the harms of tamoxifen?

Figure 10-9. Tamoxifen advertisement.

The answer is that out of every one thousand women who took tamoxifen for five years, seventeen developed invasive breast cancer, compared to thirty-three who took a sugar pill. That is, sixteen fewer women developed breast cancer. Yet the study could not show a reduction of mortality from breast cancer or from other causes. At the same time, among every one thousand women who took tamoxifen, there were five additional cases of blood clots in their legs or lungs, and six more women got invasive uterine cancer. To make the benefits look larger and harms smaller, some institutions used double-tonguing: The benefit was presented in terms of a relative risk reduction ("about 49 percent fewer diagnoses of invasive breast cancer") while the harms were framed in absolute risks, as above.[38] Besides these life-threatening side effects, hundreds of women had hot flashes and vaginal discharges, and a few needed cataract surgery. Despite the equivocal success of such drugs, virtually all funding by industry and taxpayers is spent on them. But there is a second means of prevention: to make people competent in taking their health into their own hands.

Prevention: Make People Risk Savvy

About half of all cancers have their roots in behavior. This means that changes in lifestyle and the environment can save up to half of all people who would have otherwise developed cancer. The potential is best illustrated by the fact that immigrants tend to get the local cancer of the country they move to. For example, Japanese in Osaka are much less likely than Americans (Hawaiian Caucasians) to get prostate and breast cancer, but the moment they migrate to Hawaii, the gap narrows substantially (Figure 10-10). It's not that lifestyle or the environment in Hawaii are conducive to ill health in general, but to specific cancers. In their home country, Japanese men have substantially more stomach cancers than Americans, but after they move to Hawaii, stomach cancer largely disappears. One reason for this stunning effect is the Japanese tradition of eating salted fish and other food prepared by salting, pickling, and smoking, which are not customary in Hawaii.

Many behaviors that contribute to cancer are formed in childhood and adolescence: what we eat and drink, and how physically active we are.

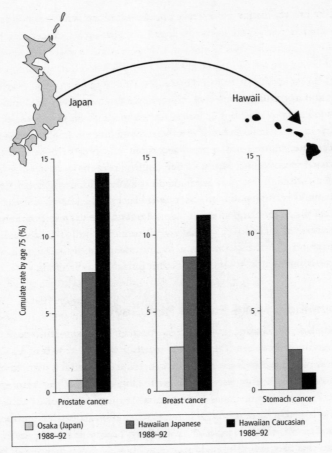

Figure 10-10. Immigrants tend to get the local cancers of their host country. Prostate and breast cancer rates in Japan (Osaka) are low compared to Hawaiian Caucasians. Among Japanese migrants to Hawaii, however, the rates became similar to the local population. In contrast, Japanese have higher rates of stomach cancer, but for those who migrated to Hawaii, the rate dropped close to that of the local population. To a large extent, cancer is due to lifestyle, including environmental factors, as opposed to genetic factors alone.

Source: Peto (2001).

Here are the major behaviors that cause cancer, with estimates for the United States:

Cigarette Smoking Causes 20 to 30 Percent of All Cancers.

At the beginning of the twentieth century, lung cancer was almost unknown. It was so rare that Isaac Adler, who wrote the first book-length review in 1912, apologized for wasting so much ink on such a trivial topic. At that time, people smoked pipes and cigars, which cause other cancers. Sigmund Freud, for one, suffered from mouth cancer the last sixteen years of his life as a result of his addiction to cigar smoking. Not until World War I did cigarettes become popular. Today, lung cancer is the leading cause of cancer death for American men and women. In total, one to three out of every ten smokers will develop it. Tobacco smoke contains poisons such as radioactive polonium-210, lead, and arsenic. It kills about 435,000 U.S. citizens each year, which is more than AIDS, traffic accidents, homicide, suicide, and terrorism combined.[39] About 90 percent of lung cancers are attributed to cigarette smoking.[40] But lung cancer is not the only cancer due to smoking. When a person smokes for thirty or forty years, carcinogens are disposed in the urine and enter the bladder; before they are disposed from the body, genes in the bladder mutate, which results in cancer of the bladder.[41]

A study that followed 35,000 British doctors for fifty years found that nonsmokers lived on average ten years longer than lifelong smokers, who died early from cancer, heart disease, and respiratory disease.[42] The deadly potential of secondhand smoke is equally established, although not always known. For instance, even in 2011 only 61 percent of Dutch adults agreed that cigarette smoking endangers nonsmokers.[43] To reduce the number one cause of cancer, there is a simple rule:

1. *Don't Start Smoking; If You Did, Stop.*

Quitting smoking is difficult if one is already addicted. The most effective remedy is to make young people risk competent before they begin. This can be done through a playful health literacy program for preteens in schools, as will be outlined in chapter 12. If such a program succeeds in making only one out of every ten children strong enough to resist the temptation, more lives will be saved from cancer than with all current screening and drug programs added together. For those who already smoke, there is also good news: If you stop smoking before age thirty, you can expect to fully regain the ten years of life otherwise lost, and stopping at age forty, fifty, and sixty, can regain nine, six, and three years, respectively.

The mighty opponents in the war against cancer are the tobacco industry and other industries that make huge profits from carcinogenic products. What is a human life worth to a cigarette manufacturer? Cigarettes cause about one death per million cigarettes smoked with a latency of several decades, and tobacco companies earn about a penny in profit for each cigarette. One million times a penny is $10,000. That is the price tag on a person who dies from smoking.[44]

Obesity, Diet, and Physical Inactivity Cause 10 to 20 Percent of All Cancers.

The following recommendations, made by cancer organizations, are easier to follow because they do not involve addiction:[45]

2. Maintain Normal Body Weight.

Ensure that body weight is not too far off the normal body mass index (BMI), most importantly throughout childhood and adolescence. The BMI is a rough measure of whether someone is too heavy for good health. It is the weight of a person (in pounds) divided by the square of their height (in inches) times 703. For instance, a man who weighs 195 pounds and is six feet tall has a body mass index of 26.4. Having a BMI above 25, this man would be called "overweight"; had it been 30 or more, he would be called "obese."[46] Being overweight or obese when young substantially shortens life, while the effect is smaller when older. The American Cancer Society estimated that excess weight could cause one out of every seven cancers, specifically cancers of the breast, cervix, colon, gall bladder, kidney, liver, esophagus, ovary, pancreas, prostate, stomach (in men), and uterus.[47] This number is on the rise.

3. Be Physically Active as Part of Everyday Life.

Limit sedentary habits such as watching TV; use stairs instead of elevators. Be moderately physically active, equivalent to walking for at least thirty minutes a day. Most people in technological societies have levels of activity below those to which the human body is adapted. Physical inactivity has been linked with increased risk of cancer of the colon, breast, pancreas, prostate, and of melanoma.[48]

4. Avoid Fast Food and Sugary Drinks.

Avoid drinks with added sugar, including colas and sodas, and readily available convenience food, such as burgers, hot dogs, fried chicken pieces, and french fries (chips). All these promote weight gain. Replace sugary drinks with water or unsweetened tea and coffee.

5. Limit Animal Food and Eat Mostly Plant Food.

Although the evidence here is much less clear, it doesn't hurt to limit intake of "red meat" and avoid processed meat—meat preserved by smoking, curing, salting, or adding chemical preservatives. People who like meat are advised to eat poultry, fish, or venison. Eggs do not seem to increase cancer. The World Cancer Research Fund's recommendation is to eat at least five portions (400 g or 14 oz) of fruit and vegetables of different colors every day, including red, green, yellow, white, purple, and orange, such as broccoli, eggplant, tomato, and garlic, and limit refined starchy vegetables such as potato products. There is evidence that red and processed meat increase the chance of colorectal cancer, and there is probable evidence that non-starchy vegetables and fruits protect against a number of cancers.

6. Avoid Salted Food.

Salt and salt-preserved food are probably causes of stomach cancer. The strong decline of stomach cancer in the Western World during the twentieth century is likely a consequence of refrigerators, not of screening or cancer drugs.

7. Avoid Dietary Supplements.

Vitamins, minerals, and other nutrients should be consumed through food and drinks, not supplements. Supplements might have unexpected adverse effects causing cancer. Supplements are only needed for people who have diseases that make it difficult to absorb naturally occurring vitamins.

8. Mothers to Breastfeed, Children to Be Breastfed.

There is evidence that lactation protects mothers against breast cancer, and probable evidence that children are protected against overweight and obesity and, thus, against cancer. Cancer societies recommend breastfeeding infants exclusively up to six months, and complementary feeding thereafter. "Exclusively" means human milk only, no water or other food and drink. Exclusive and sustained breastfeeding was commonplace until the marketing of infant formulas in the second half of the twentieth century.

Alcohol Abuse Causes About 10 Percent of All Cancers in Men (3 Percent in Women).

All types of alcoholic drinks are probable causes of cancer.[49] Some thirteen thousand cancers result every year from British drinking habits. Most of these occur in the liver, upper digestive tract, mouth and throat, and colon. In Germany, every second eighteen- to twenty-five-year-old and every fifth twelve- to seventeen-year-old drinks to the point of intoxication at least once a month. In Ireland, the situation is even worse.[50] Women who are heavy drinkers risk breast cancer: Four percent of all newly diagnosed cases of breast cancer are attributed to alcohol abuse.[51]

9. Limit Alcoholic Drinks.

Not more than two drinks a day for men and one drink a day for women. A "drink" contains about 10 to 15 grams of ethanol. Note that to prevent cancer, all alcohol should be avoided, but some alcohol is likely to protect against coronary heart disease.

CT Scans Cause About 2 Percent of All Cancers.

As mentioned before, CT scans typically have a hundred times the radiation dose of a chest X-ray. Some scans are in the interest of the patient, but others are in the interest of those who profit and market them. Should you agree to have one? The risk of dying from radiation-induced cancer from a single full-body CT is higher than the risk of dying in a traffic accident. Up to one out of every fifty cancers in the United States may be attributable to radiation from CT scans.[52]

10. *Limit Radiation Exposure, Particularly for Children.*

Use CTs and other sources of radiation more prudently and only consent to scans absolutely necessary to establish a diagnosis or plan of action, not just to be safe. When the doctor says, "let's just see what the CT shows to be sure that your child is OK," remember the SIC syndrome and your unique responsibility as a parent.

Everyone can integrate these ten simple measures into their lives. That does not mean that cancer can be prevented with certainty, but that the chances are lowered. These ten rules are far more effective in saving lives than the whole grab bag of screening and expensive cancer drugs. Even when cancer is present, lifestyle changes can be as effective as expensive drugs without their downsides by increasing the quality of life. In a study with three thousand nurses who had breast cancer, those who walked three to five hours per week died less often from cancer than those who did not.[53] And it does not seem to matter much whether it's walking, jogging, dancing, or gardening. Lifestyle can go a long way toward protection from cancer.

No Decision About Me Without Me

The two epigrams at the beginning of this chapter, one from the 1980s by the American Cancer Society and the other thirty years later by the UK Department of Health, signal a big transition. In the twentieth century, health care was not primarily for the patient, but for selling drugs, screening technology, and other goals. Patients were often treated paternalistically.

The twenty-first century should become the century of the patient.[54] Calls for better health care have been usually countered by claims that this implies one of two alternatives, which nobody wants: raising taxes or rationing care. I argue that there is a third option: by promoting health literacy of doctors and patients, we can get better care for less money.

We can all change things, each one in his or her own way. People can question their doctors about pros and cons rather than only about what to do. Doctors can provide icon boxes in their waiting rooms rather than only *Cosmopolitan* and *Newsweek*. Organizations can begin to inform patients in an understandable way rather than only trying to increase participation rates. What we can do is change our lifestyle and take our lives into our own hands.

11

Banks, Cows, and Other Dangerous Things

Any intelligent fool can make things bigger, more complex, and more violent. It takes a touch of genius—and a lot of courage to move in the opposite direction.

E. F. Schumacher

You have to work hard to get your thinking clean to make it simple.

Steve Jobs

What to do when a crisis is looming on the horizon and you are worried about your money and future? Stick your head in the sand and wait for experts to do the job? What you will likely see when you pop your head back out is more bureaucracy, more technology, and less individual freedom. What you will likely not see are more competent citizens who have learned to deal with uncertainty.

Instead of adding to the legal jungle of paperwork and restrictions, I suggest that we should first ask: Is there a simple solution to a complex problem? In other words, is there something akin to a gaze heuristic or 1/N that solves a problem faster, better, and safer?

Simple Rules for a Safer World

Banks have a social mission. They borrow money from those who don't need it in exchange for some interest, and lend the money to those who need it at a higher rate. This transfer enables people to pay for their education, to build a home, or start up a business. Communities can invest in schools, roads, airports, and concert halls. Without banks, wealth would grow much more slowly. The cozy atmosphere of traditional banking—checking accounts, bank transfers, credit cards, the ATM—is captured by the *3-6-3 business model*:

> Take in deposits at 3 percent interest,
> make loans at 6 percent interest,
> and make it to the golf course by 3:00 p.m.

Banking was safe (and boring, except for the golfing) between 1940 and 1970. In the 1970s, however, we witnessed nine banking crises around the world, and more than fifty apiece in the 1980s and 1990s.[1] Yet most of these crises did not cross the national borders; for instance, the U.S. savings and loans crisis did not reach Europe. Then, in the crisis of 2008, experts were taken by surprise. Although the initial losses were about the same as in the Japanese crisis of the 1990s, the U.S. subprime crisis went global. People lost their jobs, their fortunes, and part of their pensions all over the world. Mighty banks defaulted, and entire countries found themselves at the brink of collapse. Virtually no financial expert saw this global disaster coming, although many developed supernatural powers of hindsight. As we understand now, the global domino effect happened because financial institutions all over the world held toxic mortgage-related securities, borrowed mostly short-term, and had little capital. Suddenly, banking had gone nuclear.

The Bankers' New Clothes

In Andersen's tale "The Emperor's New Clothes" two swindlers offer to make the emperor the most beautiful suit of clothes out of the most magnificent fabric. Light as a spider web, these clothes, they say, are invisible to foolish people unfit for their positions. Impressed, the emperor orders these clothes and sends his honest old minister to monitor the weavers. The weavers explain the intricate pattern and colors to the minister, who does not see a scrap of fabric but nevertheless joins their praise for fear of being considered a fool. A second official sent to monitor their work also praises the material he does not see. The emperor finds his new attire invisible as well, but not wanting to appear stupid in front of his two officials, joins in their praise, and bestows a medal and the title of "Sir Weaver" on the swindlers. When he parades his new trousers, coat, and a train held by these noblemen, the onlookers cheer and loudly admire his costume. "But he hasn't got anything on," a little child protests. One person whispers to another, until finally everyone dares to admit that the emperor is naked.[2]

As we will see, Andersen's tale is of timely relevance. Today, bankers weave intricate, magnificent fabrics called "risk models" that promise safety that doesn't exist. These new clothes are said to measure risk precisely.

In 1988 a first international regulation was crafted to regulate the capital a bank needs so that it is unlikely to default, known as the Basel Accord (or Basel I).[3] This agreement was 30 pages long and the calculations could be done with paper and pen. It was questioned as being too simple and, based on an amendment from 1996, was revised in 2004 to something more magnificent, Basel II. With a great deal of added detail and new complex risk models, Basel II was 347 pages long. A few years after the creation of this masterpiece tailored to make the world safer, the financial crisis of 2008 broke out. The reaction was to weave an even more complex regulation, Basel III, which came to 616 pages. Whereas Basel I was translated into 18 pages of primary legislation in the United States, Basel III required more than 1,000 pages. I have asked central bank regulators: Who understands the consequences of Basel III? Their unanimous answer was probably not a soul.

When I testified before the German parliament about the illusion of certainty provided by these intricate risk models, few politicians or bank lobbyists would openly admit that they don't understand their consequences. Despite the bankers' new clothes, today's banking system is as dangerous and fragile as before. Too little has changed to prevent the next worldwide crisis. We could use some candid children in our governments.

The Turkey Illusion

Finance mathematics has its roots in games of chance; that is, in known risks. The seductive power of this mathematics is that it allows risk to be estimated with just one number. The most popular of these numbers is called "value at risk." No judgment or understanding of the assets is necessary; all you have to do is look at the number. Yet the world of money is an uncertain world, not one of known risks. This crucial difference explains why the risk numbers missed virtually every financial crisis, from Black Monday to the Asian crisis to the 2000 dot-com crisis to the 2008 credit crunch. In 2012 JPMorgan Chase lost billions even though their value at risk predicted very small risks. According to the calculations, these events should not have happened (chapter 3). Such calculations provide much greater assurance than warranted, a steady illusion of certainty. That's why they don't help to prevent disaster. Rather, they themselves are a potential hazard and cause of financial meltdowns.[4]

In 2003 Robert Lucas, probably the most distinguished macroeconomist, said that macroeconomics has succeeded to prevent economic disaster: "Its central problem of depression-prevention has been solved, for all practical purposes, and has in fact been solved for many decades."[5] Five years later, the world was shaken by the sharpest financial crisis since the Great Depression.

The turkey illusion is the belief that a risk can be calculated when it cannot. Risks can be calculated when the three conditions explained in chapter 5 hold:

- low uncertainty: the world is stable and predictable,
- few alternatives: not too many risk factors have to be estimated, and
- high amount of data available to make these estimations.

None of these conditions holds in the world of investment banking. For instance, global networks of banks generate unpredictable domino effects, and large banks need to estimate thousands of intricate risk factors in addition to millions of correlations between these. The resulting numbers are illusions of certainty, not precise risk estimates. The illusion is motivated by the desire of many regulators, financial theorists, and investors to measure and price risks exactly and thereby avoid uncertainty, not knowing how to deal with it by rules of thumb. Simple and complex rules each have their place, depending on the states of the world:

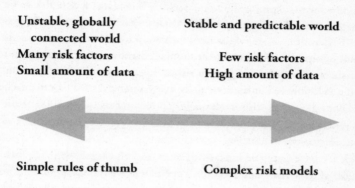

Unstable, globally connected world
Many risk factors
Small amount of data

Stable and predictable world
Few risk factors
High amount of data

Simple rules of thumb

Complex risk models

Safety Rules

So how can we minimize the risk of another financial crisis? Finance needs a scientific revolution. We need to break away from the traditional risk models and find new tools. As with the Basel regulations, the traditional way is to introduce complex regulatory systems and, if they don't work, make them more complex. This is the way taken by many governments and organizations. A different vision is to ask: Is there a set of simple rules that can solve this complex problem?

One such rule is about leverage; that is, the ratio of a bank's assets, or liabilities, to its capital. To promote change I work with the Bank of England on simple rules for a safer world of finance. When I asked Mervyn King, the governor of the Bank of England until 2013, which simple rules would reduce the danger of further crises, he did not think long. He answered with just one single rule:

Don't use leverage ratios above 10:1.

Leveraging means borrowing money in order to invest it. The more you borrow relative to the amount of capital, the higher the leverage ratio. Leverage increases potential gains, but also losses. It applies not only to banks, but to individuals as well. Here is a simplified example. Adam and Betty both guess that the housing market is on the upswing and buy rental houses to sell them in five years. Each has $100,000 to invest. Adam buys one house for that sum, while Betty buys ten houses with $10,000 down on each one and a mortgage debt of $900,000 at an interest rate of 5 percent. Betty uses leverage, while Adam does not. The leverage ratio is the amount of debt divided by the amount one actually owns. If both are right about the upswing and five years later the houses sell for $150,000 each, Adam wins $50,000 but Betty wins more. She gets $500,000 minus some $225,000 interest, which results in $275,000. And she will get ten times more rental income than Adam on top. Clearly, leverage is a great idea as long as the forecasts come true.

But if the housing market turns sour and the houses sell for only $70,000, then Adam loses $30,000—not a lucrative transaction but he at least has no debts. Betty, however, has to pay back the money borrowed plus the interest, which amounts to $1,125,000. She gets $700,000 from the sale of the houses, and thus ends up $425,000 in debt. If she is unlucky, she may have to file bankruptcy.

In the same way, banks not only invest the money they have, but money borrowed from others as well.[6] The safest banking system would be one with zero leverage, although some degree of leverage can be crucial for growth. Yet before the financial crisis of 2008 leverage ratios had risen to astronomical levels. At the height of the boom, some banks had leverage ratios of 50:1.[7] That's like financing a $100,000 mortgage with a $2,000 down payment.

The simple leverage rule would have likely saved billions of dollars lost in the financial crisis. For the future, it could create a strong safety net. Canadian banks survived the credit crunch relatively well because they were restrained by leverage ratios and had tougher lending requirements. In our studies, the leverage ratio can predict which large banks failed, but the complicated risk-based models cannot.[8] The leverage rule alone will not be enough to prevent another financial crisis, but it will prevent much harm. Banks also need to be stopped from pushing everything off the balance sheet so they can pretend to have low leverage. And leverage can be relaxed for smaller banks, where the consequences aren't as dramatic.

A leverage ratio is a rule of thumb that aims at being roughly right instead of precisely wrong. It would force banks to become less fragile by acquiring more capital. One way to acquire more capital would be to ban banks from making cash payouts to their shareholders and oblige them to instead retain the money until sufficient capital is built up. In contrast, even after the subprime crisis broke into the open, U.S. regulators allowed them to pay large dividends to shareholders, which weakened banks significantly. The amount paid to shareholders by the largest banks was about half of the sum given to them by the government subsequently through the Troubled Asset Relief Program (TARP).[9]

Why Isn't Leverage the Center of Banking Regulation?

Bank lobbyists weave a web of arguments to persuade laypeople and politicians that they should not be regulated so that they can continue taking risks as usual. To me the most striking observation is that the damage they have caused appears to have been wiped from their memory. Let's go through four arguments, and then to the real reasons.

The first argument with which bank lobbyists try to confuse the public and politicians is that banks are fully able to calculate their risks. This is the turkey illusion. As mentioned above, the complex risk models have consistently failed to predict or prevent crises. Moreover, since 1996, banks are allowed to use their own risk models, which means that risk estimates can be easily manipulated.

The next argument is that a simple rule, like leverage, could be easily exploited. The fact is that complex rules have been gamed by banks, and more complexity makes it easier to find loopholes and twist the thousands of estimates. All this has led to unproductive activities such as an adverse complexity race between bankers and regulators. Violations of simple rules are, in contrast, easier to detect.

The third, a familiar mantra, is "A dollar in capital is one less dollar working in the economy."[10] Don't fall for this trick with the term "capital." Capital is not reserve. Capital is the money a bank has received from its owners if it is a private bank, or from its shareholders if it is a corporation. Capital can be put into the economy, just as anyone's capital can be put into a house; it's not a reserve tucked underneath a pillow.

Finally, a recurrent mantra is that capital is expensive and increases the banks' costs. Let's put that into scale. Among all kinds of corporations, banks by far borrow the most. The vast majority of (nonfinancial) U.S. corporations borrow less than half of their assets, while some large banks borrow over 97 percent. Some very successful corporations, such as Apple, Bed Bath & Beyond, and Citrix, barely borrow, if at all. Corporations can in fact expand quickly without borrowing, for instance, by raising additional money by selling shares.

These flawed stories are told about clothes that don't exist. They are not told because those who weave the stories believe them. They are told because governments provide incentives for bankers to take undue risks, and bankers exploit these opportunities. Large banks can count on being bailed out by taxpayers. This is why excessive borrowing is cheap for banks as opposed to other corporations.

Survival of the Fattest

Investment banks object to leverage rules and argue that they violate free market principles. Don't they have a point? In a free market, a bank that takes on overly high risks and defaults will die, while those more prudent will survive. But many banks, such as JPMorgan Chase, Barclays, and Deutsche Bank, have grown too big to fail. They potentially enjoy a guarantee to be bailed out, which provides an incentive to take on excessive risks and high leverage. On the day that undue risk taking leads to a heavy loss, the same banks crying freedom can leave the private sector and become a socialist "state-protected" bank. This was one reason why bankers did not take enough precautions. They thought, "There is a small chance that it will go wrong, but if it does, all banks are in trouble and they'll have to bail us out." In other words, profits are pocketed by executives, and losses are compensated by taxpayers. That is not exactly a free market—it's a moral hazard.

Today, large banks no longer live in an ecosystem where the Darwinian survival of the fittest reigns. Banking has become about survival of the fattest. In fact, mergers between banks are sometimes motivated more by fatness than fitness. Too-big-to-fail institutions should not be on the market. This can be prevented by another simple rule:

> *Make sure that those who enjoy the benefits when times are good also bear the costs of periodic financial crises.*

There are several ways to make sure that banks can no longer count on being bailed out by the government; that is, the taxpayer: to make banks smaller, less interconnected, or to clearly separate the business of investment from regular banking. Then an investment bank could go bust for its hazardous behavior. Banks may object that they already take risks into consideration by calculating "value at risk." But as mentioned above, because these calculations assume known risks and cannot capture uncertainty, they are of little help. In fact, these risk measures may not be much more than an excuse to stay fat and continue indulging in a lifestyle of unhealthy risk taking.

Think for Yourself

You do not need a background in finance to understand the difference between known risks and unknown risks—or to recognize that the belief that risks can be precisely measured in an uncertain world amounts to an illusion of certainty. Instead, one needs to look for simple robust rules for a safer world. I want to encourage people to form and trust their opinions and to express doubts. We can have a safer financial system if there is more public pressure from citizens who don't want to pay for others' undue gambling. If we don't let ourselves be intimidated by mystifying jargon but instead ask politicians to implement transparency, that would be a first step. Is that all? No, we can also switch from big banks that took undue risk to smaller, more responsible ones. And we can stop being seduced by promises of especially high gains by buying risky products and settle for more modest returns that are more realistic. If everyone—companies and governments included—bought only financial products they fully understood, investment banks could do less damage. Politicians, who are surrounded by lobbyists, may be handicapped in spearheading change, and bankers are understandably hesitant as well, as long as they can pocket gains and hand down losses to taxpayers. The potential lies in courageous and risk-savvy citizens.

Dread Risks

Granted, it isn't always easy to be courageous and risk savvy when governments and media play with our fears. We are lucky to live in an age where child mortality is lower and life expectancy higher than ever. Yet many believe that the world is more dangerous and uncertain than in the past. Crisis after crisis is trumpeted in the media—mad cow disease, SARS, bird flu, swine flu, E. coli, and those yet to come. Diseases, terrorists, floods, hurricanes, and other disasters have killed many victims, but also helped governments to get reelected and the media to increase sales and viewing rates. Worst-case scenarios fuel the anxieties of voters and viewers. One trick is to exploit people's fear of dread risks and increase sales by painting horrific disasters in the headlines, real and imagined. The rise and fall of each is quite similar. In the headlines a new strain of virus or some other brand of threat appears, together with experts' warnings that many people could die. Citizens begin to worry and call for their governments to do something about it. Governments then react in a defensive way, often with drastic measures. A few months later the media stop reporting and everything is quickly forgotten. A year or so later it's the same pattern, with everyone anxious about the next crisis broadcasted by the media.

But isn't it better to be safe than sorry? Consider two famous imagined catastrophes, mad cow disease and swine flu. In both cases, worst-case thinking replaced balanced risk assessment. But they also show us how to communicate risk in a way so that people don't panic.

Beef Scare

Let's begin with a quiz.[11]

How many people were killed by mad cow disease in all of Europe in ten years?

About 150.

What other cause led to the same number of people dying in all of Europe in the same ten years?

Drinking scented lamp oil.

Who in the world drinks scented oil? Mostly children, who are attracted to the pleasant colors it comes in and the perfume. I am on the board of the German Federal Institute of Risk Assessment. It took the Institute more than ten years to get a European regulation approved that required child-proofing the bottles of lamp oil. Virtually nobody paid attention. The killing of cattle was where all the attention went.

Back in the first chapter, I defined a dread risk as a real or imagined situation in which many people suddenly die, with 9/11 as the prime example. Due to an evolved pattern of fear and flight, people tend to avoid these situations, while little anxiety is elicited when as many or more die distributed over time. That was also how mad cow disease (bovine spongiform encephalopathy; BSE for short) was presented. A *Nature* article predicted up to one hundred thousand deaths. In contrast, it is hard to evoke anxiety for causes of death where as many people die over the course of a year: motorcycles, cars, or smoking. Children who drink flavored oil don't die in sudden streaks but distributed over the years, and consequently little attention is paid. If these 150 children had died on a single day or within a short time, I am convinced that this would have made big headlines, alarming many parents.

Creutzfeldt-Jakob disease (CJD) is a rare fatal disease that turns the brain spongy. It is so rare that only about fifty people, mostly elderly, die from it every year in the UK, and about seventy in Germany. The victim may first become forgetful, sleepy, and clumsy, and eventually can no longer talk, swallow, or stand up. It is similar to mad cow disease. In the mid-1990s, a new variant of CJD was reported in ten younger adults. Experts reported to the British Government that the most likely cause of the new variant was eating BSE-infected cattle. Governments tend to make defensive decisions, and so they initiated a mass killing of cattle in the UK and in various European countries. In the United States, with fewer cases of infected cattle and people, attempts at similar scares were reported, allegedly drummed up by vegetarians, but were not successful. The economic fallout from the BSE epidemic in Europe was crushing. Not only were cattle killed and their carcasses burned but trade was also blocked because other countries worried that BSE would invade their borders. The financial damages amounted to about €38 billion.[12] This was the cost of our reaction to BSE, not of BSE itself.

In the late 1990s experts were worried that BSE might have jumped to sheep in the UK. The government was keen not to create a panic among the public about eating sheep meat and therefore kept quiet about the possibility. When Sir John Krebs (now Lord Krebs) became the first head of the new UK Food Standards Agency in 2000 he took a different approach. Despite governmental concerns, he and his colleagues decided it was better to be honest and come out and tell the public about the uncertainty. Research with focus groups of the public showed that the phrase "there is a theoretical risk of BSE in sheep" was not well understood. So instead the message was phrased as: "There could be a risk of BSE in sheep. We do not think there is and we are not advising you to stop eating sheep meat, but if you are worried here is what you could do. . . . We are working on tests to find out whether or not there is a risk, and we will get back to you as soon as we have the results." Surveys after the announcement showed that nearly two thirds of the public were aware of it and that there was no significant drop in consumption of sheep meat.

The way the BSE crisis was handled in Germany was quite different. When mad cow disease raged in Great Britain, Ireland, France, and Switzerland, the German government provided an illusion of certainty and declared its country BSE-free. "Our beef is safe"—so the reassuring tenor of a choir of governmental officials. English beef was banned. Consumers complacently asked their butcher for beef from Germany, where, unlike in Britain, one knows how to raise happy and healthy cattle. When a large number of tests were performed on cattle in 2000 and the disease was found, the nation was shocked. Few dared to bite into a steak anymore. "Is it true," a worried reader wrote to the *Rheinische Post*, "that I could get infected by BSE if I sit on my cowhide leather sofa too long?"[13] The illusion of certainty had flopped, and the ministers of health and of agriculture resigned. Now other countries banned German beef, and Germans began to slaughter and burn their cattle just like everyone else. Not a single German died from BSE or, more precisely, from the variant of Creutzfeldt-Jakob disease. Apart from the many cattle that lost their lives, the two ministers who lost their jobs were the only victims—not from eating beef, but from how they dealt with uncertainty.

Looking back at this mass slaughter and incineration of cattle, triggered by our anxieties, the evidence is not there that it was necessary at all. It may have been little more than an unwarranted fear of a dread risk. BSE illustrates how this fear can lead entire governments to fight dangers that kill only a few rather than those that kill many every year.

Pig Scare

In March 2009 five-year-old Edgar Hernández ran a high fever. Doctors discovered he was infected with the H1N1 virus, Mexico soon announced 157 deaths from swine flu, and a global crisis management machine kicked into gear. After four days Edgar recovered, and Mexico eventually corrected its estimate to only 7 deaths. But once set in motion, the global crisis management machine was unstoppable. In June the World Health Organization (WHO) declared swine flu a pandemic. Experts from the WHO estimated that up to 2 billion (!) people would be infected worldwide. This caused great dread risk anxiety. Egypt gave the order to kill all its pigs. A British headline read, "Swine flu could kill 65,000 in the UK, warns Chief medical officer." TV and newspapers started the first body counts. The worst might come during the winter, the flu season, so the message went.

As with BSE, dread risk fear was propagated across the world. Governments dedicated billions of dollars to building stockpiles of vaccines and antiviral drugs, such as Tamiflu. Once again, the recipe was "better safe than sorry." Only nobody knew how to play it safe. There was no scientific basis for the WHO's estimate of up to two billion cases of swine flu. There was also no evidence that the drugs worked when governments bought them from the industry. The FDA, for instance, had declared a year before the outbreak that Tamiflu has not been shown to prevent complications such as hospitalization or death.[14] And although Japanese regulators arrived at the same conclusion, three quarters of the worldwide drug consumption occurred there. Similarly, the British government squandered £500 million on Tamiflu and other antivirals in the absence of evidence that these were effective. The Polish minister of health, in contrast, refused to buy any. A doctor herself, she said that her job was not to fill the bank accounts of the pharmaceutical industry. Two years after the scare the German government burned the unused vaccines, literally wasting hundreds of millions of euros.

It was later confirmed that there was no evidence that Tamiflu protects people against the deadly consequences, as had been assumed.[15] All that Tamiflu can do is reduce the average time of flu from five to four days, which is what the FDA had concluded earlier. Why then did the WHO encourage governments to stockpile antivirals? The *British Medical Journal* brought one answer to light: A large number of the experts advising the WHO had financial ties to the pharmaceutical firms that produce the drugs.[16] On these experts' advice, governments wasted billions of dollars that are missing elsewhere in health care. Last but not least, the dangerous long-term effect of spreading worst-case scenarios is that people will become cynical. When it's a real emergency and antivirals and vaccinations might actually be needed, people's trust in governments and in the WHO will have eroded so deeply that too few will bother to listen and get vaccinated.

In an interview with the *British Medical Journal* I was asked whether the problem was that ordinary people don't comprehend risks, particularly during a pandemic. I responded that the problem was less the difficulty of communicating uncertainty but the fact that uncertainty was not communicated at all.[17] How is it possible to convey uncertainty openly without painting worst-case scenarios?

Figure 11-1. Remember these dread risk stories? As long as the media report on real and imagined catastrophes, fear is aroused. When they stop reporting a few months later, we tend to forget and start worrying about the next catastrophe in the headlines.

In November 2009, at the height of the swine flu scare, I used the same method that Lord Krebs did for BSE: Be transparent about the uncertainty, make comparisons with known risks, and explain what can be done. At the Max Planck Institute for Human Development in Berlin, where I am director, staff, students, and researchers met for an information session. First, I openly admitted that nobody could tell at that point in time whether the swine flu would become the big catastrophe touted in the media or a small ripple soon to disappear, as bird flu did before. But there were some facts we could use to make up our minds. First, the typical swine flu lasts about four to five days, and then it's over. Second, regular flu and influenza-like illnesses kill about ten thousand people every year in Germany, while there had only been about twenty deaths attributed to swine flu at that time. To put this number in perspective: In Germany, about twelve people die per day from motor vehicle accidents, and nine from passive smoking. Third, the argument had been made that the big catastrophe was still ahead because the flu strikes mostly in the winter. But here we also had some facts from the southern hemisphere, where the winter was already over. No swine flu catastrophe took place there. In fact, even without the vaccine, fewer people died in Australia and New Zealand from the flu than normally. Nevertheless the WHO had maintained its outrageous estimate. I also added that, unknown to many, the WHO had changed its definition of the term "pandemic" that spring. Now a pandemic no longer meant a widespread disease that kills large numbers of people, but only a widespread disease in general.

For those who were concerned I addressed the question: What can you do in this uncertain situation? Something everyone should do is prevent the virus from spreading: Cover your mouth and nose when you sneeze, wash your hands, and if you get sick, stay home. Another thing you could do is to get a vaccination, although we don't know the benefit and harms. In the end, the most important thing is to learn to live with an element of uncertainty and have the courage to form an individual opinion. No reason to panic.

After my talk, the staff members left the lecture room more relaxed than when they'd come in. Laying out the uncertainty hadn't made them nervous or unhappy. As with Lord Krebs and the BSE-infected sheep, the opposite was the case. And, in both cases, no catastrophe happened.

At the end of the day swine flu was not the big killer but plain old influenza. And the moment the media stopped reporting on it, swine flu was quickly banished from memory. Without fancy diagnostic technology and a global crisis management system it would have probably come and gone without anybody noticing.

Fear of dread risk is part of human nature. And the media exploit this fear, making us worry about things meriting little concern. My personal first law of risk communication in the media is therefore:

The more the media report on a health risk, the smaller the danger for you.

For instance, in 2003 SARS and bioterrorism were the big news in the United States. Both killed fewer than a dozen people but together generated over one hundred thousand media reports, far more than those on smoking and physical inactivity, which killed nearly a million Americans.[18] Similarly, when the Robert Koch Institute noticed that swine flu was not the big killer, the press didn't listen. So when you read about a new health risk, relax. It is most likely not what will do you in.

Governments

When we compare public policy on financial risks with dread risks a puzzling contradiction emerges. Why are governments so eager to protect their citizens against dread risks, from cows to swine, and so hesitant to protect the very same people against the risks of financial disaster from investment banking? It should certainly be easier to control banks than viruses. A possible answer is the influence of lobbying on politicians. The pharmaceutical industry has vested interest in intervention, and has pushed governments into stocking vaccines and drugs. The banking industry has little interest in intervention, and has lobbied for as little regulation as possible and resisting a "vaccination" by prudent leverage ratios. Lobbyists who represent those who pay for the consequences, the taxpayers, are few. For instance, most governments were willing to pay for Tamiflu produced by Roche, without demanding evidence for its usefulness. When the international Cochrane Collaboration, the most important evidence-based medicine organization, requested that Roche reveal the data on the benefit of Tamiflu, which it has refused to do for years, most governments suddenly had a deaf ear. We will change that mismatch only if more people don't just accept what their governments or doctors say to do, but take a critical look at the evidence and what is being done with their tax money. Becoming informed and speaking out are important steps toward a participatory democracy.

Part

III

START EARLY

A new scientific truth does not triumph by convincing
its opponents and making them see the light, but
rather because its opponents eventually die, and a
new generation grows up that is familiar with it.

Max Planck

The most interesting information comes from children,
for they tell all they know and then stop.

Mark Twain

12

Revolutionize School

Whenever the people are well-informed,
they can be trusted with their own government.

Thomas Jefferson

Tilly Smith, a ten-year-old English schoolgirl, was relaxing on the beach with her parents in Phuket, Thailand, in 2004. Suddenly, the tide rushed out. Boats bobbed up and down. While other tourists went for the fish flopping on the sand, she said, "Mummy, we must get off the beach now. I think there is going to be a tsunami." Just before their vacation Tilly had watched a video of a Hawaii tsunami in her geography class and learned the warning signs. Her parents took the little girl's warning seriously, alerted other people to leave, and notified hotel staff, who evacuated the rest of the beach. Tilly's beach was one of the few in Phuket where no one was killed or seriously injured.[1]

Billions are invested in the development of tsunami warning systems, which is a good thing. But technology alone will not help. The largest earthquake ever measured—9.5 in magnitude—happened off the coast of Chile in May 1960. It caused a huge tsunami wave that headed toward Hawaii. There, technology worked as planned: The automated alert system kicked in, and tsunami sirens went off hours before the island was hit. Yet most people who heard the sirens weren't sure what the noise meant and did not evacuate. Sixty-one people died in Hawaii that day. Technology is of limited effect when people don't understand it. A risk-savvy child can be as effective as a fancy warning system.

In October 2009 *Nature* published a four-page news feature titled "Risk School" that compared my vision of public risk literacy to the prevailing paternalistic view that people are basically hopeless at understanding risk and need to be nudged into proper behavior.[2] I have nothing against a bit of nudging, but as a philosophy of the twenty-first century it is heading in a disturbing direction. We do not want future generations of people who can manage their lives only as long they are pushed and pulled by others. Our children deserve better than that.

Modern technologies unavoidably bring new risks, and sociologists have warned that we live in a "risk society" threatened by the dangers created by the very growth of knowledge.[3] Yet new technology bestows chances as well as dangers, and instead of lamenting, we need a new generation of people who can handle them. In short, a "risk society" needs a "risk-literate society."

Teaching Risk Literacy

Centuries ago few envisioned a society where nearly everyone would be able to read and write. Such societies now exist. Today few envision a society where nearly everyone is risk literate. Yet such societies will exist very soon, if we work at it. To arrive there we have to start long before college or medical and law school. Even young children can learn to understand risk and probability when taught in a playful way. Early education in risk literacy will go a long way toward helping a new generation to deal with life's uncertainties and make paternalism a ghost of the past.

The risk literacy curriculum I envision includes three topics and three classes of skills. The three topics are:

- Health literacy
- Financial literacy
- Digital risk competence

Three skills are required for mastering each topic:

- Statistical thinking
- Rules of thumb
- Psychology of risk

Statistical thinking is about quantitative literacy, such as understanding probabilities of rain; rules of thumb are about making good decisions in an uncertain world; and the psychology of risk concerns the emotional and social forces that guide our behavior, alone and in groups. The three skills should not be taught in the abstract, but as tools for everyday problem solving, such as taking care of health, money, and the digital media. Good teaching begins with stories that motivate and connect to children's life, and only later moves on to abstract principles.

What will be the result? For one, reduced obesity, cancer, and health problems in general. The new generation will better know how to deal with money, as opposed to racking up cell phone bills and credit card debt. And they will be able to use and control digital media instead of being controlled by them. With these assets children can grow into mature citizens who are used to asking questions and taking on responsibility for their decisions.

But is this just a naive dream from the ivory tower? For illustration, let's consider one of the hardest statistical tasks, Bayesian inference, which we have already encountered several times.

Fourth Graders Can Solve It

Can children reason correctly about problems that stump doctors? When I proposed that they could if given information in natural frequencies, some teachers found it a ludicrous thought, since children ten years or younger have not yet learned proportions or percentages. A professor of education expressed similar disbelief and insisted that we not test children in the fourth grade or below, who were much too young to solve such difficult problems.

But educators sometimes underestimate what their pupils can do. Of course we couldn't question children on genetic screening tests because they might not be familiar with the subject or with three-digit numbers. Instead, we had a fun time thinking up other problems that would capture a child's imagination. Here is one about more magical things. We gave 176 second-graders and fourth-graders from Berlin schools six problems in natural frequencies, with and without using icons (Figure 12-1).[4] Here is one:

The Ravenclaw School of Magic

- *Out of every 20 pupils in the Ravenclaw School of Magic, 5 have a wand.*
- *Of these 5 pupils, 4 also wear a magical hat.*
- *Of the other 15 without wands, 12 also wear a magical hat.*

Imagine a group of pupils from the Ravenclaw School who wear a magical hat. Here are two questions
1. Are there more with a wand?
More likely yes.
More likely no.
2. How many of those with a magical hat also have a wand? ____ of ____

The first question is the easier one. Among the second graders, 88 percent correctly said the answer is "more likely no." Among fourth graders, virtually everyone (96 percent) got the answer right. The second question is more difficult and requires quantitative reasoning. If you look at it closely, you will see that it is the same type of question that few physicians could answer when asked about a medical condition rather than a wand. Note that none of these children had yet been taught percentages or proportions. Nevertheless, 14 percent of the second graders and 51 percent of the fourth graders gave the right answer: that only 4 out of every 16 pupils with a magical hat also have a wand.

Each child worked on six problems altogether. With icons, second graders solved 22 percent of the problems (Figure 12-2), a number that equals the percentage of doctors who solved the screening problem given in conditional probabilities (see Figure 9-1 top). Fourth graders were already able to solve 60 percent of the problems. Even when the text was provided without icons, the younger children could solve 11 percent of the problems and the older ones 40 percent.

Fourth to sixth graders in Beijing were just as good, even though they too hadn't yet learned proportions in school. Not all children are able to answer correctly, but development is fast from second to fourth grade. All in all, with the help of icons, the majority of fourth graders can

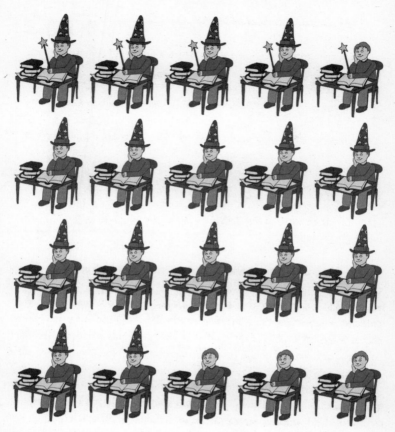

Figure 12-1. Natural frequencies can be represented in numbers or icons. For children and not-so-numerate adults, icons help make solutions more transparent.

successfully solve problems that many doctors cannot. Do natural frequencies and icons also help children who have unusual learning disabilities in acquiring arithmetic skills? Surprisingly, these children could solve the problems with equal ease and profited from icons almost as well as other children did. This indicates that the problem is less a question of abnormal genes than of how the information is communicated.

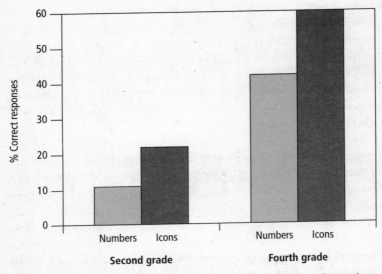

Figure 12-2. What is the probability that a pupil at the Ravenclaw School of Magic has a wand if he has a magical hat? Children can solve complex problems (so-called Bayesian problems) if these are framed in natural frequencies. When icons (as in Figure 12-1) are added to the numbers, one fifth of second graders and more than half of fourth graders understand. With this technique, children are able to solve diagnostic problems that challenge doctors.

Now both you and your fourth grader have a tool to understand the probabilities of medical tests or magical wands. Children can learn efficient tools for thinking, as soon as we revise the way we teach.

Two First Principles for Teaching

Teach Problem Solving in the Real World

Our children are taught algebra, geometry, precalculus, and calculus. In other words, we teach them the mathematics of certainty, not of uncertainty; that is, statistical thinking. How many of us need to solve quadratic equations, calculate the intersection of a cube with a plane, or think about irrational numbers at work or at home? Training in abstract disciplines such as algebra and geometry has been claimed to improve thinking and problem-solving skills. If that were true, we would not have so many doctors who do not understand health statistics or lawyers who do not understand DNA evidence.[5] And neither the psychologist E. L. Thorndike back in the 1920s nor contemporary studies found any evidence of such positive effects.[6] This suggests that if we want a new generation capable of solving the problems ahead, we'd better teach them the necessary cognitive skills rather than abstract principles.

To that purpose, statistical thinking is the most useful branch of mathematics for life—and the one that children find most interesting. Teaching statistical thinking means giving people tools for problem solving in the real world. It should not be taught as pure mathematics. Instead of mechanically solving a dozen problems with the help of a particular formula, children and adolescents should be asked to find solutions to real-life problems. That's what teaches them how to solve problems, and also shows that there may be more than one good answer in the first place. Equally important is encouraging curiosity, such as asking for answers to questions by doing experiments. For instance, "Can someone who is doing a headstand drink water?" Don't tell children; let them discover the answer themselves. And you can bet that they will. What's important for everyday life needs to be taught first, what's important for mathematicians later. The orientation toward real-world problem solving as opposed to abstract math makes transparent framing, hands-on tools, and smart rules of thumb essential.[7] To implement these changes, we need to teach the teachers.

Don't Teach for Tests, Teach for Life

The Roman statesman Seneca, who was Nero's tutor, said some two thousand years ago, "Non vitae, sed scholae discimus." We don't learn for life, but for school. Not much has changed since then: Teachers, parents, and pupils prepare for SATs instead of for life. Children first memorize, then pass the test, and finally forget. The cycle repeats itself over and over again at school and on throughout college.

Similar to many other policymakers, people behind education-reform movements typically assume that teachers and pupils alike need carrots and sticks to persuade or nudge them into doing their best. A new breed of corporate-world managers assume that business plans are the road toward better schools, replacing experienced teachers by less experienced ones with lower salaries or by online instruction, or by paying teachers according to the average test scores of their pupils.

The Finnish school system is based on a quite different vision.[8] In Finland, the profession of teachers is highly esteemed, as it should be in every country. Very few universities are permitted to train teachers, and admission to these elite programs is highly competitive: Only one out of every ten applicants is accepted. There is little room for incompetence. Teachers have a strong sense of professional responsibility and are driven by intrinsic motivation, not by the hope of a bonus or fear of being fired. They have a wide choice of what to teach and would refuse to prepare students for standardized tests. Instead, they design their own tests to ascertain their students' needs, although even these tests are rare. Finnish schools consistently outperform European and American ones in almost every respect, embodying the ideal of excellence. They also have the least variation in quality, embodying the ideal of equality.

Perhaps the most important feature is that the Finnish system places responsibility before accountability. Part of its success is based on a rule of thumb that we encountered in the toolbox of successful leaders:

Hire well and let them do their jobs.

This rule helps to create a climate of excellence and trust. In a system where the emphasis is on testing, there are other ways to avoid having students learn just for the test and then mentally trash what they learned. Here is a candidate:

Don't just test last month's topic; include what was learned before and what has not yet been learned.

This simple rule would provide an incentive not to forget, as well as to learn to think creatively about new problems. It can also create a domino effect. Schools would signal that solving unknown problems is an important skill. After all, rote learning has become definitively outdated since the advent of the Internet, which provides access to facts faster than ever. Children now need to learn to think independently and to evaluate the ocean of facts available online.

When risk-savvy kids grow up, we will finally have doctors, finance experts, and lawyers who understand uncertainties. And we will have clients and patients who are not fooled and know what questions to ask. They will form a society that can deal with risks in an informed and relaxed way.

Health Literacy

In the twenty-first-century Western world, we can expect to live longer than ever, meaning that cancer will become more prevalent as well. We deal with cancer like we deal with other crises: We bet on technology. The Holy Grail of cancer research is finding a pill that delays, cures, or prevents cancer. Emphasis is on chemotherapy, drugs, and vaccines. An aspirin a day will keep colorectal cancer away, so they say. Will it? Probably not.[9] As we have seen in chapter 10, early detection of cancer also is of very limited benefit: It saves none or few lives while harming many.

The best weapon we have against cancer is risk-savvy citizens. Here is why.

An estimated 50 percent of all cancers are due to behavior: smoking, obesity, alcohol abuse, eating fast food, lack of physical activity, and unnecessary CT scans. Cigarette smoking is the leading cause, although obesity is catching up. These cancers could be prevented by a healthy lifestyle. But there is no point in telling a fifteen-year-year old to stop smoking; by then it's usually too late. At that age, humans are more dependent than ever on the opinion of their peers. Promoting healthy lifestyles needs to begin earlier, before puberty. How to go about it? Instead of pointing fingers we need to make young people competent in understanding the risks of an unhealthy lifestyle, and how their desires are steered by the industry. This will not only decrease the incidence of cancer but also increase health in general.

A program of health literacy should be based on two psychological principles:

- Children should be age five to ten when the program starts, before puberty.
- Children should be taught health literacy at school together with their classmates so that peer influence is turned into a positive rather than negative effect when they reach puberty.

The content of the curriculum should include:

- Skills such as cooking and sports.
- Knowledge such as how cigarettes cause lung cancer, what poisons cigarettes contain, and how heavy smoking can damage the appearance of a person's face and teeth and intensify body odor.
- Psychological principles such as how kids are manipulated by profit-interested companies into harmful lifestyles and what techniques advertisers use to control their desires.

Skills and hands-on experience are essential. Eating habits are formed early, and the joy of cooking is the best antidote to obesity and fast food. Resurrect Julia Child! Children might even take over the cafeteria a day per week and cook for their peers. Psychological principles are crucial: While campaigns typically focus on the long-term harms of smoking, adolescents smoke because of the short-term benefits, such as feeling grown-up and looking cool. A health literacy program called ScienceKids found that participating children took more control of their health. At home they talked about health topics and influenced their parents' health as well.[10]

Here is my cancer bet:

If we spent the same amount of money on developing a health literacy program to make children risk savvy as on developing new cancer drugs, I wager that the health literacy program would save many more lives from cancer.

We may not save every child from an unhealthy lifestyle, but if we save as few as 10 to 20 percent of the next generation, we will be more successful than further research on new drugs in the fight against cancer. We would also see more teenagers without obesity, smoking, and alcohol problems, as well as more healthy adults in general.[11] We do not have to wait until the children grow old to see if it's successful. The efficacy of such a health literacy program can already be measured when the children are adolescents, by the number of those who smoke, get drunk, are obese, or have other health problems. And the skills children learn cannot only increase health in general but also help to lead a more self-controlled life.

Financial Literacy

You are $3,000 in debt. You pay a nominal interest rate of 12 percent per year. Each month you pay a sum of $30. When will you have paid off the debt? In

a. less than five years [15 percent]
b. five to ten years [31 percent]
c. eleven to fifteen years [18 percent]
d. sixteen to twenty years [10 percent]
e. never [26 percent]

We asked this question to more than a thousand Germans age eighteen or older.[12] The numbers in the brackets show what percentage of those chose each answer. Almost half thought the debt would be settled in less than five or ten years. In reality, after signing this clever deal, the borrower would never manage to pay off the debt. That shouldn't be too difficult to work out. The bank charges twelve percent interest on the total debt, adding up to $360 every year. The customer pays $30 per month, which amounts to $360 per year. Both sums are equal, meaning that the borrower pays off only the interest and will never be able to begin paying back the debt itself. Only a quarter of Germans understood that they would be paying forever. The young were as clueless as the old; the sole difference was found in TV consumption. For every hour in front of the television per day, people were less likely to know the answer.

When considering investments, bank customers frequently don't know anything but simply trust their financial advisers, jeopardizing their fortune in a consultation that takes less time than they'd spend watching a football game. Many of the NINJAs (no income, no job, no assets) who lost everything but the shirts on their backs in the subprime crisis didn't realize that their interest rates were variable, not fixed, and their initial low rates only teasers. They may have assumed that their mortgages were like car loans, whose rates are fixed. They were easy prey for the greed of some bankers, who could talk them into taking a loan on a house that they could not repay. But as we have seen in this book, not only ordinary people but quite a few professionals could benefit from more financial literacy.

Not until we teach the next generation how to think with money can we protect them from being easily exploited. So why don't we teach financial literacy in school? A curriculum can be organized around the same principles as health literacy: teaching skills such as how to budget pocket money, knowledge about mobile phone bills and debt traps, and psychological insights about the value of money in the students' lives and in other cultures.

Digital Risk Competence

Digital communication technology—from the Internet to Facebook to digital eyewear to technologies we cannot yet imagine—deeply influences what we spend our time on, what privacy means, and how we think. The question is not whether the digital media will change our mental lives; they do. The question is how. Digital technology provides huge opportunities and is not the problem. The problem lies in us, whether we remain at the helm or are instead remote-controlled by new technology. Digital media have already changed the way people conduct their social relations and the risks they are willing to take. In an interview, three Connecticut high school students explained why they send text messages while driving.[13]

Roman says he is not going to stop: "I know I should, but it's not going to happen. If I get a Facebook message or something posted on my wall . . . I have to see it. I have to." Similarly, Maury does not give reasons but expresses a need to connect: "I interrupt a call even if the new call says

*'unknown' as an identifier—I just have to know who it is. So I'll cut off
a friend for an 'unknown.' I need to know who wanted to connect. . . .
And if I hear my phone, I have to answer it. I don't have a choice. I have
to know who it is, what they are calling for." Marilyn adds: "I keep the
sound on when I drive. When a text comes in, I have to look. No matter
what. Fortunately, my phone shows me the text as a pop up right up
front . . . so I don't have to do too much looking while I'm driving."*

These three students are willing to risk a car accident in order to gratify
their need to connect digitally. When asked when was the last time they
didn't want to be interrupted, there was silence. "I am waiting to be interrupted right now," one said. Interruption has become connection. Even in
the physical company of real friends, there is a strong urge to be contacted
by someone else online.

Digital technology has taken control over these young people's risk taking and social relations. It has also changed some parents' relations to their
children. Because it enables constant monitoring, parents often do so; the
result is higher parental anxiety. As one mother agonized:

*"I've sent a text. Nothing back. And I know they have their phones.
Intellectually, I know there is little reason to worry. But there is something about this unanswered text."*

The same mother envied her own mother, who didn't worry back then.
Children went to school, came home. Her mother worked and returned
around six. Today some children have a fantasy of their parents simply
waiting for them, expectantly—without having called them twice on the
way home. "I'd like to make a call" has changed to "I need to make a call."
The ability to be alone and to reflect on one's emotions in private runs
counter to the spirit of digital networking; teenagers confess to discomfort
when they are without their cell phones. A study reported that two thirds
of Britons concentrate so hard on their mobile phone when texting that
they lose peripheral vision.[14] According to legend, after pedestrians started
walking into lampposts, some cities padded the posts.

Are teens hooked to digital media at least happy? A study with over one hundred fourteen- to seventeen-year-olds with excessive Internet use reported that only 10 percent were very happy with their leisure time (compared to 39 percent in a control group of peers), 13 percent with their friends (versus 49 percent), 3 percent with themselves (26 percent), and only 2 percent with their life in general (29 percent).[15] These teens had virtually stopped reading and completely stopped going to events and being engaged with society.

Digital risk competence is the ability to harvest the benefits of digital technology while avoiding harm. It has a cognitive and a motivational component: risk literacy and self-control.

Digital Risk Literacy

In order to be risk literate, we need to have a basic understanding of facts and psychological principles relevant in a digital world. One such fact concerns the potential harms from using a cell phone while driving. As mentioned in the introduction, the reaction time of a twenty-year-old who talks on a cell phone is slowed down to that of a seventy-year-old without one. While listening to the radio does not impair driving, drivers distracted by cell phone conversations fail to "see" traffic lights and other objects even if they gaze at them, have more rear-end collisions, and end up with as many or more accidents as drunk drivers with 0.08 percent blood alcohol. This holds for both handheld and hands-free cell phones. As a consequence, an estimated 2,600 people die every year in the United States, and about 330,000 are injured in accidents that result from distracted drivers.[16] Knowing that thousands are killed every year, however, may not be sufficient to change everyone's behavior; we also need digital self-control.

Despite many unknowns in how digital media will change our mental lives, there are psychological principles that help us to see what will possibly happen and what will not.

Early language learning. Competitive parents want to give their children an early edge in order to get them into an Ivy League school. Until recently every third infant in the United States was trained with a "baby DVD" to learn English earlier, faster, and better. Programs such as Baby Einstein and

Brainy Baby teach new words to build up vocabulary. But gung ho parents appear not to know a basic psychological principle of first-language learning. Learning a mother tongue relies to a large extent on social interaction, such as eye contact with parents. Quite a few babies are glued to the screen, some even ignoring their parents, yet tests show that the babies learn nothing. For instance, when parents read to their eight- to sixteen-month-olds daily, it was found that the babies' score on a language test increased by seven points. In contrast, for every hour of watching a baby DVD per day, scores decreased by seventeen points.[17] Learning without social interaction can turn Baby Einstein into Baby Homer Simpson.

Multitasking. The digital revolution has offered new possibilities for multitasking. Teenagers read e-mails, write texts, and listen to their favorite music while doing homework. One might assume that experience with multitasking makes it easier to master. But this ignores the psychological principle that we can focus our conscious attention on one task only, and if we try several tasks simultaneously, all of them suffer. In fact, studies indicate that multitasking devotees, compared to those who rarely practice it, are more easily distracted by irrelevant information, can remember less, and are slower at switching between tasks.[18] All these are skills at which die-hard multitaskers should excel.

Multitasking succeeds only if all tasks but one are taken over by the unconscious, that is, when these are all performed on autopilot. This is why we can drive and talk, but only if driving is automatized by our unconscious or by devices such as auto speed control. If something unexpected happens on the road, we abruptly stop talking to focus on the problem. Successful multitasking would require even more tasks to be taken over by the unconscious. That might become our future. In the words of the English philosopher Alfred North Whitehead, "Civilization advances by extending the number of operations which we can perform without thinking about them."[19] The unconscious may become quite busy in the course of the digital revolution.

Digital Self-Control

By digital self-control I mean the ability to control digital technologies rather than being controlled by them. Media should serve people, but it is often the other way around. Some get hooked on a technology. Even in 2005 an AOL survey reported that one out of four people could not be without e-mail for more than three days. Almost half wake up and begin their day by reading e-mail, and continue throughout work reading personal e-mails.[20] According to the Kaiser Foundation half of American eight- to eighteen-year-olds mix homework with entertainment, mostly by simultaneously surfing on the Internet. "I need to stop this and do my homework," some say, "but I can't." Digital addiction can result in social techno-stress: the longer the time spent on the Internet, the less people are capable of maintaining existing friendships. To avoid being controlled by the medium and reduce negative consequences, early development of personal control is essential.

The Internet is a huge store of information. Increasingly users rely on it more often than on their own memories. We "outsource" search, memory, and other cognitive capacities. Most of us can no longer recall long poems or stories, just as we have lost the ability to do mental calculation since the advent of the pocket calculator. Digital media will continue to amplify this process. In the best of all worlds both mind and media are enriched, and are better adapted to each other. The new abilities will create new tools, which in turn will inspire new abilities, and so forth.

As with health literacy, it is likely too late to tell an eighteen-year-old not to text while driving. Instead of pointing fingers, we need to begin teaching digital literacy and self-control much earlier. The goal is a new generation that has the knowledge and the will to take their lives into their own hands.

Everyone Can Learn to Deal with Risk and Uncertainty

I began this book with the observation that when things go wrong, we are told that we need better technology, more laws, and bigger bureaucracy. One idea is absent from that list: risk-savvy citizens. Instead, paternalism is seen as the solution.

The term "paternalism" stems from the Latin *pater*, for father, and means treating adults like children. Paternalism limits the liberty of people, whether they like it or not, allegedly for their own good. *Hard* paternalism, like antismoking legislation, coerces people into behaving a particular way and can be morally defended as long as it protects people from being hurt by others. *Soft* paternalism, such as automatically enrolling people into organ donation programs unless they opt out, nudges people into behaving a particular way. The idea is that governments should steer people's choices without coercing them. As a general policy, coercing and nudging people like a herd of sheep instead of making them competent is not a promising vision for a democracy.

This book's message is more optimistic about human liberty. People are not doomed to be at the mercy of governments and experts who know what is best for you and me. As I have shown for health and wealth, those are a rare breed: The average doctor or financial adviser has conflicting interests, practices defensive decision making, or does not understand the evidence. That's why we have to think for ourselves and take responsibility into our own hands. As we've seen, it is possible to improve competence in dealing with risk and uncertainty. And it's not difficult. Even fourth graders can learn to do what adults supposedly can't.

There is a third way to sustain a democracy, beyond both hard and soft paternalism: to invest in people. As John Adams, the second American president, said in 1765, "Liberty cannot be preserved without a general knowledge among the people"—all the people, male and female, rich and poor. This vision is known as participatory democracy. Adams's words still ring true for our technological societies. Critical thinking requires knowledge. To get it running we need courage, the courage to make our own decisions and take on the responsibility. Dare to know.

ACKNOWLEDGMENTS

This book tells the story of how we make—or don't make—decisions in an uncertain world. It is purposely not written as an academic textbook. I have been extremely fortunate to have the resources of the Max Planck Society for my research, and with this book I want to give something back to the taxpayers who fund our society, as well as to people in other countries. Some of my academic colleagues frown on writing in a way that the general public understands. I believe it is a duty, at least for those who share the vision that science should not become more estranged from people than it already is. Mixing real stories and psychological concepts, I hope to provoke readers and motivate them to take their lives into their own hands and make decisions in a more informed and relaxed way. For those who get hooked on the topic and would like to learn more about the underlying research, I recommend *Rationality for Mortals* (Gigerenzer 2008) and *Heuristics* (Gigerenzer et al. 2011) as a start. Further references to the scholarly literature are provided in the references list of this book.

Many dear friends and colleagues have read, commented on, and helped shape the many versions of this book manuscript: David Aikman, Gerd Antes, Hal Arkes, Sylvia Arkes, Peter Arnold, Lucas Bachmann, Jürgen Baumert, Will Bennis, Nathan Berg, Gaby-Fleur Böl, Kyle Chan, Lorraine Daston, Wendy Doniger, Markus Feufel, Wolfgang Gaissmaier, Mirta Galesic, Atul Gawande, Mike Gazzaniga, Thalia Gigerenzer, Sophie Hartmann, Cora Haselbeck, Günther Jonitz, Sujit Kapadia, Mervyn King, John Krebs of Wytham, Mota Kremnitzer, Kevin Laland, Ilana Lowy, Modesto Maidique, Julian Marewski, Laura Martignon, Kevin McConway, Jan Multmeier, Eileen Munro, Emma Murphy, Rick Peevey, Linda Pickney, Jürgen Rossbach, Matthias Rothmund, Heide Sattler, Sascha Schroeder, Lisa Schwartz, Birgit Silberhorn, Özgür Simsek, Johann Steurer, Nassim Taleb, Peter Todd, Rona Unrau, Oliver Vitouch, Georg von Wintzingerode, Odette Wegwarth, Maren Wöll, and Steven Woloshin.

Last but not least, I thank my graduate students, post-docs, and researchers in the ABC Research Group who keep challenging and shaping my ideas.

My special thanks go to Rona Unrau, who has edited the entire book manuscript, including the footnotes. She helped much in achieving clarity of exposition. Rona has been a wonderful support. My thanks also go to Brittney Ross from Viking for her immense help in giving the book a clear structure. I am also grateful to Jürgen Rossbach, who designed the figures, and to Christel Fraser for editing the references. Lorraine Daston, my wife, and Thalia Gigerenzer, my daughter, provided intellectual and emotional support during the years I was working on this book. I am grateful for the help of family, friends, and colleagues.

Despite the generous support of the Max Planck Society, the "transport" of knowledge to the general public requires private donors. The research reported in this book is partly based on research by the Harding Center for Risk Literacy. The center is named after David Harding, a London investment banker. After reading my book *Calculated Risks* (UK edition: *Reckoning with Risk*), he bought copies for all his employees, and over dinner one day donated a substantial sum to fund a center dedicated to increasing risk literacy in the world.

People are crucial, but so is the environment. *Risk Savvy* is inspired by the research I conducted at the Max Planck Institute for Human Development, where I have been director for more than a decade. I was lucky to have the unique support of the Max Planck Society, and to profit from its outstanding resources and splendid intellectual atmosphere. It's research paradise.

GLOSSARY

1/N: Allocate your resources equally to each of N alternatives. Also known as *equality heuristic.*

Absolute risk reduction. A measure of the efficacy of a treatment in terms of the absolute number of people saved or lost. For instance, if a treatment reduces the number of people who die of a disease from six to four in one thousand, then the absolute risk reduction is two in one thousand, or 0.2 percent.

Accuracy-effort trade-off. The view that the price to be paid for using less effort (such as a heuristic that does not take the time to search for all the information) is less accuracy. This trade-off is true in a world of known risks, but not when some of the risks are unknown. Under uncertainty, simple heuristics can save effort yet be more accurate at the same time. See *Less is more.*

Adaptive toolbox. The repertoire of heuristics (rules of thumb) that a person, institution, or culture has at its disposal to deal with uncertainty intelligently.

Aspiration level. A stopping rule that defines when an alternative is good enough and search can be terminated. For instance, in *satisficing*, one sets an aspiration level and then chooses the first alternative that meets this level. See *Satisficing.*

Base rate. The base rate of an attribute (or event) in a population is the proportion of individuals manifesting that attribute (such as having breast cancer). Also known as prevalence.

Bayes' rule. A rule for updating the probability of hypotheses in the light of new evidence. Its origin is attributed to the Reverend Thomas Bayes. For the simple case of a binary hypothesis (H and not-H, such as cancer and not cancer) and data D (such as a positive test), the rule is:

$$p(H|D) = p(H)p(D|H)/[p(H)p(D|H) + p(not\text{-}H)p(D|not\text{-}H)]$$

where $p(D|H)$ is the posterior probability, $p(H)$ is the prior probability, $p(D|H)$ is the probability of D given H, and $p(D|not\text{-}H)$ is the probability of D given not-H.

Many have problems understanding this rule. But there is help. The interesting point is that the calculation of $p(H|D)$ becomes more intuitive when the input is stated in natural frequencies rather than probabilities. For natural frequencies, the rule is:

$$p(H|D) = a/(a + b)$$

where a is the number of D and H cases, and b the number of D and not-H cases. See *Natural frequencies*.

Bias-variance dilemma. A statistical theory that explains less-is-more effects; that is, when and why simple heuristics can lead to more accurate predictions than more complex methods. The key idea is that the total error consists of three components:

Total error = bias² + variance + noise

Noise is irreducible (measurement) error, while the other two kinds of error can be influenced. Bias is the difference between mean estimate and true state, and variance is the variability (instability) of individual estimates (based on different samples) around the mean estimate. For instance, 1/N has no free parameters and therefore has bias only (it makes the same allocation independent of specific samples). Models with many free parameters tend to have less bias, but more variance. Too much variance is one reason why "less can be more."

Biological preparedness. Allows vicarious learning of what is dangerous when personal experience would be lethal. A prepared object (or situation) is one that was dangerous in human history, such as snakes, spiders, and darkness. If a child watches another person exhibiting fear of a prepared object, then this fear is often acquired in a single encounter. For instance, in many species, fear of venomous snakes is not inborn, but the concept of a snake is prepared, and fear of snakes is acquired by watching another person exhibiting it. This fast learning does not occur with objects that are not biologically prepared, such as guns. In modern environments where the object no longer poses a danger, biological preparedness can make us fear the wrong things.

Conditional probability. The probability that an event A occurs given event B, usually written as p(A|B). An example of a conditional probability is the probability of a positive first-trimester test given that the fetus has Down syndrome, which is around 0.90. The probability p(A), for instance, is not a conditional probability. Conditional probabilities are notoriously misunderstood, and in two different ways. One is to confuse the probability of A *given* B with the probability of A *and* B; the other is to confuse the probability of A given B with the probability of B given A. One can reduce this confusion by replacing conditional probabilities with natural frequencies. See *Natural frequencies*.

Conflicts of interest. A person or institution has two or more interests that are in conflict with one another. Consider health care and banking. On the one hand, doctors and bank advisers would like to do the best for patients or clients; on the other hand, this may entail losing money. As a consequence, patients may receive unnecessary surgery or expensive imaging, and bank customers are persuaded into investments that are more profitable for the bank than for them. Conflicts of interest (C) are part of the SIC syndrome, a key dilemma in modern health care. See *SIC syndrome.*

Defensive decision making. A person or group ranks option A as the best, but chooses an inferior option B to protect itself in case something goes wrong. This form of self-defense (S) is part of the SIC syndrome, a key dilemma in modern health care. *See SIC syndrome.*

Degrees of belief. One of the three interpretations of probability (besides *relative frequencies* and *physical design*). The probability of an event is the subjective degree of belief a person has in that event. Historically degrees of warranted belief entered probability theory from applications in the courtroom, such as the credibility of witnesses. Degrees of belief are constrained by the laws of probability (such as the rule that probabilities need to add up to one), which means beliefs need to follow these laws to qualify as subjective probabilities.

Diversification. A resource-allocation principle. The goal is to avoid damage caused by putting everything into one basket. In financial investment, *1/N* is a simple diversification heuristic, while the mean-variance portfolio is a complex one.

Double-tonguing. A trick to make the benefit of a drug (treatment) appear larger and its harms smaller. Typically, benefits are reported in relative risks (big numbers) and harms in absolute risks (small numbers). For instance, consider a drug that reduces mortality from stroke from two to one in one hundred patients, but increases mortality from cancer from one to two in one hundred. Double-tonguing means to report that the drug reduces mortality from stroke by 50 percent, while it increases mortality from cancer by only one in one hundred, or 1 percent. Another form of double-tonguing is to report the benefit of screening for one's hospital in terms of increasing survival rates (which are big numbers but misleading), and that of competitors in terms of mortality rates (which are small numbers but correct). Double-tonguing is not used in advertisements alone; it has been reported in every third article in top medical journals.

Dread-risk fear. It is easy to make people fear real or imagined situations in which many people suddenly die, such as the 9/11 attacks. Due to an evolved pattern of fear and flight, people tend to avoid these situations. In contrast, it is hard to make people fear situations in which as many or more people die distributed over the year, such as by driving and smoking. Dread-risk fear may have been adaptive in human history when our ancestors lived in small groups, where the sudden death of a substantial part threatened the survival of the rest.

Early detection. The use of screening tests for non-symptomatic people for the purpose of reducing morbidity or mortality. Early detection (screening) is not the same as prevention. Screening is meant to detect a disease that is already there, while prevention means to lower the chance of getting the disease in the first place. The confusion between the two terms is amplified by the use of the term "secondary prevention" for screening. Early detection may or may not reduce mortality. For instance, if there is no effective therapy, then early detection, including treatment, will not reduce mortality.

Error. A test can result in one of two errors, a false positive or a false negative. These errors can result from various sources, including human error (the laboratory assistant confuses two samples or enters the wrong result into the computer) and medical conditions (a positive HIV test as a result of rheumatological diseases and liver diseases that have nothing to do with HIV). Errors can be reduced but not completely eliminated, and they may even be positive errors, indispensable to adaptation and survival, as the copying errors (mutations) in DNA illustrate.

Error culture. The way an individual or institution deals with error. A positive error culture admits errors in order to learn about their causes and create a safer environment. A negative error culture hides errors in order to protect itself, focuses on blame instead of on eliminating their causes, and tends to repeat the errors in the future. See *Defensive decision making.*

Fact box. A table for transparent risk communication, summarizing the scientific evidence for a drug, treatment, or screening method. The box shows benefits and harms for people with and without treatment. All numbers are in plain frequencies. Fact boxes do not use misleading statistics, such as relative risks, double-tonguing, and five-year survival rates for screening.

False negative. A false negative or miss occurs when a test is negative (a pregnancy test that finds no sign of pregnancy) but the condition is actually present (the woman is pregnant).

False-negative rate. The proportion of negative tests among people with the condition (disease) is called the false-negative rate. It is typically expressed as a conditional probability or a percentage. For instance, mammography screening has a false-negative rate of 5 to 20 percent, depending on age; that is, 5 to 20 percent of women with breast cancer receive a negative test result. The false-negative rate and the sensitivity (hit rate) of a test add up to 100 percent.

False positive. A false positive or false alarm occurs when a test is positive (a positive pregnancy test) but the condition is not extant (the woman is not pregnant).

False-positive rate. The proportion of positive tests among people without the disease is called the false-positive rate. It is typically expressed as a conditional probability or a percentage. For instance, mammography screening has a false-positive rate of 5 percent to 10 percent depending on age; that is, 5 percent to 10 percent of women without breast cancer nevertheless receive a positive test result. The false-positive rate and the specificity (the probability of a negative result given no disease) of a test add up to 100 percent. The rates of the two errors are dependent: Decreasing the false-positive rate of a test increases the false-negative rate, and vice versa.

Franklin's law. Nothing is certain but death and taxes. A reminder that in all human conduct, uncertainty is ubiquitous due to human and technical errors, limited knowledge, unpredictability, deception, and a plethora of other causes.

Frequency. A number of observations in a class of events. Frequencies can be expressed as relative frequencies, absolute frequencies, or natural frequencies. Relative frequencies are one of the three interpretations of probability (besides *degrees of belief* and *physical design*).

Gaze heuristic: Fix your gaze on an object and adjust your speed so that the angle of gaze remains constant. A fast and frugal heuristic for navigation, such as safe landing, catching balls, and intercepting objects.

Good errors. Errors that speed up learning and lead to innovation.

Gut feeling. An intuition, or gut feeling, is a judgment (i) that appears quickly in consciousness, (ii) whose underlying reasons we are not fully aware of, yet (iii) is strong enough to act upon. A gut feeling is neither caprice nor a sixth sense, nor is it clairvoyance or God's voice. It is a form of unconscious intelligence.

Heuristic. A rule of thumb, or *heuristic*, is a conscious or unconscious strategy that ignores part of the information to make better judgments. It enables us to make a decision fast, with little search for information, but nevertheless with high accuracy. Heuristics are indispensable in a world where not all risks are known ("uncertainty"), while probability theory is sufficient in a world where all risks are known ("risk"). A rational mind needs both sets of tools. Classes of heuristics include (i) recognition-based heuristics such as the recognition heuristic, (ii) one-good-reason heuristics such as the gaze heuristic, (iii) sequential heuristics such as take-the-best, and (iv) social heuristics such as imitate-your-peers. The widespread idea that heuristics are always second best and more information and computation are always better is incorrect. See *Less is more* and *Bias-variance dilemma*.

Hiatus heuristic: If a customer has not made a purchase for nine months or longer, classify as inactive, otherwise as active. The rule belongs to the class of one-good-reason heuristics. It is used by managers to predict which customers will buy in the future. It has been shown to outperform complex optimization methods. The number of months can vary.

Icon box. A visual tool for transparent risk communication, summarizing the scientific evidence for a drug, treatment, or screening method. An icon box shows two groups of individuals: those who underwent a treatment and those who did not (control). Each individual is represented by an icon indicating benefits and harms. Icon boxes do not use misleading statistics such as relative risks, double-tonguing, and five-year survival rates for screening. They are transparent like fact boxes, only visually more appealing. Fact boxes are more adequate for rare diseases or small effects that would need thousands of icons. See *Fact box*.

Illusion of certainty. The belief that an event is absolutely certain although it is not. The illusion can have benefits, such as reassurance, but also costs, such as suicide after a false positive HIV test. It is sometimes socially enforced. For instance, becoming accepted as a member of a social group may require the newcomer to share illusions of certainty concerning moral and political values.

Innumeracy. The inability to think with numbers. Statistical innumeracy is the inability to think with numbers that represent risks. Like illiteracy, innumeracy is curable. It is not simply a mental defect inside an unfortunate mind, but due to lack of education and promoted by misleading risk communication. Innumeracy (I) is part of the SIC syndrome among doctors, a key problem in modern health care. See *SIC syndrome*.

Intuition. See *Gut feeling*.

Lead time bias. One of two reasons why survival rates are misleading about the benefits of screening (the other is *overdiagnosis*). Even if the time of death is not changed by screening—that is, no life is saved or prolonged—early detection advances the time of diagnosis and thus results in increased survival rates.

Less is more. The apparent paradoxical phenomenon that using less information, less computation, or less time can lead to better judgments. Note that less is more does not mean that no information is best, but that there is a point where more information (computation) hurts, even when it is for free. According to the *accuracy-effort trade-off*, there should be no less-is-more effects. This is true for a world of known risk, but not for a world of partially unknown risks. Heuristics can lead to less is more; for when and why it happens see the *Bias-variance dilemma*.

Leverage. A technique to increase the amount of gains (and losses) by borrowing money and investing it. Leverage is used by individuals and banks. The leverage ratio can be roughly defined as assets divided by capital. For instance, a person who owns $10,000 and buys a house that costs $100,000 has a leverage of ten to one.

Maximizing. Determining the best value; that is, the maximum (or minimum) of a curve. In a world of unknown risks, however, one cannot calculate the best. Treating uncertainty as if it were known risk (the turkey illusion) can lead to fragile solutions and failure. The alternative is satisficing; that is, trying to find an alternative that meets an aspiration level or, in other words, is good enough. See *Satisficing* and *Heuristics*.

Mortality reduction. A measure of the benefit of a treatment in terms of lives saved. The mortality reduction can be represented in many ways, including relative risk reduction, absolute risk reduction, and increased life expectancy. In the context of screening, mortality rates are the proper statistics, not survival rates. See *Survival rate*.

Natural frequencies. Frequencies that correspond to the way humans encountered information before the invention of books and probability theory. Unlike probabilities and relative frequencies, they are "raw" observations that have not been normalized with respect to the base rates of the event in question. For instance, a physician has observed one hundred persons, ten of whom show a new disease. Of these ten, eight show a symptom, whereas four of the ninety without disease also show the symptom. Breaking these one hundred cases down into four numbers (disease and symptom: 8; disease and no symptom: 2; no disease and symptom: 4; no disease and no symptom: 86) results in four natural frequencies: 8, 2, 4, and 86. Natural frequencies facilitate Bayesian inferences. For instance, a physician who observes a new person with the symptom can easily see that the chance that this patient also has the disease is 8/(8 + 4), that is, two thirds. This probability is called the posterior probability. If the physician's observations, however, are transformed into conditional probabilities or relative frequencies (for example, by dividing the natural frequency 4 by the base rate 90, resulting in a false positive rate of 0.044 or 4.4 percent), the computation becomes more difficult. Natural frequencies help people to "see" the posterior probabilities, whereas conditional probabilities tend to cloud minds. *See Bayes' rule.*

Negative test result. Typically good news. That is, no sign of a disease has been found.

Number needed to treat (NNT). A transparent measure of the benefit of a treatment. For instance, consider patients at high risk of heart disease who take the cholesterol-lowering drug Lipitor for four years. Studies show that among every one hundred patients, one was saved from a stroke. Here the NNT to save one life is one hundred. In other words, ninety-nine patients do not benefit. The absolute risk reduction is one in one hundred, which is the inverse of the NNT. NNT makes quite transparent how many or few patients profit from a drug or treatment.

Overdiagnosis. Overdiagnosis is the detection of pseudo-disease. For instance, screening can detect cancers that meet the pathological definition of cancer but will never progress to cause symptoms in the patient's lifetime. Given that technological progress leads to more sensitive screening techniques, overdiagnosis has become a huge problem in health care. It increases unnecessary testing, anxiety, and health care costs. It is one of the two reasons (the other being *lead time bias*) why five-year survival rates are misleading information in the context of screening: the detection of pseudo-disease inflates the five-year survival statistics. See *Survival rates.*

Overtreatment. Overtreatment is a consequence of *overdiagnosis.* It means unnecessary surgery, radiation therapy, or other interventions for conditions that are technically disease but of no clinical relevance. It provides no benefit but possible harm for the patient. Overtreatment is motivated by the *SIC syndrome.*

Percentages. Relative frequencies multiplied by one hundred are called percentages. Their range is between zero and one hundred, while the range of probabilities and relative frequencies is between zero and one. Most people find it easier to talk in terms of percentages. Consider the statement "About 80 percent of American women who smoke before they become pregnant continue to do so during pregnancy." Contrast this with "American women have a probability of 0.8 to continue smoking during pregnancy." The probability statement is more awkward and less transparent to the general public. That's why percentages are used throughout this book.

Physical design. One of the three interpretations of probability (besides *relative frequencies* and *degrees of belief*). In this interpretation, probability is about constructing, not counting (as with relative frequencies). For instance, electronic slot machines are programmed to deliver a certain probability of winning. Physical design is also called propensity. Historically, physical design entered probability theory from the domain of gambling, such as from the design of dice and roulette wheels.

Positive test result. Typically not good news: A possible sign of a disease has been found.

Posterior probability. The probability of an event after new evidence; that is, the updated prior probability. It is also called post-test probability. It can be calculated from the prior probability using *Bayes' rule* and, more intuitively, using *natural frequencies.*

Prevalence. See *Base rate.*

Prior probability. The probability of an event prior to new evidence. Bayes' rule specifies how prior probabilities are updated in the light of new evidence. Base rates are often used as prior probabilities.

Probability. A measure that quantifies the uncertainty associated with an event. A probability is a number between 0 and 1. If an event A cannot happen, the probability $P(A)$ is zero; if the event is certain to happen, $P(A)$ is one; otherwise the values of $P(A)$ are between zero and one. For a set of events, A and B, that are mutually exclusive and exhaustive, the probabilities of the individual events add up to one.

Propensities. See *Physical design.*

Randomized trial. A study designed for estimating the benefits and harms of a treatment using randomization as a method of control. Participants are randomly assigned to either a treatment group or to a control group. After a certain period of time, the two groups are compared on a criteria, such as mortality, to determine whether the treatment has been effective. Randomization makes it possible to control for variables—such as age, education, and health—that could be alternative explanations (besides the treatment) for an observed difference between groups.

Recognition heuristic: If one of two alternatives is recognized and the other is not, then infer that the recognized alternative has the higher value with respect to the criterion. This heuristic leads to accurate inferences when a correlation exists between recognition and the criterion (like the size of a city).

Reference class. The class of events or objects to which a relative frequency refers. In the frequency interpretation of the concept of probability, there is no probability without a specified reference class. This view excludes single-event probabilities that by definition do not specify a reference class.

Relative frequencies. One of the three interpretations of probability (the others are *degrees of belief* and *physical design*). The probability of an event is defined as its relative frequency in a reference class. Historically frequencies entered probability theory through mortality tables that provided the basis for calculating life insurance rates. Relative frequencies are constrained to repeated events that can be observed in large numbers.

Relative risk reduction. A measure of the benefit of a treatment in terms of the relative number of people saved or lost. For instance, if a treatment reduces the number of people who die from six to four in one thousand, then the relative risk reduction is 33.3 percent. Reporting relative risks is popular because the numbers look larger than the absolute risk reduction (which would be two in one thousand or 0.2 percent). Relative risks do not convey how large the risk is in absolute terms, and are therefore often misunderstood. For instance, if a treatment reduces the number of people who die from six to four in *ten thousand*, the relative risk reduction is still the same (33.3 percent), although the absolute risk reduction has decreased to 0.02 percentage points.

Risk. If the uncertainty associated with an event can be quantified on the basis of empirical observations or causal knowledge (physical design), the uncertainty is called risk. Relative frequencies and probabilities are ways to express risks. Contrary to the everyday use of the term, a risk need not be associated with harm; it can refer to a positive, neutral, or negative event. The classical distinction between known risks ("risk") and unknown risks ("uncertainty") is attributed to the economist Frank Knight. See *Uncertainty*.

Risk aversion. The tendency to prefer a sure option over a less certain one. It is sometimes believed that risk aversion is a personality trait. Yet few if any people are generally risk averse or risk seeking. Most turn out to practice both, but in different domains, like the carefree chain smoker who is concerned about getting cancer from genetically modified corn. Risk aversion is not a general trait, but domain specific. The *social imitation of fear* explains that there is a specific pattern of socially acquired risks individuals are willing to take or anxious to avoid.

Rule of succession. Probability that something happens again if it happened *n* times before = $(n+1)/(n+2)$. The rule can be derived from Bayes' rule assuming equal prior probabilities.

Rule of thumb. See *Heuristic.*

Satisficing. A heuristic for choosing one alternative (such as a house or spouse) from a large set of objects. An aspiration level is set, and search is stopped when the first object is found that meets that level. The aspiration level can be lowered when time passes by and one still has not found a good-enough alternative.

Screening. See *Early detection.*

Sensitivity. The sensitivity of a test is the percentage of individuals who are correctly classified as having the disease. Formally, the sensitivity is the *conditional probability* P(positive|disease) of a positive test result given the disease. The sensitivity and the false negative rate add up to 100 percent. The sensitivity is also called the hit rate.

SIC syndrome. A key problem in health care every patient should be aware of. Many physicians:

1. practice defensive medicine (Self-defense),
2. do not understand health statistics (Innumeracy), or
3. pursue profit instead of virtue (Conflicts of interest).

The three troubles go hand in hand, resulting in second-best care, *overdiagnosis*, and *overtreatment* harmful to patients.

Single-event probabilities. A probability associated with a singular event for which no reference class is specified. Single-event probabilities can lead to misunderstandings because people tend to fill in different reference classes. For instance, based on an FDA report the Mayo Clinic issued a warning that antidepressants are increasingly marketed to children: "The analysis showed that children taking antidepressants had about a 4 percent chance of developing suicidal thoughts or behavior, compared with only a 2 percent chance in children taking a sugar pill (placebo)." What does it mean for a child to have a 4 percent chance of suicidal thoughts or behavior? Some parents might think:

1. My child will have suicidal thoughts 4 percent of the time,

2. 4 percent of the pills are flawed, causing suicidal thoughts, or
3. 4 percent of children taking antidepressants developed suicidal thoughts.

What the FDA intended to say was (3), but parents can only guess. This miscommunication can be avoided by using frequencies instead of single-event probabilities because frequencies spell out a reference class (as in options 1–3: time, pills, or children).

Social imitation of fear. The psychological principle "fear whatever your social group fears" enables us to learn about dangers without experiencing these in the first place. It protects us when personal experience might be lethal. At the same time, it can also make us fear the wrong things.

Specificity. The specificity of a test is the percentage of individuals who are correctly classified as not having the disease. Formally, the specificity is the *conditional probability* P(negative|no disease) of a negative test result given no disease. The specificity and the false-positive rate add up to 100 percent.

Survival rate. A measure of the benefit of a treatment: five-year survival rate = number of patients diagnosed with cancer who are still alive five years after diagnosis divided by the number of patients diagnosed with cancer. In the context of screening, changes in survival rates are misleading about the benefit because they do not correspond to changes in mortality rates. The reasons are lead time bias and overdiagnosis. Nevertheless, many institutions advertise screening with survival rates, misleading the public about its usefulness. See *Lead time bias* and *Overdiagnosis.*

Take-the-best. A heuristic for inferring which of two alternatives has the better value on some criterion. It consists of three building blocks: Search rule: Look up cues in order of validity. Stopping rule: Stop search when the first cue is found that allows for a decision. Decision rule: Infer that the object with the higher cue value has the higher criterion value.

Turkey illusion. The *calculable risk* illusion (or turkey illusion) mistakes uncertainty for known or calculable risks. The result is an illusion of certainty. Among others, it stems from the mistaken belief that every problem should be solved with probability theory, such as Bayes' rule.

Uncertainty. Uncertainty means that some risks are unknown. The classical distinction between known risks ("risk") and unknown risks ("uncertainty") is attributed to the economist Frank Knight. Uncertainty, as used here, refers to more than unknown probabilities ("ambiguity"); it can extend to not knowing all alternatives and consequences. Uncertainty requires tools beyond probability theory, such as smart rules of thumb. Optimization (finding the best course of action) is by definition unfeasible in an uncertain world; thus the goal is to find a robust course of action, one that has a good chance of surviving in the unknown future.

Zero-risk illusion. Whenever known risks are mistaken for absolute certainty, the *zero-risk* illusion occurs.

NOTES

1

Are People Stupid?

1. Bagehot, "Wink, Wink," *The Economist*, July 26, 2008.
2. The science magazine *Nature* covered the debate between those who believe that people are basically hopeless at dealing with risk and those who have a more positive view of human nature, such as myself (Bond 2009). On the pessimistic side, economist Richard Thaler (1991, p. 4) asserted that "mental illusions should be considered the rule rather than the exception," cognitive scientist Massimo Piatelli-Palmarini (1991, p. 35) that "our species is uniformly probability-blind," evolutionary biologist Stephen Jay Gould (1992, p. 469) that "our minds are not built (for whatever reason) to work by the rules of probability," and economist Dan Ariely (2008) that "we are not only irrational, but *predictably irrational*—that our irrationality happens the same way, again and again" (p. xx), while psychologist Daniel Kahneman (2011, p. 417) went even further and attributed mental illusions to a biologically old "System 1" that is "not readily educable." I disagree with this dismal picture. Cognitive illusions are not hard-wired. There are simple tools to deal with risk and uncertainty that can be quickly learned by everyone (Gigerenzer 2000, 2008; Gigerenzer et al. 2012). More about these in this book.
3. Paulos 1988. What is the actual chance of rain on the weekend? If the two events are independent, then the probability that it will rain on the weekend is 0.75 or, expressed in percentages, 75 percent. To arrive at this number, one first calculates the probability that it won't rain on Saturday (0.5) and multiplies it by the probability that it won't rain on Sunday (0.5), which is 0.25 (25 percent). That's the probability that it won't rain on either day. The probability that it *will* rain is therefore 75 percent. To simplify, I will express probabilities in terms of percentages throughout the rest of this book.
4. Gigerenzer, Hertwig, et al. 2005.
5. Yet even meteorologists do not always agree. For instance, in 2003 the Royal Dutch Meteorological Institute confusingly explained what a probability of rain means by using the "region" interpretation together with a "meteorologist's degree of certainty" interpretation:

> If the chance exceeds 90 percent, then one can count on rain in every region in Holland. The higher the percentage, the more certain the meteorologist is that it will rain. Some examples:

10–30% Almost none	Almost nowhere
30–70% Possible	In some places
70–90% There's a fair chance	In almost all the regions.

As Robert Mureau of the Royal Dutch Meteorological Institute explained, "We are aware of the fact that probabilities are not very well understood by the general public. We ourselves have not been very clear about the terminology definitions either, which might have caused even more confusion" (Gigerenzer, Hertwig, et al. 2005, p. 627).

6. Furedi 1999. This scare happened in 1995.

7. See Gigerenzer, Wegwarth, and Feufel 2010.

8. Gigerenzer 2004, 2006. Gaissmaier and Gigerenzer (2012) provide a regional analysis of the traffic fatalities. The case of Justin Klabin is described in his book *9/11: A Firefighter's Story* (2003, Imprintbooks) and cited in Ripley 2009, p. 35. At the Society for Risk Analysis Annual Meeting, 6–8 Dec 2009, Robert G. Ross pointed out that the peaks in fatal crashes in Figure 1-2 follow the terrorism alerts after 9/11.

9. Daveed Gartenstein-Ross, "Bin Laden's 'war of a thousand cuts' will live on." *The Atlantic*, May 3, 2011.

10. Paul Slovic (1987) proposed the term "dread risk" for perceived lack of control, dread, catastrophic potential, and inequitable distribution of risks and benefits. I use the term in the more restricted sense given in the text.

11. Consistent with this explanation, young adults report that they are more afraid of incidents (disease, factory accident, or earthquake) that could kill one hundred people rather than those killing ten people, but their fear remains the same for incidents that cause one hundred or one thousand deaths. This psychological limit of around one hundred is characteristic for fear of deaths but does not apply to monetary loss, where a loss of $1,000 is feared more than losing $100 (Galesic and Garcia-Retamero 2012).

12. Joseph Stiglitz, *Frankfurter Allgemeine Zeitung*, September 10, 2011, p. 19.

13. Schneider 2010.

14. Old-style "hard" paternalism argued that people are selfish and need to be guided to serve society's best interests, such as obey laws and pay taxes. In *Nudge*, Thaler and Sunstein (2008) proposed a version of "soft" paternalism that gently "nudges" people into making decisions in their own interest. While soft paternalism does not use force, it is more radical than hard paternalism in assuming that people don't even know what their best interests are (Rebonato 2012). The new argument is that because people have systematic cognitive illusions, paternalism is needed to change their behavior. But that argument is not correct: Cognitive biases do *not* imply paternalism (Berg and Gigerenzer 2007). Most important, poor cognitive abilities are not written into our genes, but are largely a consequence of the lack of an intellectually stimulating environment, including schools. As a consequence poor IQ, often regarded as innate, can be substantially improved by training (Nisbett 2009). Why, for instance, do children born before September 15 have higher IQs than those born after? The answer is that most countries have a cutoff

date around September 15, meaning that children born afterward have to wait another year before being admitted to school. This fact made it possible to conduct a natural experiment. When the intelligence of kids who had the advantage of being almost a year older when beginning school was compared with the intelligence of those who had the advantage of a year's extra schooling, a year of school was found to be worth about twice as much as a year of age (p. 42).

15. Kant 1784. Enlightenment is largely still a task of the future.
16. Mill 1869; Berlin 1967.

2

Certainty Is an Illusion

1. Gigerenzer, Gaissmaier, et al. 2007.
2. Gigerenzer 2002, pp. 11–13.
3. Dijksterhuis et al. 1996; Neuberg and Newsom 1993.
4. Dewey 1929.
5. Cited by Sherden 1998, p. 259.
6. Tetlock 2005.
7. Gigerenzer, Swijtink, et al. 1989. On the probabilistic revolution see Krüger, Daston, and Heidelberger 1987; Krüger, Gigerenzer, and Morgan 1987. Highly recommended is David Spiegelhalter's website on statistical thinking: http://understandinguncertainty.org/.
8. Let me correct at once a widespread misconception about the nature of heuristics. According to the heuristics-and-biases view (e.g., Kahneman 2011), our thinking can be explained by two systems, described by a list of opposing characteristics. System 1 is said to be unconscious, work by heuristics, and make errors. In contrast, System 2 is conscious, works by logical and statistical rules, and does not seem to make errors. This picture does not fit the facts. First, every heuristic we have studied can be used both unconsciously *and* consciously (Kruglanski and Gigerenzer 2011); thus, heuristics do not stand in opposition to consciousness. Second, heuristics are not the general source of errors but can lead to *more* accurate inferences than logical or statistical methods (e.g. Figures 6-3 and 6-4). Heuristics and errors are therefore also not aligned. The two-system view has overlooked the distinction between risk and uncertainty: Statistical methods are required when dealing with known risks, heuristics when dealing with uncertainty. Rather than spending our time knocking heuristics, we need to study their ecological rationality; that is, to find out when they work and when they don't (Gigerenzer et al. 2011; Todd et al. 2012).

In contrast to this negative view, rules of thumb have always had a positive connotation in fields that deal with uncertainty, such as artificial intelligence and animal behavior. Originally, the Greek term "heuristic" meant "serving to find out or discover." The Stanford mathematician G. Polya (1954) distinguished between heuristic and analytic thinking. For instance, heuristic thinking is indispensable for finding a mathematical proof, whereas analytic thinking is necessary for checking the steps of a proof. Polya introduced Herbert Simon to heuristics, on whose work I draw.

9. The distinction between risk and uncertainty is attributed to the University of Chicago economist Frank Knight (Knight 1921, section I.I.26). Some scholars reject the distinction between risk and uncertainty on the grounds that it is always possible to form subjective probabilities, which would allow uncertainty to be reduced to risk. I do not think that this is a fruitful move, and nor did Jimmy Savage, the father of modern Bayesian decision theory, to whom this reductionist view is often attributed. Savage (1954) restricted his theory to "small worlds"; that is, well-defined tasks where everything is known, such as lotteries. But he thought it would be "utterly ridiculous" (p. 16) to apply his theory to large worlds, even to simple questions such as planning a family picnic or playing a game of chess. I personally think of the mind as an adaptive toolbox with many tools, including rules of thumb and Bayes' rule, each for its own purpose. Although it is a beautiful dream to think of every problem as one of probabilities, it is like using only a hammer for every household repair.

10. Gigerenzer, Swijtink, et al. 1989.

11. Daston 1988, chapter 6.

12. *The Charlie Rose Show*, February 11, 2009. The pilots also considered Teterboro airport but concluded that they could not make it. The passenger stories are from Firman and Quirk 2009.

13. The rule works when the ball is already high up in the air; otherwise it can be easily adjusted. See Gigerenzer 2007, chapter 1. The same rule helps sailors to avoid collisions: *Fix your gaze on the other boat. If the angle of gaze remains constant, turn away quickly.*

14. E.g., Kahneman 2011. It is sometimes said that for Kahneman, the glass of rationality is half-empty, and for Gigerenzer, the glass is half-full. One is a pessimist, the other an optimist. That characterization misses the point. We differ in what the glass of rationality is in the first place. Kahneman and followers take logic or probability theory as a general, "content-blind" norm of rationality. In their thinking, heuristics can never be more accurate, only faster. That, however, is true only in a world of known risk. In an uncertain world, simple heuristics often can do better. The real research question is to understand why and when. The answers we know today are based on the bias-variance dilemma (chapter 5; Gigerenzer and Brighton 2009) and the general study of ecological rationality (Todd, Gigerenzer, and the ABC Research Group 2012).

15. See Gigerenzer, Hertwig, and Pachur 2011; Hertwig, Hoffrage, and the ABC Research Group 2013.

16. Gigerenzer, Todd, and the ABC Research Group 1999; Todd, Gigerenzer, and the ABC Research Group 2012.

17. The Welch quote is from Akerlof and Shiller 2009, p. 14.

18. Stine 1996, pp. 333–38. I use the term HIV here for HIV-1, which is the most common type worldwide, while HIV-2 is rarely found outside West Africa.

19. Munro 2004.

20. This prevalence corresponds to that of U.S. women who were Red Cross first-time blood donors: Centers for Disease Control and Prevention. http://www.cdc.gov/hiv/topics/testing/resources/reports/hiv_prevalence/low-risk.htm (retrieved Nov 3, 2012).

21. Gigerenzer 2002, chapter 7. In 2013 we tested AIDS counselors again, only to find the same illusion of certainty among most of them. The two trees in Figure 2-5 use "natural frequencies," which help counselors and clients to intuitively understand Bayes' rule (see chapter 9). HIV tests illustrate our limits in calculating risks precisely: the false positive rate (as well as the true positive rate, i.e., sensitivity) varies between different tests, and both rates appear to be even dependent on the prevalence of HIV in the population.

22. www.idph.state.il.us/aids/materials/10questions.htm.

23. For cases of false positives in HIV testing see Gigerenzer 2002, chapters 1 and 7; the case of the construction worker is reported on pp. 231–32.

24. Taleb and Blyth 2011. The idea orginated with Bertrand Russell in *The Problems of Philosophy* (1912), chapter VI on induction. I added the formal analysis in terms of the rule of succession. This rule is a special version of Bayes' rule (Gigerenzer 2002, p. 212).

25. Quoted in Makridakis et al. 2009, p. 796.

26. The value-at-risk calculations here are based on assuming a normal distribution. See Haldane, A. G. 2009. Why banks failed the stress test. www.bankofengland.co.uk/publications/Documents/speeches/2009/speech374.pdf.

27. Stiglitz 2010, p. 243; emphasis added. Despite Stiglitz's insight, most studies of decision making, including in neuroeconomics, investigate behavior in worlds of risk, not of uncertainty. The pretty colors of these neuroimaging studies show us a brain reacting to known risks, not to the real world of uncertainty (Volz and Gigerenzer 2012). Such devotion to lotteries and social gambling is puzzling given that few researchers buy lottery tickets themselves. The reason appears to be the desire to use the mathematics of optimization. For a philosophical analysis of the limits to the idea of optimization in a humane society, see Nida-Rümelin 2011.

28. Leibniz 1690/1951.

29. See Sherden 1998, pp. 174–75, also for the quote on lightbulbs, and the *Süddeutsche Zeitung* (T. Fromm, Für die Zukunft nur das Beste, January 28, 2011) on Daimler. On Aiken, who is often misquoted out of context, see Cohen 1998.

3

Defensive Decision Making

1. Letter from Max Wertheimer to Albert Einstein 1934. See also Luchins and Luchins 1979; the old-car brain teaser is on pp. 186–87. The text is translated directly from the original and varies from Luchins and Luchins's translation.

2. Einstein wrote in German: "*Erst durch Rechnung* merkte ich, dass für den Herunterweg keine Zeit mehr verfügbar bleibt! . . . Solche Witzchen zeigen

einem, wie blöd man ist!" Letter from Albert Einstein to Max Wertheimer. Albert Einstein Duplicate Archive, Princeton University Library.

3. Goldstein and Gigerenzer 2002. The serendipity story is in Gigerenzer and Goldstein 2011.

4. Mervyn King: "What fates impose: Facing up to uncertainty." The Eighth British Academy Annual Lecture 2004.

5. Kohn 2000.

6. Emanuel 2008, p. 2.

7. *Ten facts on patient safety* (2012): www.who.int/features/factfiles/patient _safety/en/index.html.

8. Reported in Atul Gawande's article "The Checklist" in the *New Yorker*, December 10, 2007.

9. Pronovost et al. 2006.

10. Gawande 2009.

11. Brochure from Aktionsbündnis Patientensicherheit: Aus Fehlern lernen, 2008.

12. Gigerenzer and Goldstein 2011.

13. Domenighetti et al. 1993.

14. Trunkey 2010, p. 421. On prophylactic removal of ovaries see Larson 2011.

15. Steurer et al. 2009.

16. Studdert et al. 2005.

17. Brenner 2010; Picano and Matucci-Cerinic 2011.

18. Brenner 2010; Brenner and Hall 2007; Schwartz 2007. The survivors of the atomic bomb were exposed to radiation throughout the body, whereas a CT targets a specific organ. There is little evidence that the risk of cancer for a specific organ is substantially increased by exposure of other organs to radiation. For comparison, the mean dose absorbed by an average person from natural sources, such as radon in the home, is around 3 mSv.

19. Berrington de González et al. 2009 estimated seventy-two million CT scans in the United States in 2007, and the numbers have been rising from year to year.

20. Brenner and Hall 2007. The estimate is based on an ad hoc survey during a panel discussion at a meeting of pediatric radiologists. Lin (2010) presents similar estimates that one out of every three to four CT and MRI scans were unnecessary.

21. American Dental Association and U.S. Department of Health and Human Services 2004.

22. TAP Study Group 2001.

4

Why Do We Fear What's Unlikely to Kill Us?

1. LeDoux 1996.

2. U.S. hospital emergency rooms treat about thirteen hundred injuries per year related to electric lights on Christmas trees, resulting in about ten deaths and more than $15 million in property loss and damage. As a consequence, in 2007 the U.S. Consumer Product Safety Commission ordered a recall of Prelit Trees for hazards of overheating and electrical shocks. Even earlier, in

2000 Walgreens recalled artificial Christmas trees with fiber optic lights because they overheated and caught fire. There is no such thing as zero risk. (German statistics: Feuerwehr und Rettungsdienst Landeshauptstadt Düsseldorf, 2001, www.duesseldorf.de/feuerwehr/pdf/alle/histbra.pdf).

3. For this and the following stories, including references, see Quigley 1996.
4. Cited in Quigley 1996, p. 187.
5. T. Gigerenzer, "Teaching the foreign teacher how to travel." *The Caravan*, January 2011.
6. Survey by Associated Press and Ipsos, October 2008. A Gallup poll in 2005 reported a similar figure of 32 percent, as well as that 28 percent of Canadians believe in haunted houses.
7. Gaskell et al. 2006. This belief has remained stable over the years. Earlier Eurobarometers since 1996 showed a constant 35–36 percent who believe that ordinary tomatoes have no genes.
8. Payer 1996.
9. Nisbett 2003, p. 12.
10. Leeman, Fischler, and Rozin 2011.
11. Seligman 1970.
12. Öhman and Mineka 2001.
13. Yamamoto 1979.
14. Muris et al. 1997.
15. For this and the following studies see Twenge et al. 2010.

Part II
Getting Risk Savvy

1. There is a long story to this short quote. In the classic *How to Lie with Statistics* (Huff 1959), one epigraph reads: "Statistical thinking will one day be as necessary for efficient citizenship as the ability to read and write." The quote is attributed to Wells but without any reference. In fact, hundreds of authors use this quote without providing a source. When I myself used it in my book *Calculated Risks* (UK edition: *Reckoning with Risk*), I added a footnote explaining that I had been unable to locate its source (Wells wrote more than a hundred books) and that it might have even been fabricated. In response, I received various letters, including an article by J. W. Tankard (1979) arguing that Wells's prediction was about the role of mathematics, not statistics, and that statisticians might have misrepresented this to promote their own cause. Tankard quotes Wells calling for "sound training in mathematics" and saying: "It is as necessary to be able to compute, to think in averages and maxima and minima, as it is now to be able to read and write" (pp. 30-31). Tankard also cites Lovat Dickson, one of Wells's biographers, who could not recall another place in his writings that dealt specifically with statistics.

Just as I was prepared to accept this account, I received a letter from a British librarian, Geoffrey Hunt, with a copy of Wells's *World Brain* (1938/1994). And here it was: "A certain elementary training in statistical method is becoming as necessary for everyone living in this world of today as reading and writing" (p. 141). That verifies the essence, if not the exact wording, of this popular quote.

5

Mind Your Money

1. DiPrete 2007. DiPrete notes that the wording of the questions was ambiguous.
2. Based on ConsensusEconomics 2001–2010. Some of the banks have changed their names. To avoid confusion, I use the present name.
3. Orrell 2010.
4. www.abendblatt.de/wirtschaft/article95679/DAX-Prognose.
5. Twain 1894, chapter 13.
6. Sherden 1998, p. 96. For the case of Elaine Garzarelli see Malkiel 2007, p. 143.
7. Taleb 2004.
8. Törngren and Montgomery 2004.
9. Markowitz interviewed by Bruce Bower 2011, p. 26. Markowitz used 1/N for his TIAA/CREF fund and split his money equally between stocks and bonds. The study reported here uses 1/N for stocks only.
10. DeMiguel, Garlappi, and Uppal 2009. The conditions under which 1/N is superior to optimization methods are still debated; see Kritzman, Page, and Turkington 2010.
11. Gigerenzer and Brighton 2009; Gigerenzer, Hertwig, and Pachur 2011; Haldane 2012.
12. The key idea is that the total error when making a prediction consists of three components:
   $$Total\ error = bias^2 + variance + noise.$$
   Noise (in other words, meaningless or misleading information such as measuring something incorrectly) is the component we have to live with, while the other two sources of error can be influenced. Bias is the difference between mean estimate and true state, and variance is the variability of individual estimates (based on different samples) around the mean estimate. For instance, 1/N has no free parameters, and therefore has bias only (it makes the same allocation independent of specific samples). For details, see Geman, Bienenstock, and Doursat 1992; Gigerenzer and Brighton 2009.
13. Vitouch et al. 2007. The interviewer's name has been changed. The Austrian banks are legally required to invest 40:60 into stocks and bonds, respectively, which is the basis of the interest they pay in addition to the premium.
14. Goldstein and Taleb 2007.
15. Monti et al. 2012.
16. Buffett in his chairman's letter to the shareholders of Berkshire Hathaway Inc., February 21, 2002, printed in *Berkshire Hathaway Inc., 2002 Annual Report*, p. 14.
17. Lewis 2010.

18. E. L. Andrews. "Greenspan concedes error on regulation," *New York Times*, October 23, 2008.
19. In a column for the *New York Post* titled "The only useful thing banks have invented in 20 years is the ATM," December 13, 2009.
20. Monti et al. 2012.
21. Mandelbrot and Taleb 2005, p. 100.

6
Leadership and Intuition

1. See Gigerenzer and Selten 2001 and Gigerenzer, Hertwig, and Pachur 2011 for an academic version of decision making under uncertainty.
2. Mintzberg 2009, p. 19.
3. Maidique 2012. He is now executive director of the Center for Leadership at FIU. The following discussion is based on this article.
4. Bingham and Eisenhardt 2011.
5. For those interested in the technicalities: The Pareto/NBD (negative binomial distribution) model assumes that while active customers make purchases according to a Poisson process with purchase rate λ, customer lifetime has an exponentially distributed duration with a dropout rate μ, and that across customers, individual purchase rates and dropout rates are distributed according to gamma distributions. For more details, see Wübben and Wangenheim 2008.
6. Wübben and Wangenheim 2008. For the CD retailer, the hiatus was six months.
7. Czerlinski et al., 1999. Take-the-best is a sequential rule that compares two options on the most valid cue, and if they differ, ignores all other cues and makes the decision. If the options do not differ, the same process is repeated with the second best cue, and so on, until a decision can be made. For a comparison between simple rules and complex nonlinear methods see Gigerenzer and Brighton 2009.

7
Fun and Games

1. "Ask Marilyn," *Parade*, September 9, 1990, p. 15, and December 2, p. 25. The Monty Hall problem was first stated by Steve Selvin 1975. See also Krauss and Wang 2003. The following passages draw on John Tierney's July 21, 1991 *New York Times* article "Behind Monty Hall's doors: Puzzle, debate and answer?"
2. In his book *Inevitable Illusions* (1994), Piatelli-Palmarini singled out the Monty Hall problem as *the* cognitive illusion in which "even the finest and best-trained minds get trapped" (p. 161).
3. Compare this solution with the standard solution in terms of probabilities using Bayes' rule. Take the situation where the contestant first chooses door 1 and then Monty opens door 3 and shows a goat. Here, we want to know the probability $p(\text{Car1}|\text{Monty3})$ that the car is behind door 1 after Monty opened door 3:

$p(\text{Car1}|\text{Monty3}) = p(\text{Car1})p(\text{Monty3}|\text{Car1})/[\,p(\text{Car1})p(\text{Monty3}|\text{Car1})+p(\text{Car2})$
$p(\text{Monty3}|\text{Car2})+p(\text{Car3})p(\text{Monty3}|\text{Car3})]= \frac{1}{3} \times \frac{1}{2} /[\frac{1}{3} \times \frac{1}{2} + \frac{1}{3} \times 1 + \frac{1}{3} \times 0]= \frac{1}{3}.$

That is, the probability that the car is behind door 1 remains unchanged, and thus the probability that it is behind door 2 has increased to 2/3. The probabilities $p(\text{Car1})$, $p(\text{Car2})$, and $p(\text{Car3})$ are called the *prior probabilities*, and $p(\text{Car1}|\text{Monty3})$ is called the *posterior probability*. The *conditional probability* $p(\text{Monty3}|\text{Car1})$ that Monty opens door 3 if the car is behind door 1 is 1/2 because Monty has a choice between doors 2 and 3, and is assumed to choose randomly. The conditional probability $p(\text{Monty3}|\text{Car2})$ that Monty opens door 3 if the car is behind door 2 is 1 because Monty has no choice given that he cannot open door 1. Finally, $p(\text{Monty3}|\text{Car3})$ is zero because Monty cannot show the car to the contestant. This amount of explanation and calculation illustrates why people tend to be confused when thinking in terms of conditional probabilities.

4. This assumption can be weakened to the following: Monty does not always open the door, but he does not make this offer dependent on which door the guest picked. Interviews in the next paragraphs are reported in Friedman 2004.

5. Dan Friedman and Aadhi Nakhoda, Monty Hall Problem 2008.

6. This card problem is also known as Bertrand's box problem. It is logically equivalent to the Monty Hall problem and the Three Prisoners problem (Gigerenzer 2002). How natural frequencies work is explained in more detail in chapter 9.

7. This and the next section are based on Bennis et al. 2012. The "digital" machines described here are already becoming a thing of the past, being replaced by animated screens that often have five reels and many more combinations to win. Coin and token payouts also have been replaced by paper vouchers in many casinos, so that soon new ways to manipulate subjective experience may emerge.

8. Beilock et al. 2004.

9. Galesic et al. 2014. On fast and frugal food choice see Todd and Minard, in press.

10. Schwartz et al. 2002.

8

Getting to the Heart of Romance

1. Darwin 1887/1969, pp. 232–33. For a more detailed analysis of Darwin's decision making see also Gigerenzer and Todd 1999, pp. 7–15.

2. See Gigerenzer, Hertwig, and Pachur 2011.

3. Billari et al. 2007.

4. Benjamin Franklin was a scientist, statesman, and one of the great figures of the Enlightenment. His "moral algebra" is an early version of modern utilitarianism. In his ethics, the rake and the drunkard are no different from other people except in that they did not calculate their risks correctly. Franklin 1779.

5. Finkel et al. 2012.
6. Franklin 1745.
7. Bearden, Rapoport, and Murphy 2006.
8. Miller 2000.
9. Todd, Billari, and Simao, 2005; Todd and Miller 1999.
10. Gigerenzer, Galesic, and Garcia-Retamero 2013.
11. Quoted in Gigerenzer 2007, pp. 70–71.
12. Ortmann et al. 2008; Barber and Odean 2001.
13. Becker 1991.
14. Hertwig, Davis, and Sulloway 2002.
15. Gigerenzer and Galesic (2012).
16. We asked seventy-three adults aged sixty to seventy-seven years (Gigerenzer and Galesic 2012).

9
What Doctors Need to Know

1. A Trabi (Trabant) is a tiny East German car with cult status. It's a mobile museum that brings back the joy of driving the old way with its vibrations and noisy motor.
2. Donner-Banzhoff et al. 2011, p. 227.
3. Steinman et al. 2001.
4. See Gøtzsche and Nielsen 2011.
5. Bramwell et al. 2006; Ghosh and Ghosh 2005; Hoffrage and Gigerenzer 1998; Hoffrage, Lindsey, et al. 2000; Labarge et al. 2003. For an overview see Gigerenzer, Gaissmaier, et al. 2007. For instance, most (67–82 percent) of 1,361 Swiss physicians from all specialties selected a positive predictive value of 95–99.9 percent, regardless of the prevalence of the disease and even when no information on prevalence was provided (Agoritsas et al. 2011).
6. Young et al. 2002.
7. As with most discoveries it is uncertain who actually discovered Bayes' rule. According to Stigler's law of eponymy, no scientific discovery is named after its original discoverer. In an ironic detective story, Stigler (1983) concluded that the odds are three to one that the blind Nicholas Saunderson rather than Thomas Bayes discovered Bayes' rule. At the age of twenty-nine, Saunderson held the prestigious Lucasian chair of mathematics in Cambridge, which Newton had held before him. There is also an impolite interpretation of Stigler's law: "Every scientific discovery is named after the last individual too ungenerous to give credit to his predecessors" (Stigler 1980). Bayes cannot be accused of such unsportsmanlike behavior, since he never published his treatise. The eminent statistician Ronald Fisher congratulated him postmortem for leaving it unpublished, since in his eyes Bayes' rule was absolutely useless in science (see Gigerenzer, Swijtink, et al. 1989).
   Natural frequencies, like conditional probabilities, refer to joint events, such as nine people with positive test and disease, and should not be confused with simple frequencies, such as that one out of one hundred people has

a disease. On the difference between natural frequencies and relative frequencies see Hoffrage and Gigerenzer 1998 and Gigerenzer 2011.

8. This claim goes back to Kahneman and Tversky (1972), who argued that "In his evaluation of evidence, man is apparently not a conservative Bayesian: he is not Bayesian at all" (p. 450). In their book *Nudge*, Thaler and Sunstein put forward a "libertarian" program of paternalism that aims at correcting for this and other "inevitable" cognitive illusions.

9. Kurz-Milcke et al. 2008.

10. Siegrist, Cousin, and Keller 2008, figure 1. There are now noninvasive blood tests (LifeCodexx) that carry no risk of miscarriage, but like all tests, they are not perfect and the problem of interpreting what a positive test means remains essentially the same.

11. Bramwell et al. 2006. Five to ten percent of a sample of women and obstetricians shared this illusion of certainty. Although invasive testing is also not certain, a majority of Swiss women who were pregnant or had already delivered believed that it was (Siegrist et al. 2008).

12. Siegrist et al. 2008.

13. Bramwell et al. 2006. They were given a 1 percent false-positive rate, which does not correspond to the available data. To avoid confusion, I have used the 5 percent rate here. The authors also used ten thousand pregnant women for the natural frequency version, as opposed to one thousand here. These large numbers complicate the calculations unnecessarily.

14. Hewlett and Waisbren 2006.

15. Gurian et al. 2006.

16. McManus et al. 1998.

17. Garcia-Retamero and Galesic 2012.

18. Chen 2007.

19. Sirovich and Welch 2004.

20. Good Stewardship Working Group 2011.

21. Gibson and Singh 2010, p. 136.

22. Kattah et al. 2009.

23. Bachmann et al. 2003.

24. A fast-and-frugal tree with *n* binary attributes (or questions) has $n+1$ exits, while a full tree has 2^n exits (Martignon et al. 2011). For teaching materials on the ankle rule and other fast and frugal rules see www.ohri.ca/emerg/cdr/.

25. Graham et al. 2001.

26. Hale 1996.

27. Krogsboll et al. 2012.

10

Health Care: No Decision About Me Without Me

1. Reported in Michael Dobbs, "Rudy wrong on cancer survival chances," *Washington Post*, October 30, 2007. Giuliani apparently used data from the year 2000, when forty-nine British men per one hundred thousand were diagnosed with prostate cancer, twenty-eight of whom died within five

years—about 44 percent. More recent figures (which differ from those cited by Giuliani) are 98 percent five-year survival in the United States versus 71 percent in Britain.

2. About twenty-six prostate cancer deaths per one hundred thousand American men versus twenty-seven per one hundred thousand in Britain (Shibata and Whittemore, 2001).

3. The correlation coefficient is exactly 0.0 (Welch et al. 2000). The five-year survival rate is defined as the number of patients alive five years after diagnosis divided by the number of patients diagnosed. The mortality rate, in contrast, is defined as the number of people who died from cancer divided by *all* people in the group (not just those who were diagnosed). Figures 10-1 and 10-2 are adapted from Gigerenzer, Gaissmaier, et al. 2007.

4. Scientists have begun to uncover biological mechanisms that halt the progression of cancer (Folkman and Kalluri 2004; Mooi and Peeper 2006).

5. U.S. Preventive Services Task Force 2012. Screening for prostate cancer. www.uspreventiveservicestaskforce.org.

6. These rough estimates are based on autopsies (Delongchamps et al. 2006) and vary between populations. Note that estimates based on incidence rates are lower and less reliable because they do not include men with smaller or undetected cancers or those who did not attend screening.

7. Steimle 1999, p. 1189.

8. The icon box is based on Djulbegovic et al. 2010. Arkes and Gaissmaier (2012) provide a version with one thousand people. To simplify, nonsignificant differences are represented by the same number. All numbers are "abouts." Icon boxes are particularly effective for people with low numeracy (Galesic et al. 2009).

9. Schroeder et al. 2012.

10. Welch et al. 2011, p. 50.

11. Harris and Lohr 2002.

12. Ablin, "The great prostate mistake," *New York Times*, March 10, 2010, p. A27. In contrast to routine screening, PSA tests do have a place in other contexts, as when checking for the return of the disease after treatment for prostate cancer.

13. Stiftung Warentest 2004.

14. Enserink 2010, p. 1738.

15. Wegwarth et al. 2012.

16. See Welch et al. 2011, chapter 5.

17. Wegwarth et al. 2011. Unlike the U.S. sample, the German doctors were a convenience sample.

18. Welch et al. 2011, p. 156.

19. An ACS campaign poster from the 1980s: http://comedsoc.org/Breast _Cancer_Screening.htm?m=66&=447.

20. "Why should I have a mammogram?" brochure from the Arkansas Department of Human Services and Arkansas Foundation of Medical Care.

21. Fact boxes were developed and tested by two brilliant researchers from Dartmouth Medical School, Lisa Schwartz and Steven Woloshin. See Schwartz et al. 2009 and Schwartz and Woloshin 2011.

22. Based on the Cochrane Review by Gøtzsche and Nielsen 2011. The authors distinguished between better (adequately randomized) studies and suboptimal ones. The better studies found only a nonsignificant absolute reduction of 0.3 deaths from breast cancer in every 1,000 women, while the suboptimal studies found a reduction of 2.1 in 1,000. Favoring the better studies, the authors estimated an overall reduction of 0.5 in 1,000. My more generous estimate in the fact box is 1 in 1,000, which is the middle (rounded) of reductions reported by the better and suboptimal studies. This is also consistent with Nyström (2002), who reported a reduction from 5.0 to 3.9 deaths from breast cancer in 1,000 women. The size of the reduction varies slightly from study to study. It is often said that modern technology and new treatment save more lives and that these estimates are therefore overly pessimistic. However, the benefits actually get *smaller* the more recent the study and the better the mammography equipment is. Total costs for breast cancer screening in the United States amount to around $3 billion and in Germany €300 to €400 million per year, or 0.1 percent of the total expenditure of the health system (www.news. doccheck.com/de/article).

23. Schwartz, Woloshin, and Welch 2009.

24. Schwartz and Woloshin 2011.

25. Ehrenreich 2010.

26. Gigerenzer, Gaissmaier, et al. 2007.

27. Knaul and Frenk 2010.

28. Posted by Gary Schwitzer on www.healthnewsreview.org. "What doctors don't know and journalists don't convey about screening may harm patients," March 8, 2012. Wikipedia lists other sources of funding in its entry on Susan G. Komen for the Cure. See also Woloshin and Schwartz 2012.

29. Deutsche Krebshilfe in their 2007 brochure *Brustkrebs* (pp. 15–16).

30. Gigerenzer, Mata, and Frank 2009.

31. This study is covered by the icon box: When one looks at all studies even this small effect disappears. To err on the conservative side, I have counted both "zero in one thousand" and "one in one thousand" as a realistic estimate for PSA tests in Figure 10-7.

32. Hoffman et al. 2010.

33. See Woloshin et al. 2008, p. 129; Gigerenzer, Gaissmaier, et al. 2007, Table 1.

34. Nass-Griegoleit et al. 2009. The basis for the confusion is in medical terminology, where screening is called "secondary prevention."

35. Rampura, Hapani, and Wu 2011.

36. Begley 2012. On the causes for lack of replication see Ioannidis 2005.

37. Based on Woloshin et al. 2008.

38. Speaking double-tongue occurs not only in marketing but earlier on, in the medical journals. In the three top medical journals, *British Medical Journal* (*BMJ*), the *Journal of the American Medical Association* (*JAMA*), and *The Lancet*, double-tonguing was used in one out of every three articles between 2004 and 2006 (Sedrakyan and Shih 2007). On double-tongue for tamoxifen see Schwartz et al. 1999.

39. Brandt 2007.

40. Hecht, Kassie, and Hatsukami 2009.
41. Willyard 2011.
42. Doll et al. 2004.
43. Cited in Proctor 2012.
44. Proctor 2012.
45. These recommendations are largely based on the report by the World Cancer Research Fund/American Institute for Cancer Research 2007. *Food, nutrition, physical activity, and the prevention of cancer: A global perspective.* Washington DC: AICR.
46. For adults, the BMI is only a crude measure. In fact, before 1998, the cutoff was different in the United States: Only men with 28 and women with 27 or more were considered overweight. Lowering the cutoff had the effect that 25 million Americans who had been "normal" were suddenly "overweight." Studies reported that those classified as "normal" with a BMI from 18.5 to 25 had a slightly higher risk of mortality than those labeled "overweight," while those below 18.5 and above 35 had the highest risk (Orpana et al. 2008; Flegal et al. 2005). For men, a BMI around 26 was associated with the lowest risk of death. For women, the lowest risk was between 23 and 24. Thus, those millions who became overweight overnight appear to be those who can relax and enjoy eating again.
47. Willyard 2011.
48. Liu et al. 2011.
49. Schütze et al. 2011.
50. *Frankfurter Allgemeine Zeitung,* June 4, 2011.
51. Longnecker et al. 1995.
52. Brenner and Elliston 2004; Brenner and Hall 2007.
53. Holmes et al. 2005. See also Tengs et al. 1995.
54. Gigerenzer and Muir Gray 2011.

11

Banks, Cows, and Other Dangerous Things

1. Reinhart and Rogoff 2009, Table A.3.1. Cited in Admati and Hellwig 2013.
2. See Admati and Hellwig 2013. Part of the following analysis is based on this excellent book.
3. The following is based on Haldane 2012.
4. Orrell 2010.
5. Cited in Posner 2009, p. 287.
6. Banks use leverage in many other ways than described here. The leverage ratio is generally calculated as Debt/Equity. There are different ways to calculate it, but I will not deal with these here.
7. *Risk Off,* speech held by A. G. Haldane on August 18, 2011, p. 4. Available at www.bankofengland.co.uk/publications/speeches/default.aspx.
8. See Haldane 2012. Leverage ratio does not weight risks, not even in the crude way that Basel I does; thus, it is a version of $1/N$.
9. Admati and Hellwig 2013.

10. Admati and Hellwig 2013, footnote 24.
11. Renn 2007.
12. Ortwin Renn, "Riskante Wahrnehmung," guest commentary in *Der Tages spiegel* (January 31, 2010). The story about BSE in sheep in the next section is based on Lord Krebs, personal communication, July 2012.
13. Krämer 2011, p. 178.
14. Doshi 2009. The conclusion that Tamiflu reduces complications was based on a single article that reviewed ten studies. All of these were funded by Roche, the manufacturer of Tamiflu. Interestingly, the positive conclusion was based on the unpublished studies among the ten, while the two published ones showed no benefit. When Peter Doshi and the Cochrane Collaboration repeatedly tried to obtain the unpublished data in order to verify the claim, Roche either didn't respond or sent incomplete data containing a host of inconsistencies. At the beginning of 2013, Roche had yet to reveal the data. In reaction, the *British Medical Journal* announced that it would no longer publish studies without the data being made available to other researchers.
15. Jefferson et al. 2012.
16. Cohen and Carter 2010.
17. Cohen and Carter 2010.
18. Bomlitz and Brezis 2008.

12

Revolutionize School

1. Ripley 2009, p. 49.
2. Bond 2009.
3. Beck 1992.
4. Multmeier 2012 and Zhu and Gigerenzer 2006. For earlier studies with adults and icon arrays see Cosmides and Tooby 1996.
5. For an overview of the relationship between innumeracy and poor health see Reyna and Brainerd 2007. On lawyers' and judges' confusion about DNA evidence see Gigerenzer 2002.
6. Similarly, it has been argued that learning Latin helps to learn Romance languages. Yet pupils who had first learned French made fewer errors when learning Spanish than pupils who had first learned Latin. Nor does Latin improve test intelligence; its only benefit appears to be better grammatical skills in the mother tongue (Haag and Stern 2003).
7. Kurz-Milcke et al. 2008, 2011; Zhu and Gigerenzer 2006.
8. Sahlberg 2011. Critics argue that Finland is too small to serve as a model for other countries, although around thirty states in the United States have a population close or smaller in size.
9. Berg and Søreide 2011.
10. www.sciencekids.de.
11. I am currently working on such a health literacy program for young kids in the Netherlands with the Dutch Cancer Society.

12. Wobker et al. 2012. Note that at the time of the study German banks first applied the monthly payments to the interest, not the principle. The OECD has launched a clearinghouse for financial education programs: www.financial-education.org.

13. Turkle 2011, p. 171.

14. Sorrel, C. Padded lampposts cause fuss in London. March 10, 2008. www.wired.com/gadgetlab/2008/03/padded-lamposts/.

15. Kammerl et al. 2012.

16. Strayer et al. 2006.

17. Zimmerman et al. 2007.

18. Ophir et al. 2009.

19. Cited in Egidi and Marengo 2004, p. 335. On digital society see also Schirrmacher 2009.

20. Hair et al. 2007.

REFERENCES

Admati, A., and Hellwig, M. (2013). *The bankers' new clothes: What's wrong with banking and what to do about it*. Princeton, NJ: Princeton University Press.

Agoritsas, T., Courvoisier, D. S., Combescure, C., Deom, M., and Perneger, T. V. (2011). Does prevalence matter to physicians in estimating post-test probability of disease? A randomized trial. *Journal of General Internal Medicine* 26, 373–78.

Akerlof, G. A., and Shiller, R. J. (2009). *Animal spirits*. Princeton, NJ: Princeton University Press.

American Dental Association, U.S. Department of Health and Human Services. (2004). *The selection of patients for dental radiographic examinations*. Report. Retrieved from www.fda.gov/downloads/Radiation-EmittingProducts/RadiationEmittingProducts andProcedures/MedicalImaging/MedicalX-Rays/ucm116505.pdf.

Ariely, D. (2008). *Predictably irrational*. London: HarperCollins.

Arkes, H. R., and Gaissmaier, W. (2012). Psychological research and the prostate-cancer screening controversy. *Psychological Science* 23, 547–53.

Bachmann, L. M., Kolb, E., Koller, M. T., Steurer, J., and ter Riet, G. (2003). Accuracy of Ottawa ankle rules to exclude fractures of the ankle and mid-foot: Systematic review. *British Medical Journal* 326, 417–19.

Barber, B. M., and Odean, T. (2001). Boys will be boys: Gender, overconfidence, and common stock investment. *The Quarterly Journal of Economics* 1, 261–92.

Bearden, J. N., Rapoport, A., and Murphy, R. O. (2006). Sequential observation and selection with rank-dependent payoffs: An experimental test of alternative decision rules. *Management Science* 52, 1437–49.

Beck, U. (1992). *Risk society: Toward a new modernity* (M. Ritter, Trans.). London: Sage. (Original work published 1986.)

Becker, G. S. (1981). *A treatise on the family*. Cambridge, MA: Harvard University Press.

Begley, C. G. (2012, March 28). In cancer science, many "discoveries" don't hold up. *Reuters*. Retrieved from www.reuters.com.

Beilock, S. L., Bertenthal, B. I., McCoy, A. M., and Carr, T. H. (2004). Haste does not always make waste: Expertise, direction of attention, and speed versus accuracy in performing sensorimotor skills. *Psychonomic Bulletin and Review* 11, 373–79.

Bennis, W. M., Katsikopoulos, K. V., Goldstein, D. G., Dieckmann, A., and Berg, N. (2012). Designed to fit minds: Institutions and ecological rationality. In P. M. Todd, G. Gigerenzer, and the ABC Research Group, *Ecological rationality. Intelligence in the world* (pp. 409–27). New York: Oxford University Press.

Berg, M., and Søreide, K. (2011). Prevention: Will an aspirin a day keep the colorectal cancer away? *Nature Reviews Clinical Oncology* 8, 130–31.

Berg, N., and Gigerenzer, G. (2007). Psychology implies paternalism? Bounded rationality may reduce the rationale to regulate risk taking. *Social Choice and Welfare* 28, 337–59.

Berlin, I. (1967). Two concepts of liberty. In A. Quinton (Ed.), *Political philosophy* (pp. 141–52). Oxford, UK: Oxford University Press.

Berrington de González, A., Mahesh, M., Kim, K. P., Bhargavan, M., Lewis, R., Mettler, F., and Land, C. (2009). Projected cancer risk from computed tomography scans performed in the United States in 2007. *Archives of Internal Medicine* 169, 2071–77.

Billari, F. C., Prskawetz, A., Fent, T., and Aparicio Diaz, B. (2007). The "Wedding-Ring": An agent-based marriage model based on social interaction. *Demographic Research* 17, 59–82.

Bingham, C. B., and Eisenhardt, K. M. (2011). Rational heuristics: The "simple rules" that strategists learn from process experience. *Strategic Management Journal* 32, 1437–64.

Bomlitz, L. J., and Brezis, M. (2008). Misrepresentation of health risks by mass media. *Journal of Public Health* 30, 202–4.

Bond, M. (2009). Risk school. *Nature* 461, 1189–92.

Bower, B. (2011, June 4). Simple heresy. *Science News* 179, 26–29.

Bramwell, R., West, H., and Salmon, P. (2006). Health professionals' and service users' interpretation of screening test results: Experimental study. *British Medical Journal* 333, 284–86.

Brandt, A. M., (2007). *The cigarette century.* New York: Basic Books.

Brenner, D. J. (2010). Slowing the increase in the population dose resulting from CT scans. *Radiation Research* 174, 809–15.

Brenner, D. J., and Elliston, C. D. (2004). Estimated radiation risk potentially associated with full-body CT screening. *Radiology* 232, 735–38.

Brenner, D. J., and Hall, E. J. (2007). Computed tomography—An increasing source of radiation exposure. *New England Journal of Medicine* 357, 2277–84.

Chen, X.-Y. (2007). Defensive medicine or economically motivated corruption? A Confucian reflection on physician care in China today. *Journal of Medicine and Philosophy* 32, 635–48.

Chou, R. et al. (2005). Screening for HIV: A review of the evidence for the U.S. Preventive Services Task Force. *Annals of Internal Medicine* 143, 55–73.

Cohen, D., and Carter, P. (2010). WHO and the pandemic flu "conspiracies." *British Medical Journal* 340, 1274–79.

Cohen, I. B. (1998). Howard Aiken on the number of computers needed for the nation. *IEEE Annals of the History of Computing* 20, 27–32.

Covey, J. (2007). A meta-analysis of the effects of presenting treatment benefits in different formats. *Medical Decision Making* 27, 638–54.

Cosmides, L., and Tooby, J. (1996). Are humans good intuitive statisticians after all? Rethinking some conclusions from the literature on judgment under uncertainty. *Cognition* 58, 1–73.

Czerlinski, J., Gigerenzer, G., and Goldstein, D. G. (1999). How good are simple heuristics? In G. Gigerenzer, P. M. Todd, and the ABC Research Group, *Simple heuristics that make us smart* (pp. 97–118). New York: Oxford University Press.

Daston, L. J. (1988). *Classical probability in the Enlightenment.* Princeton, NJ: Princeton University Press.

Doll, R., Peto, R., Boreham, J., and Sutherland, I. (2004). Mortality in relation to smoking: 50 years' observations on male British doctors. *British Medical Journal* 328, 1519.

Delongchamps, N. B., Sing, A., and Haas, G. P. (2006). The role of prevalence in the diagnosis of prostate cancer. *Cancer Control* 13, 158–68.

DeMiguel, V., Garlappi, L., and Uppal, R. (2009). Optimal versus naive diversification: How inefficient is the 1/*N* portfolio strategy? *Review of Financial Studies* 22, 1915–53.

Dewey, J. (1929). *The quest for certainty.* New York: Minton, Balch and Co.

Dijksterhuis, A., van Knippenberg, A., Kruglanski, A. W., and Schaper, C. (1996). Motivated social cognition: Need for closure effects on memory and judgments. *Journal of Experimental Social Psychology* 32, 254–70.

DiPrete, T. A. (2007). Is this a great country? *Research in Social Stratification and Mobility* 25, 89–95.

Djulbegovic, M., Beyth, R. J., Neuberger, M. M., Stoffs, T. L., Vieweg, J., Djulbegovic, B., and Dahm, P. (2010). Screening for prostate cancer: Systematic review and meta-analysis of randomized controlled trials. *British Medical Journal* 341, c4543.

Doll, R., Peto, R., Boreham, J., and Sutherland, I. (2004). Mortality in relation to smoking: 50 years' observations on male British doctors. *British Medical Journal* 328, 1519.

Domenighetti, G., Casabianca, A., Gutzwiller, F., and Martinoli, S. (1993). Revisiting the most informed consumer of surgical services: The physician-patient. *International Journal of Technology Assessment in Health Care* 9, 505–13.

Donner-Banzhoff, N., Bastian, H., Coulter, A., Elwyn, G., Jonitz, G., Klemperer, D., and Ludwig, W. D. (2011). How can better evidence be delivered? In G. Gigerenzer and J. A. Muir Gray (Eds.), *Better doctors, better patients, better decisions* (pp. 215–32). Cambridge, MA: MIT Press.

Doshi, P. (2009). Neuraminidase inhibitors: The story behind the Cochrane review. *British Medical Journal* 330, 1348–51.

Egidi, M., and Marengo, L. (2004). Near-decomposability, organization, and evolution: Some notes on Herbert Simon's contribution. In M. Augier and J. J. March (Eds.), *Models of a man: Essays in memory of Herbert A. Simon* (pp. 335–50). Cambridge, MA: MIT Press.

Ehrenreich, B. (2010). *Bright-sided: How positive thinking is undermining America.* New York: Picador.

Einstein, A. (undated). Letter to Max Wertheimer. Albert Einstein Archive, Princeton University Library.

Emanuel, E. J. (2008). *Healthcare, guaranteed: A simple, secure solution for America.* New York: Public Affairs.

Enserink, M. (2010, December 24). What's next for disease eradication? *Science* 330, 1736–39. doi: 10.1126/science.330.6012.1736.

Finkel, E. J., Eastwick, P. W., Karney, B. R., Reis, H. T., and Sprecher, S. (2012). Online dating: A critical analysis from the perspective of psychological science. *Psychological Science in the Public Interest* 13, 3–66.

Firman, D., and Quirk, K. (2009). *Brace for impact.* Deerfield Beach, FL: Health Communications, Inc.

Flegal, K. M., Graubard, B. I., Williamson, D. F., and Gail, M. H. (2005). Excess deaths associated with underweight, overweight, and obesity. *Journal of the American Medical Association* 293, 1861–67.

Folkman, J., and Kalluri, R. (2004). Cancer without disease. *Nature* 427, 787. doi: 10.1038 /427787a

Franklin, B. (1745). Letter to a friend (Philadelphia, June 25, 1745). Retrieved from www .bibliomania.com/2/9/77/124/21473/1/frameset.html.

———(1779). Letter to Jonathan Williams (Passy, April 8, 1779). In A. H. Smyth (Ed.), *The writings of Benjamin Franklin* (Vol. VII, pp. 281–82). New York: Macmillan.

Friedman, D. (2004). Monty Hall's three doors: Construction and deconstruction of a choice anomaly. *American Economic Review* 88, 933–46.

Friedman, D., and Nakhoda, A. (2008, August). *Monty Hall Problem.* Learning and Experimental Economics Projects of Santa Cruz (LEEPS), University of Santa Cruz. Retrieved from leeps.ucsc.edu/misc/page/monty-hall-puzzle/.

Furedi, A. (1999). The public health implications of the 1995 "pill scare." *Human Reproduction Update* 5, 621–26. doi: 10.1093/humupd/5.6.621.

Gaissmaier, W., and Gigerenzer, G. (2012). 9/11, act II: A fine-grained analysis of regional variations in traffic fatalities in the aftermath of the terrorist attacks. *Psychological Science* 23, 1449–54.

Galesic, M., and Garcia-Retamero, R. (2012). The risks we dread: A social circle account. *PLoS ONE*, 7, e32837.

Galesic, M., Garcia-Retamero, R., and Gigerenzer, G. (2009). Using icon arrays to communicate medical risks to low-numeracy people. *Health Psychology* 28, 210–16.

Galesic, M., Garcia-Retamero, R., and Gigerenzer, G. (2014). *Maximizing and satisficing: Personality trait or adaptive strategies?* Manuscript, Max Planck Institute for Human Development: Berlin.

Garcia-Retamero, R., and Galesic, M. (2012). Doc, what would you do if you were me? On self-other discrepancies in medical decision making. *Journal of Experimental Psychology: Applied* 18, 38–51.

Gaskell, G., Allansdottir, A., Allum, N., Corchero, C., Fischler, C., Hampel, J., et al. (2006). Europeans and biotechnology in 2005: Pattern and trends. *Eurobarometer* 64.3.

Gawande, A. (2009). *The checklist manifesto.* New York: Metropolitan Books.

Ghosh, A. K., and Ghosh, K. (2005). Translating evidence-based information into effective risk communication: Current challenges and opportunities. *Journal of Laboratory and Clinical Medicine* 145, 171–80. doi: 10.1016/j.lab.2005.02.006.

Gibson, R., and Singh, J. P. (2010). *The treatment trap.* Chicago, IL: Dee.

Gigerenzer, G. (2000). *Adaptive thinking: Rationality in the real world.* New York: Oxford University Press.

———. (2002). *Calculated risks: How to know when numbers deceive you.* New York: Simon and Schuster (UK version: *Reckoning with risk: Learning to live with uncertainty.* London: Penguin).

———. (2004). Dread risk, September 11, and fatal traffic accidents. *Psychological Science* 15, 286–87 doi: 10.1111/j.0956-7976.2004.00668.x.

———. (2006). Out of the frying pan into the fire: Behavioral reactions to terrorist attacks. *Risk Analysis* 26, 347–51. doi: 10.1111/j.1539-6924.2006.00753.x.

———. (2007). *Gut feelings: The intelligence of the unconscious.* New York: Viking (UK version: London: Allen Lane/Penguin).

———. (2008). *Rationality for mortals: How people cope with uncertainty.* New York: Oxford University Press.

———. (2011). What are natural frequencies? Doctors need to find better ways to communicate risk to patients. *British Medical Journal* 343:d6386.

Gigerenzer, G., and Brighton, H. (2009). Homo heuristicus: Why biased minds make better inferences. *Topics in Cognitive Science* 1, 107–43.

Gigerenzer, G., Fiedler, K., and Olsson, H. (2012). Rethinking cognitive biases as environmental consequences. In P. M. Todd, G. Gigerenzer, and the ABC Research Group, *Ecological rationality: Intelligence in the world* (pp. 80–110). New York: Oxford University Press.

Gigerenzer, G., Gaissmaier, W., Kurz-Milcke, E., Schwartz, L. M., and Woloshin, S. (2007). Helping doctors and patients to make sense of health statistics. *Psychological Science in the Public Interest* 8, 53–96.

Gigerenzer, G., and Galesic, M. (2012). Why do single event probabilities confuse patients? *British Medical Journal* 344, e245. doi:10.1136/bmj.e245.

Gigerenzer, G., Galesic, M., and Garcia-Retamero, R. (2013). Stereotypes about men's and women's intuitions: A study of two nations. *Journal of Cross Cultural Psychology.* doi:10.1177/0022022113487074.

Gigerenzer, G., and Goldstein, D. G. (2011). The recognition heuristic: A decade of research. *Judgment and Decision Making* 6, 100–121.

Gigerenzer, G., Hertwig, R., van den Broek, E., Fasolo, B., and Katsikopoulos, K. V. (2005). "A 30% chance of rain tomorrow": How does the public understand probabilistic weather forecasts? *Risk Analysis* 25, 623–29.

Gigerenzer, G., Hertwig, R., and Pachur, T. (Eds.) (2011). *Heuristics: The foundations of adaptive behavior.* New York: Oxford University Press.

Gigerenzer, G., Mata, J., and Frank, R. (2009). Public knowledge of benefits of breast and prostate cancer screening in Europe. *Journal of the National Cancer Institute* 101(17), 1216–20. doi: 10.1093/jnci/djp237.

Gigerenzer, G., and Muir Gray, J. A. (Eds.) (2011). *Better doctors, better patients, better decisions: Envisioning health care 2020.* Cambridge, MA: MIT Press.

Gigerenzer, G., and Selten, R. (2001). *Bounded rationality: The adaptive toolbox.* Cambridge, MA: MIT Press.

Gigerenzer, G., Swijtink, Z., Porter, T., Daston, L., Beatty, J., and Krüger, L. (1989). *The empire of chance: How probability changed science and everyday life.* Cambridge, UK: Cambridge University Press.

Gigerenzer, G., Todd, P. M., and the ABC Research Group (1999). *Simple heuristics that make us smart.* New York: Oxford University Press.

Gigerenzer, G., Wegwarth, O., and Feufel, M. (2010). Misleading communication of risk: Editors should enforce transparent reporting in abstracts. *British Medical Journal* 341, 791–92. doi: 10.1136/bmj.c4830.

Goldstein, D. G., and Gigerenzer, G. (2002). Models of ecological rationality: The recognition heuristic. *Psychological Review* 109, 75–90. doi: 10.1037/0033-295X.109.1.75.

Goldstein, D. G., and Taleb, N. N. (2007). We don't quite know what we are talking about when we talk about volatility. *Journal of Portfolio Management* 33, 84–86.

Good Stewardship Working Groups (2011). The "top 5" lists in primary care. *Archives of Internal Medicine* 171, 1385–90.

Gøtzsche, P. C., and Nielsen, M. (2011). Screening for breast cancer with mammography. *Cochrane Database of Systematic Reviews* 1, Article CD001877. doi: 10.1002/14651858 .CD001877.pub4.

Gould, S. J. (1992). *Bully for brontosaurus: Further reflections in natural history.* New York: Penguin Books.

Graham, I. D., Stiell, I. G., Laupacis, A., et al. (2001). Awareness and use of the Ottawa ankle and knee rules in 5 countries: Can publication alone be enough to change practice? *Annals of Emergency Medicine* 37, 259–66.

Gurian, E. A., Kinnamon, D. D., Henry, J. J., and Waisbren, S. E. (2006). Expanded newborn screening for biomedical disorders: The effect of a false-positive result. *Pediatrics* 117, 1915–21.

Haag, L., and Stern, E. (2003). In search of the benefits of learning Latin. *Journal of Educational Psychology* 95, 174–78.

Hair, M., Renaud, K. V., and Ramsay, J. (2007). The influence of self-esteem and locus of control on perceived email-related stress. *Computers in Human Behavior, 23*, 2791–03.

Haldane, A. G. (2012). The dog and the Frisbee. Speech, Jackson Hole, August 31, 2012. www.bankofengland.co.uk/publications/Pages/speeches/2012/596.aspx.

Hale, W. R. (1996). Can the Ottawa ankle decision rules be applied in the United States? *Western Journal of Medicine* 164, 363.

Harris, R., and Lohr, K. N. (2002). Screening for prostate cancer: An update of the evidence for the U.S. Preventive Services Task Force. *Annals of Internal Medicine* 137, 917–29.

Hecht, S. S., Kassie, F., and Hatsukami, D. K. (July 2009). Chemoprevention of lung carcinogenesis in addicted smokers and ex-smokers. *Nature Reviews Cancer* 9, 476–88.

Hertwig, R., Davis, J. N., and Sulloway, F. (2002). Parental investment: How an equity motive can produce inequality. *Psychological Bulletin* 128, 728–45.

Hertwig, R., Hoffrage, U., and the ABC Research Group. (2013). *Simple heuristics for a social world.* New York: Oxford University Press.

Hewlett, J., and Waisbren, S. E. (2006). A review of the psychosocial effects of false-positive results on parents and current communication practices in newborn screening. *Journal of Inherited Metabolic Disease* 29, 677–82.

Hoffman, R. M., Lewis, C. L., Pignone, M. P., Couper, M. P., Barry, M. J., Elmore, J. G., et al. (2010). Decision making processes for breast, colorectal, and prostate cancer screening: The DECISIONS survey. *Medical Decision Making* 30, 53S–64S.

Hoffrage, U., and Gigerenzer, G. (1998). Using natural frequencies to improve diagnostic inferences. *Academic Medicine 73*, 538–40. doi: 10.1097/00001888-199805000-00024.

Hoffrage, U., Lindsey, S., Hertwig, R., and Gigerenzer, G. (2000). Communicating statistical information. *Science* 290, 2261–62. doi: 10.1126/science.290.5500.2261.

Holmes, M. D., Chen, W. Y., Feskanich, D., Kroenke, C. H., and Colditz, G. A. (2005). Physical activity and survival after breast cancer diagnosis. *Journal of the American Medical Association* 293, 2479–86.

Huff, D. (1959). *How to lie with statistics*. New York: Norton.

Ioannidis, J. P. A. (2005). Why most published research findings are false. *PLoS Medicine* 2, 696–701.

Jefferson, T., Jones, M. A., Doshi, P., Del Mar, C. B., Heneghan, C. J., Hama, R., and Thompson, M. J. (2012). Neuraminidase inhibitors for preventing and treating influenza in healthy adults and children. *Cochrane Database of Systematic Reviews* 1. Art. No.: CD008965. doi: 10.1002/14651858.

Kahneman, D. (2011). *Thinking, fast and slow*. London: Allen Lane.

Kahneman, D., and Tversky, A. (1972). Subjective probability: A judgment of representativeness. *Cognitive Psychology* 3, 430–54.

Kammerl, R., Hirschäuser, L., Rosenkranz, M., Schwinge, C., Hein, S., Wartberg, L. (2012). *EXIF—Excessive Internetnutzung in Familien [Excessive Internet use in families]*. Berlin: Bundesministerium für Familie, Senioren, Frauen und Jugend.

Kant, E. (1784). Beantwortung der Frage: Was ist Aufklärung? *Berlinische Monatsschrift*, *Dezember-Heft* 481–94.

Kattah, J. C., Talkad, A. V., Wang, D. Z., Hsieh, Y.-H. and Newman-Toker, D. E. (2009). HINTS to diagnose stroke in the acute vestibular syndrome. *Stroke* 40, 3504–10.

Knaul, F., and Frenk, J. (2010). Latin America's silent breast cancer epidemic. Harvard School of Public Health, Office of the Dean. Retrieved from http://134.174.190.199/administrative-offices/deans-office/julio-frenk-dean/silent-breast-cancer-epidemic/index.html.

Knight, F. (1921). *Risk, uncertainty and profit*. Boston, MA: Houghton Mifflin Co.

Kohn, L. T., Corrigan, J. M., and Donaldson, M. S. (Eds.) (2000). *To err is human: Building a safer health system*. Washington, DC: National Academy Press.

Krämer, W. (2011). *Die Angst der Woche: Warum wir uns vor den falschen Dingen fürchten*. Munich: Piper.

Krauss, S., and Wang, X. T. (2003). The psychology of the Monty Hall problem: Discovering psychological mechanisms for solving a tenacious brain teaser. *Journal of Experimental Psychology: General* 132, 3–22.

Kruglanski, A., and Gigerenzer, G. (2011). Intuitive and deliberate judgments are based on common principles. *Psychological Review* 118, 97-109.

Kritzman, M., Page, S., and Turkington, D. (2010). In defense of optimization: The myth of 1/N. *Financial Analysis Journal* 66, 31–39.

Krogsbøll, L. T., Jørgensen, K. J., Grønhøj Larsen, C., and Gøtzsche, P. C. (2012). General health checks in adults for reducing morbidity and mortality from disease. *Cochrane Database of Systematic Reviews* 10, CD009009. doi: 10.1002/14651858. CD009009.pub2.

Krüger, L., Daston, L., and Heidelberger, M. (Eds.) (1987). *The probabilistic revolution, Vol. 1: Ideas in history*. Cambridge, MA: MIT Press.

Krüger, L., Gigerenzer, G., and Morgan, M. S. (Eds.) (1987). *The probabilistic revolution: Vol. II: Ideas in the sciences*. Cambridge, MA: MIT Press.

Kurz-Milcke, E., Gigerenzer, G., and Martignon, L. (2008). Transparency in risk communication: Graphical and analog tools. *Annals of the New York Academy of Sciences* 1128, 18–28.

———. (2011). Risiken durchschauen: Graphische und analoge Werkzeuge. *Stochastik in der Schule* 31, 8–16.

Labarge, A. S., McCaffrey, R. J., and Brown, T. A. (2003). Neuropsychologists' ability to determine the predictive value of diagnostic tests. *Clinical Neuropsychology* 18, 165–75.

Larson, C. A. (2011). Evidence-based medicine: An analysis of prophylactic bilateral oophorectomy at time of hysterectomy for benign conditions. *Current Oncology* 18, 13–15.

LeDoux, J. E. (1996). *The emotional brain*. New York: Simon and Schuster.

Lee, C. I., Haims, A. H., Monico E. P., Brink, J. A., and Forman, H. P. (2004). Diagnostic CT scans: Assessment of patient, physician, and radiologist awareness of radiation dose and possible risk. *Radiology* 231, 393–98.

Leeman, R. F., Fischler, C., and Rozin, P. (2011). Medical doctors' attributes and beliefs about diet and health are more like those of their lay countrymen (France, Germany, Italy, UK, and U.S.A) than those of doctors in other countries. *Appetite* 56, 558–63.

Leibniz, G. W. (1951). The horizon of human doctrine. In P. P. Wiener (Ed.). *Selections* (pp. 73–77). New York: Scribner's Sons. (Original work published 1690.)

Lewis, M. (2010). *The big short*. New York: Norton.

Lin, E. C. (2010). Radiation risk from medical imaging. *Mayo Clinic Proceedings* 85, 1142–46.

Liu, Y., Hu, F., and Li, D. (2011). Does physical activity reduce the risk of prostate cancer? *European Urology* 60, 1029–44.

Longnecker, M. P., Newcomb, P. A., Mittendorf, R., Greenberg, E. R., Clapp, R. W., Bogdan, G. F., et al. (1995). Risk of breast cancer in relation to lifetime alcohol consumption. *Journal of the National Cancer Institute* 87, 923–29.

Luchins, E. H., and Luchins, A. S. (1979). Introduction to the Einstein-Wertheimer correspondence. *Methodology and Science* 12, 165–202.

MacDonald, K. L., Jackson, J. B., Bowman, R. J., Polesky, H. F., Rhame, F. S., Balfour, H. H., et al. (1989). Performance characteristics of serologic tests for human immunodeficiency virus type 1 (HIV-1) antibody among Minnesota blood donors. Public health and clinical implications. *Annals of Internal Medicine* 110, 617–21.

Maidique, M. (2012). The leader's toolbox: A deconstruction of high-stakes CEO decision making. Poster presentation at the meeting of the Society of Judgment and Decision making, Seattle. Retrieved from onlineappsdev.fiu.edu/lead/news/article/38.

Makridakis, S., Hogarth, R. M., and Gaba, A. (2009). Forecasting and uncertainty in the economic and business world. *International Journal of Forecasting* 25, 794–812.

Malkiel, B. G. (2007). *A random walk down Wall Street*. New York: Norton.

Mandelbrot, B., and Taleb, N. N. (2005, July 11). How finance gurus get risk all wrong. *Fortune* 99–100.

Martignon, L., Vitouch, O., Takezawa, M., and Forster, M. R. (2011). Naive and yet enlightened: From natural frequencies to fast and frugal trees. In G. Gigerenzer, R. Hertwig, and T. Pachur (Eds.), *Heuristics: The foundations of adaptive behavior* (pp. 134–50). New York: Oxford University Press.

McCollough, C. H. (2011). Defending the use of medical imaging. *Health Physics* 100, 318–21.

McManus, I. C., Richards, P., Winder, B. C., and Sproston, K. A. (1998). Clinical experience, performance in final examinations, and learning style in medical students: Prospective study. *British Medical Journal* 316, 345–50.

Mill, J. S. (1869). *On liberty*. London: Longman, Roberts and Green.

Miller, G. (2000). *The mating mind: How sexual choice shaped the evolution of human nature*. London: William Heinemann.

Mintzberg, H. (2009). *Managing*. San Francisco: Berrett-Koeler.

Monti, M., Martignon, L., Pelligra, V., and Gugliemetti, C. (2012). *The insurance by my side: Better risk assessment for smarter insurance decisions* (CAREFIN Working Paper No. 3/2011). Milan: Università Commerciale Luigi Bocconi.

Mooi, W. J., and Peeper, D. S. (2006). Oncogene-induced cell senescence—Halting on the road to cancer. *New England Journal of Medicine* 355, 1037–46.

Multmeier, J. (2012). *Representations facilitate Bayesian reasoning: Computational facilitation and ecological design revisited* (Unpublished doctoral dissertation). Free University: Berlin.

Munro, E. (2004). A simpler way to understand the results of risk assessment instruments. *Children and Youth Services Review* 25, 873–83.

Muris, P., Merckelbach, H., Meesters, C., and Van Lier, P. (1997). What do children fear most often? *Journal of Behavior Therapy and Experimental Psychiatry* 28, 263–67.

Nass-Griegoleit, I., Schultz-Zehden, B., Klusendick, M., Diener, J., and Schulte, H. (2009). Studie belegt hohe Akzeptanz des Mammographie-Screenings bei Frauen: Ergebnisse der ersten repräsentativen Studie in Deutschland. *Frauenarzt* 50, 494–501.

Neuberg, S. L., and Newsom, J. T. (1993). Personal need for structure: Individual differences in the desire for simple structure. *Journal of Personality and Social Psychology* 65, 113–31.

Nida-Rümelin, J. 2011. *Die Optimierungsfalle*. Munich: Irisiana.

Nisbett, R. E. (2003). *The geography of thought: How Asians and Westerners think differently . . . and why*. New York: Free Press.

———. (2009). *Intelligence and how to get it*. New York: Norton.

Nyström, L. (2002). Long-term effects of mammography screening: Updated overview of the Swedish randomized trials. *Lancet* 359, 909–19.

Öhman, A., and Mineka, S. (2001). Fears, phobias, and preparedness: Toward an evolved module of fear and fear learning. *Psychological Review* 108, 483–522.

Ophir, E., Nass, C., and Wagner, A. D. (2009). Cognitive control in media multitaskers. *Proceedings of the National Academy of Sciences of the United States of America* 106, 15583–87.

Orpana, H. M, Berthelot, J. M., Kaplan, M. S., Freny, D. H., McFarland, B., and Ross, N. A. (2008). BMI and mortality: Results from a national longitudinal study of Canadian adults. *Obesity* 18, 214–18.

Orrell, D. (2010). *Economyths*. London: Icon Books.

Ortmann, A., Gigerenzer, G., Borges, B., and Goldstein, D. G. (2008). The recognition heuristic: A fast and frugal way to investment choice? In C. R. Plott and V. L. Smith (Eds.), *Handbook of experimental economics results: Vol. 1* (pp. 993–1003). Amsterdam: North-Holland.

Paulos, J. A. (1988). *Innumeracy: Mathematical illiteracy and its consequences*. New York: Vintage Books.

Payer, L. (1996). *Medicine and culture*. New York: Holt.

Peto, J. (2001). Cancer epidemiology in the last century and the next decade. *Nature* 411, 390–95.

Piatelli-Palmarini, M. (1991). Probability blindness: Neither rational nor capricious. *Bostonia*, March/April, 28–35.

———. (1994). *Inevitable illusions: How mistakes of reason rule our minds*. New York: Wiley.

Picano, E., and Matucci-Cerinic, M. (2011). Unnecessary radiation exposure from medical imaging in the rheumatology patient. *Rheumatology* 50, 1537–39.

Polya, G. (1954). *Mathematics and plausible reasoning* (Vol. 1). Princeton, NJ: Princeton University Press.

Posner, R. A. (2009). *A failure of capitalism*. Cambridge, MA: Harvard University Press.

Proctor, R. N. (2012). The history of the discovery of the cigarette–lung cancer link: Evidentiary traditions, corporate denial, global toll. *Tobacco Control* 21, 87–91.

Pronovost, P., Needham, D., Berenholtz, S., Sinopoli, D., Chu, H., Cosgrove, S., et al. (2006). An intervention to decrease catheter-related bloodstream infections in the ICU. *New England Journal of Medicine* 355, 2725–32.

Quart, A. (2003). *Branded: The buying and selling of teenagers*. Cambridge, MA: Perseus Publishing.

Quigley, C. (1996). *The corpse: A history*. London: McFarland.

Rampura, V., Hapani, S., and Wu, S. (2011). Treatment-related mortality with Bevacizumab in cancer patients: A meta-analysis. *Journal of the American Medical Association* 305, 487–94.

Rebonato, R. (2012). *Taking liberties: A critical examination of libertarian paternalism*. Basingstoke, UK: Palgrave Macmillan.

Renn, O. (2007). Die Multidisziplinarität des Themas Risiko [The multidisciplinarity of the topic "risk"]. In Berlin-Brandenburgische Akademie der Wissenschaften (Ed.). *Risiko* (pp. 71–75). Berlin.

Reyna, V. F., and Brainerd, C. J. (2007). The importance of mathematics in health and human judgment: Numeracy, risk communication, and medical decision making. *Learning and Individual Differences* 17, 147–59.

Ripley, A. (2009). *The unthinkable: Who survives when disaster strikes—and why*. New York: Three Rivers Press.

Sahlberg, P. (2011). *Finnish lessons: What can the world learn from educational change in Finland?* New York: Teachers College Press.

Savage, L. J. (1954). *The foundations of statistics*. NY: Dover.

Schirrmacher, F. (2009). *Payback*. Munich: Blessing.

Schneider, S. (2010, June 29). Homo economicus—or more like Homer Simpson? *Deutsche Bank Research*. Retrieved from www.dbresearch.com.

Schroeder, F. H., et al. (2012). Prostate-cancer mortality at 11 years of follow-up. *New England Journal of Medicine* 366, 981-90.

Schütze, M. (2011). Alcohol attributable burden of incidence of cancer in eight European countries based on results from prospective cohort study. *British Medical Journal* 342, d1584.

Schwartz, D. T. (2007). Counter-point: Are we really ordering too many CT scans? *Western Journal of Emergency Medicine* 9, 120–22.

Schwartz, B., Ward, A., Monterosso, J., Lyubomirsky, S., White, K., and Lehman, D. R. (2002). Maximizing versus satisficing: Happiness is a matter of choice. *Journal of Personality and Social Psychology* 83, 1178–97.

Schwartz, L. M., and Woloshin, S. (2011). The drug facts box: Making informed decisions about prescription drugs possible. In G. Gigerenzer and J. A. Muir Gray (Eds.). *Better doctors, better patients: Envisioning health care 2020* (pp. 233–42). Cambridge, MA: MIT Press.

Schwartz, L. M., Woloshin, S., and Welch, H. G. (1999). Risk communication in clinical practice: Putting cancer in context. *Monograph of the National Cancer Institute* 25, 124–33.

———. (2009). Using a drug facts box to communicate drug benefits and harms. *Annals of Internal Medicine* 150, 516–27.

Schwartz, L. M., Woloshin, S., Fowler, F. J., and Welch, H. G. (2004). Enthusiasm for cancer screening in the United States. *Journal of the American Medical Association* 291, 71–78.

Sedrakyan, A., and Shih, C. (2007). Improving depiction of benefits and harms: Analyses of studies of well-known therapeutics and review of high-impact medical journals. *Medical Care* 45, 523–28.

Seligman, M. E. P. (1970). On the generality of the laws of learning. *Psychological Review* 77, 406–18.

Selvin, S. (1975). A problem in probability [Letter to the editor]. *American Statistician* 29, 67.

Shah, N. B., and Platt, S. L. (2008). ALARA: Is there a cause for alarm? Reducing radiation risk from computed tomography scanning in children. *Current Opinion in Pediatrics* 20, 243–47.

Sherden, W. A. (1998). *The fortune sellers.* New York: Wiley.

Shibata, A., and Whittemore, A. S. (2001). Re: Prostate cancer incidence and mortality in the United States and the United Kingdom. *Journal of the National Cancer Institute* 9, 1109–10.

Siegrist, M., Cousin, M.-E., and Keller, C. (2008). Risk communication, prenatal screening, and prenatal diagnosis: The illusion of informed decision making. *Journal of Risk Research* 11, 87–97.

Sirovich, B. E., and Welch, H. G. (2004). Cervical cancer screening among women without a cervix. *Journal of the American Medical Association* 291, 2990-93.

Slovic, P. (1987). Perception of risk. *Science* 236, 280–85. doi: 10.1126/science.3563507.

Smith-Bindman, R., Lipson, J., Marcus, R., Kim, K.-P., Mahesh, M., Gould, R., et al. (2009). Radiation dose associated with common computed tomography examinations and the associated lifetime attributable risk of cancer. *Archives of Internal Medicine* 169, 2078–86.

Steimle, S. (1999). UK's Tony Blair announces crusade to fight cancer. *Journal of the National Cancer Institute* 91, 1189.

Steinman, M., Shlipak, M. G., and McPhee, S. J. (2001). Of principles and pens: Attitudes and practices of medical house staff toward pharmaceutical industry promotions. *American Journal of Medical Genetics* 110, 551–57.

Stephen, A. E., Segev, D. L., Ryan, D. P., Mullins, M. E., Kim, S. H., Schnitzer, J. J., and Doody, D. P. (2003). The diagnosis of acute appendicitis in a pediatric population: To CT or not to CT. *Journal of Pediatric Surgery* 38, 367–71.

Steurer, J., Held, U., Schmidt, M., Gigerenzer, G., Tag, B., and Bachmann, L. M. (2009). Legal concerns trigger prostate-specific antigen testing. *Journal of Evaluation in Clinical Practice* 15, 390–92. doi: 10.1111/j.1365-2753.2008.01024.x.

Stiftung Warentest (2004, February). Urologen im Test: Welchen Nutzen hat der PSA-Test? *Stiftung Warentest*, 86–89.

Stigler, S. M. (1980). Stigler's law of eponymy. *Transactions of the New York Academy of Sciences* 39, 147–57.

———. (1983). Who discovered Bayes' Theorem? *American Statistician* 37, 290–96.

Stiglitz, J. E. (2010). *Freefall: America, free markets, and the sinking of the world economy.* New York: Norton.

Stine, G. J. (1996). *Acquired immune deficiency syndrome: Biological, medical, social, and legal issues* (2nd ed.). Englewood Cliffs, NJ: Prentice Hall.

Strayer, D. L., Drews, F. A., and Crouch, D. J. (2006). Comparing the cell-phone driver and the drunk driver. *Human Factors* 48, 381–91.

Studdert, D. M., Mello, M. M., Sage, W. M., DesRoches, C. M., Peugh, J., Zapert, K., and Brennan, T. A. (2005). Defensive medicine among high-risk specialist physicians in a volatile malpractice environment. *Journal of the American Medical Association* 293, 2609–17.

Studdert, D. M., Mello, M. M., Gawande, A. A., Gandhi, T. K., Kachalla, A., Yoon, C., et al. (2006). Claims, errors, and compensation payments in medical malpractice litigation. *New England Journal of Medicine* 354, 2024–33.

Taleb, N. N. (2004). *Fooled by randomness: The hidden role of chance in life and in the markets.* London: Thomson.

Taleb, N. N., and Blyth, M. (2011). The black swan of Cairo. *Foreign Affairs* 90, 33–39.

Tankard, J. W. (1979). The H. G. Wells quote on statistics: A question of accuracy. *Historia Mathematica* 6, 30–33.

TAP Study Group (2001). Photodynamic therapy of subfoveal choroidal neovascularization in age-related macular degeneration with verteporfin. *Archives of Ophthalmology* 119, 198–207.

Tengs, T. O., Adams, M. E., Pliskin, J. S., Safran, D. G., Siegel, J. E., Weinstein, M. C., and Graham, J. D. (1995). Five-hundred life-saving interventions and their cost-effectiveness. *Risk Analysis* 15, 369–90.

Tetlock, P. E. (2005). *Expert political judgment.* Princeton, NJ: Princeton University Press.

Thaler, R. H. (1991). *Quasi rational economics.* New York: Russell Sage Foundation.

Thaler, R. H., and Sunstein, C. R. (2008). *Nudge.* New Haven, CT: Yale University Press.

Todd, P. M., Billari, F. C., and Simão, J. (2005). Aggregate age-at-marriage patterns from individual mate-search heuristics. *Demography* 42, 559–74.

Todd, P. M., Gigerenzer, G., and the ABC Research Group. (2012). *Ecological rationality: Intelligence in the world.* New York: Oxford University Press.

Todd, P. M., and Miller, G. F. (1999). From pride and prejudice to persuasion: Satisficing in mate search. In G. Gigerenzer, P. M. Todd, and the ABC Research Group. *Simple heuristics that make us smart* (pp. 287–308). New York: Oxford University Press.

Todd, P. M., Knutson, B., and Minard, S. L. (in press). Simple heuristics for deciding what to eat. In S. Preston, M. Kringelbach, and B. Knutson (Eds.). *Interdisciplinary science of consumption.* Cambridge, MA: MIT Press.

Törngren, G., and Montgomery, H. (2004). Worse than chance? Performance and confidence among professionals and laypeople in the stock market. *Journal of Behavioral Finance* 5, 148–53.

Trunkey, D. D. (2010). Health care reform: What went wrong. *Annals of Surgery* 252, 417–25.

Tu, X. M., Litvak, E., and Pagano, M. (1992). Issues in human immunodeficiency virus (HIV) screening programs. *American Journal of Epidemiology* 136, 244–55.

Turkle, S. (2011). *Alone together.* New York: Basic Books.

Twain, M. (2005). *Pudd'nhead Wilson.* New York: Bantam Classics. (Original work published 1894.)

Twenge, J. M., Gentile, B., DeWall, N., Ma, D., Lacefield, K., and Schurtz, D. R. (2010). Birth cohort increases in psychopathology among young Americans, 1938–2007. *Clinical Psychology Review* 30, 145–54.

Vazquez, F., and Federico, P. (2012). *Bank funding structures and risk* (IMF Working Paper 12/29). International Monetary Fund.

Vitouch, O., Strauss, S., and Lading, O. (2007). *Kognitive Täuschungen durch Prozentangaben: Der Fall der staatlich geförderten Pensionsvorsorge* (Final Report, OeNB Project No. 11109). Department of Psychology, University of Klagenfurt.

Volz, K. G., and Gigerenzer, G. (2012). Cognitive processes in decision under risk are not the same as in decisions under uncertainty. *Frontiers in Decision Neuroscience*, 6: 05. doi: 10.3389/fnins.2012.00105.

Wegwarth, O., Gaissmaier, W., and Gigerenzer, G. (2011). Deceiving numbers: Survival rates and their impact on doctors' risk communication. *Medical Decision Making* 31, 386–94. doi: 10.1177/0272989X10391469.

Wegwarth, O., Schwartz, L. M., Woloshin, S., Gaissmaier, W., and Gigerenzer, G. (2012). Do physicians understand cancer screening statistics? A national survey of primary care physicians in the United States. *Annals of Internal Medicine* 156, 340–49.

Welch, H. G., Schwartz, L. M., and Woloshin, S. (2000). Are increasing five-year survival rates evidence of success against cancer? *Journal of the American Medical Association* 283, 2975–78.

———. (2011). *Overdiagnosed: Making people sick in the pursuit of health.* Boston, MA: Beacon Press.

Wells, H. G. (1938/1994). *World Brain.* London: Adamantine Press.

Wertheimer, M. (1934, Summer). Letter to Albert Einstein. (Summer, 1934). Albert Einstein Archive, Princeton University Library.

Willyard, C. (2011). Lifestyle: Breaking the cancer habit. *Nature* 471, S16–S17.

Wobker, I., Lehmann-Waffenschmidt, M., Kenning, P., and Gigerenzer, G. (2012). *What do people know about the economy? A test of minimal economic knowledge in Germany.* Manuscript. Zeppelin University, Friedrichshafen.

Woloshin, S., and Schwartz, L. M., (2012). How a charity oversells mammography. *British Medical Journal* 345, e5132. doi: 10.1136/bmj.e5132.

Woloshin, S., Schwartz, L. M., and Welch, H. G. (2008). *Know your chances: Understanding health statistics.* Berkeley: University of California Press.

Wübben, M., and Wangenheim, F. v. (2008). Instant customer base analysis: Managerial heuristics often "get it right." *Journal of Marketing* 72, 82–93. doi: 10.1509/jmkg.72.3.82.

Yamamoto, K. (1979). Children's ratings of the stressfulness of experiences. *Developmental Psychology* 15, 581–82.

Young, J. M., Glasziou, P., and Ward, J. E. (2002). General practitioners' self rating of skills in evidence based medicine: A validation study. *British Medical Journal* 324, 950–51.

Zhu, L., and Gigerenzer, G. (2006). Children can solve Bayesian problems: The role of representation in mental computation. *Cognition* 98, 287–308.

Zimmerman, F. J., Christakis, D. A., and Meltzoff, A. N. (2007). Associations between media viewing and language development in children under age 2 years. *Journal of Pediatrics* 151, 364–68.

INDEX

ILLUSTRATION CREDITS

1-1 Max Planck Institute for Human Development
1-2 Gigerenzer
2-1 Gigerenzer
2-2 Bridgeman Art Library
2-3 Max Planck Institute for Human Development
2-4 Max Planck Institute for Human Development
2-5 Gigerenzer
3-1 Max Planck Institute for Human Development
3-2 ©1995, Edward H. Adelson. These checkershadow images may be repro-
    duced and distributed freely. http://web.mit.edu/persci/people/adelson/
    checkershadow_illusion.html
4-1 Max Planck Institute for Human Development
5-1 Gigerenzer
5-2 Gigerenzer
5-3 Max Planck Institute for Human Development
6-1 Gigerenzer
6-2 Gigerenzer
6-3 Gigerenzer
6-4 Gigerenzer
7-1 Max Planck Institute for Human Development
7-2 Max Planck Institute for Human Development
7-3 Gigerenzer
7-4 Max Planck Institute for Human Development
7-5 Gigerenzer
8-1 Gigerenzer
8-2 Gigerenzer
9-1 Gigerenzer
9-2 Gigerenzer
9-3 Gigerenzer
9-4 Gigerenzer
9-5 Gigerenzer
10-1 Gigerenzer
10-2 Gigerenzer
10-3 Gigerenzer
10-4 Harding Center for Risk Literacy
10-5 Gigerenzer
10-6 Gigerenzer
10-7 Harding Center for Risk Literacy

ALLEN LANE
an imprint of
PENGUIN BOOKS

Recently Published

Dana Thomas, *Gods and Kings: The Rise and Fall of Alexander McQueen and John Galliano*

Steven Weinberg, *To Explain the World: The Discovery of Modern Science*

Jennifer Jacquet, *Is Shame Necessary?: New Uses for an Old Tool*

Eugene Rogan, *The Fall of the Ottomans: The Great War in the Middle East, 1914-1920*

Norman Doidge, *The Brain's Way of Healing: Stories of Remarkable Recoveries and Discoveries*

John Hooper, *The Italians*

Sven Beckert, *Empire of Cotton: A New History of Global Capitalism*

Mark Kishlansky, *Charles I: An Abbreviated Life*

Philip Ziegler, *George VI: The Dutiful King*

David Cannadine, *George V: The Unexpected King*

Stephen Alford, *Edward VI: The Last Boy King*

John Guy, *Henry VIII: The Quest for Fame*

Robert Tombs, *The English and their History: The First Thirteen Centuries*

Neil MacGregor, *Germany: The Memories of a Nation*

Uwe Tellkamp, *The Tower: A Novel*

Roberto Calasso, *Ardor*

Slavoj Žižek, *Trouble in Paradise: Communism After the End of History*

Francis Pryor, *Home: A Time Traveller's Tales from Britain's Prehistory*

R. F. Foster, *Vivid Faces: The Revolutionary Generation in Ireland, 1890-1923*

Andrew Roberts, *Napoleon the Great*

Shami Chakrabarti, *On Liberty*

Bessel van der Kolk, *The Body Keeps the Score: Mind, Brain and Body in the Transformation of Trauma*

Brendan Simms, *The Longest Afternoon: The 400 Men Who Decided the Battle of Waterloo*

Naomi Klein, *This Changes Everything: Capitalism vs the Climate*

Owen Jones, *The Establishment: And How They Get Away with It*

Caleb Scharf, *The Copernicus Complex: Our Cosmic Significance in a Universe of Planets and Probabilities*

Martin Wolf, *The Shifts and the Shocks: What We've Learned - and Have Still to Learn - from the Financial Crisis*

Steven Pinker, *The Sense of Style: The Thinking Person's Guide to Writing in the 21st Century*

Vincent Deary, *How We Are: Book One of the How to Live Trilogy*

Henry Kissinger, *World Order*

Alexander Watson, *Ring of Steel: Germany and Austria-Hungary at War, 1914-1918*

Richard Vinen, *National Service: Conscription in Britain, 1945-1963*

Paul Dolan, *Happiness by Design: Finding Pleasure and Purpose in Everyday Life*

Mark Greengrass, *Christendom Destroyed: Europe 1517-1650*

Hugh Thomas, *World Without End: The Global Empire of Philip II*

Richard Layard and David M. Clark, *Thrive: The Power of Evidence-Based Psychological Therapies*

Uwe Tellkamp, *The Tower: A Novel*

Zelda la Grange, *Good Morning, Mr Mandela*